BRIAN MASTERS

The Shrine of Jeffrey Dahmer

HODDER &
STOUGHTON

First published in Great Britain in 1993 by Hodder & Stoughton
Hachette UK company

This paperback edition published in 2020

1

A CIP catalogue record for this title is available from the British Library

B format ISBN 9781529338911
eBook ISBN 9781529338935

Printed and bound in Great Britain by Clays Ltd, Elcograf S.p.A.

Hodder & Stoughton policy is to use papers that are natural, renewable
and recyclable products and made from wood grown in sustainable forests.
The logging and manufacturing processes are expected to conform to the
environmental regulations of the country of origin.

Hodder & Stoughton Ltd
Carmelite House
50 Victoria Embankment
London EC4Y 0DZ

www.hodder.co.uk

Dedicated to the late
James Crespi

Acknowledgments

A book of this nature depends for its content upon the co-operation and trust of a number of people, and for its conclusions alone upon the author. I have been fortunate in having been offered assistance where it was most valuable, and would like heartily to acknowledge my many debts before the text gets under way.

Mr Gerald Boyle, Jeffrey Dahmer's attorney both before and during his trial, was ever courteous and patient with my enquiries so long as I was careful not to allow them to intrude upon professional confidentiality, and helped clarify the burden of his defence effort. His entire staff were likewise tolerant of my frequent interruptions of their working day. I am grateful to District Attorney E. Michael McCann for a long interview in which he graciously set forth his view of the legal and moral implications of the case he had prosecuted.

Mr Dan Patrinos of the *Milwaukee Journal* made me welcome in Milwaukee at a time when he was besieged by journalists with a far more obvious right to attend the trial than I, and I am beholden to him for his good nature and practical assistance. Mr James Shellow explained to me the intricacies of the Wisconsin Statute with regard to criminal responsibility, which he helped to frame, as well as giving me the benefit of his reflections upon Anglo-Saxon jurisprudence. His wife Gilda and daughter Robin, both in legal practice, were unfailingly obliging in putting up with my questions and encouraging my undertaking.

My sojourn in Milwaukee on several occasions, and over many weeks, was made agreeable by the cheerful staff of the Milwaukee Athletic Club, where I stayed, and the Wisconsin Club, where I repaired every day to ruminate, both welcoming me with the courtesy they would accord to a member of long standing.

The Forensic Unit at the Safety Building became my office over a long period, thanks to the tolerance of the two ladies who run it, Lois Schmidt and Karen Marzion, to both of whom I am most grateful. The doctors who work there additionally accepted my presence among them. I am also indebted to Dr George Palermo and Dr Samuel Friedman for various opinions and views freely expressed. Dr John Pankiewicz was especially helpful in pointing me towards important essays in psychiatric journals which would otherwise have escaped my attention. Similarly, in England, Dr Christopher Cordess alerted me to other articles germane to my task, for which I wish to express my indebtedness.

I made it a point not to descend upon the families of those who died, out of respect for their privacy; despite this, the brothers and sisters of Eddie Smith made me welcome in their home and shared some of their memories with me, which I appreciate with full heart. It is to Theresa Smith that I owe the use of a photograph of Eddie not previously published. For similar reasons, I did not attempt to impose myself upon Dr Lionel and Mrs Shari Dahmer, father and stepmother of the defendant, and yet they always treated me with warmth and understanding in the most difficult circumstances. I shall long cherish the meals we had together, in which they spoke of their attitude towards the crimes and trial off the record, with a confidence which I have respected and not betrayed in these pages.

Photographs of court exhibits, notably the interior of Dahmer's apartment and portraits of his victims, were taken for me by Greg Gent Studios.

My editor, Bill Massey, has been so scrupulous and thorough in his analysis of the text as to improve it beyond a point at which mere gratitude would suffice, and my agents, Jacintha Alexander and Julian Alexander, have been entirely supportive at times when my very purpose has been questioned.

In the pages which follow, all quotations from family, schoolfriends and acquaintances of Jeffrey Dahmer are taken from statements made to Milwaukee or Ohio police officers in the course of their enquiries, and contained in file 2472 of the Milwaukee Police Department. In addition to this, Detective Dennis Murphy allowed me the privilege of a personal interview.

I reserve until the last my appreciation to Jeffrey L. Dahmer for the permission he granted to Dr Kenneth Smail (and, by extension, to myself) for his interviews with Dr Smail to be used for professional purposes. Except for a few instances specifically indicated, wherever I have quoted Mr Dahmer's words directly they have been taken from these interviews and are identified in source notes by the letters J.L.D. and the date of the interview. It follows from this that my deepest debt is to Dr Smail himself, who has not only entrusted me to treat the material with proper respect and restraint, but has himself contributed a postscript to the book, explaining for the first time why he felt unable to support the case for the defence.

In view of the above, it must be obvious that the opinions I express in this book, and the tentative conclusions I posit, are mine and mine alone, while Dr Smail is responsible only for the views he has put forward in his postscript.

Brian Masters, London, 1992

Contents

'And hence one master-passion in the breast,
Like Aaron's serpent, swallows up the rest'

Alexander Pope, *An Essay on Man*, Epistle 2, line 131

Chapter One

The Charges

'Ladies and gentlemen of the jury, you are about to embark upon an odyssey.'

So began Gerald Boyle's opening statement at the trial of Jeffrey Dahmer on 30 January, 1992. They were heavy, ominous words to use in a cosy courtroom in Milwaukee, where lawyers habitually lounge and banter, and in summer address the judge in shirt-sleeves. But this was not summer, and there was nothing remotely cosy or comforting about the case which Mr Boyle had to present. His voice presaged a distinct warning. From months of preparation, he knew what lay ahead. His task was to open a window upon depths of iniquity and perversion as could scarcely be imagined, and still protect his, and the jury's, capacity to reason without prejudice, to understand without disgust. Boyle seemed almost to apologise for what he was about to demand of his audience, to identify with them in wishing to avoid contamination by the evidence he would have to display before them. To some extent, he distanced himself from his own client. By the end of the day, it was not difficult to see why.

The odyssey had begun, for the public at least, at 11.30 on the evening of 22 July, 1991, on the corner of Kilbourn Avenue and North 25th Street in Milwaukee. It was a sultry night and a dangerous hour, for this was a somewhat tense part of town, the scene of many a late-night argument and fight. Police Officers Rolf Mueller and Robert

Rauth were driving along in their squad car, alert but relaxed, certainly not anticipating any significant incidents, when they were flagged down by a thirty-two-year-old black man, Tracy Edwards, who had a handcuff dangling from his left wrist. The squad car stopped and officers Rauth and Mueller got out. Edwards told them that some 'freak' had placed the handcuffs on him, and could they please remove them. 'I just want to get it off,' he said. The officers tried to unlock the handcuffs, but their keys did not fit that particular brand. Had they fitted, Edwards would most likely have thanked them for their help and made his way home (he lived on Kilbourn Avenue and could have walked). The story of Jeffrey Dahmer's distorted dramas may have remained hidden from the world for several more weeks, or even months.

Since Tracy Edwards appeared to be stuck with the handcuffs, and since the officers were curious, though not yet overtly suspicious, Edwards took them to the apartment where the 'freak' lived, at 924 North 25th Street. It was a block of apartments mostly inhabited by black or Asian families. The tenant of No. 213, however, was white, and it was with him that Edwards had spent the evening, since about 6.30 p.m. The three men knocked on the door. It was opened by Jeffrey L. Dahmer, thirty-one years old, sandy hair, glasses, six feet tall with regular features, but a pallid complexion and stark lack of cheerfulness. He invited them in, holding the door open. The living-room was small but pleasantly furnished, with a large comfortable arm-chair, a healthy pot-plant on a tall pedestal, an oriental rug, blue curtains at the window, some fine pictures on the wall, and one framed picture of a naked male model. There was nothing seedy or squalid about the room; rather did it appear surprisingly neat and tidy for the neighbourhood.

Dahmer was vague but co-operative at first. He said he worked as a mixer at the Ambrosia Chocolate Factory downtown. What was the problem with the handcuffs, he was asked; why not unlock them, was he some kind of

2

psycho? He acknowledged that he had placed the handcuffs on Edwards, but could not say why. Edwards now went further. Dahmer had brandished a large knife at him, he said. Dahmer did not react to this, but told the officers he thought the key to the handcuffs must be in the bedroom, and pointed to the door. He invited Officer Mueller to go into the bedroom himself and retrieve the key, but then moved towards the door, as if he had suddenly remembered something, and was intercepted by Officer Rauth, who told him to 'back off'.

Meanwhile, Mueller immediately noticed that there was indeed a large knife lying just beneath the bed, and that the top drawer of a chest was open, revealing scores of polaroid photographs of naked men. He looked further and realised, with some shock, that many of them were pictures of severed heads, dismembered limbs, decomposing torsos, and from the evidence of the décor in the pictures, it was clear that they were not commercially produced fakes, but had actually been taken in that same bedroom. Incredulous, Mueller came back into the livingroom with photographs in his hand. 'These are real pictures,' he told Rauth.

At this point, Dahmer seemed to come to his senses. Rauth went to restrain him, and the two men fell to the floor, struggling. The policeman was on top of Dahmer, holding one arm, but Dahmer was able to reach behind him and pinch Rauth's thigh. Rauth then shouted in pain, and Mueller joined him to subdue Dahmer. They called another squad car, and Officer Schoessow turned up at 11.50 p.m. to find the suspect being pinned to the ground. He went back to his car for handcuffs, and Jeffrey Dahmer was duly placed under arrest.

For him it was the end of a very long road, but for the police it had scarcely begun. Tracy Edwards told them that Dahmer had clapped his own handcuffs on him as he was approaching the refrigerator to get himself a beer, and had told him that there was something in there which he would not believe. Rolf Mueller thereupon opened the

3

door of the refrigerator, and saw, on the bottom shelf, a cardboard box containing the severed head of a black man, face upwards. He closed the door quickly. Dahmer, still being held to the ground, turned his head and muttered, 'For what I did I should be dead.' The officers then called the Criminal Investigation Bureau, and by soon after midnight Dahmer's tiny apartment was crammed with policemen, medical officers, and firemen.

First to arrive was Detective James Devalkenaere at 12.05 a.m. He proceeded to inspect the bedroom more thoroughly and begin the laborious task of compiling an inventory, while Detectives Michael Dubis and Patrick Kennedy, who were on the scene by 12.15 a.m., questioned the suspect. It was Kennedy who would read out the first part of the confession to an utterly silent courtroom six months later. At 12.30 a.m. the office of the Milwaukee County Medical Examiner, Dr Jeffrey Jentzen, was notified, and he immediately alerted his staff. Shirley Gaines arrived at the apartment by 12.45 a.m., Dr Allen Stormo joined her at 1 a.m., and Dr Jentzen himself, with the Assistant Medical Examiner Dr John Teggatz, were there shortly afterwards. Another police officer, James Schoenecker, also arrived with an expert in identification, Ralph Basile. It was these two who spent the night taking one hundred and six photographs of the scene and of items to be removed. Finally, the Chief of the Fire Brigade, Kevin Clarke, came with an engine and ladder, and a so-called Hazardous Material Unit, specifically to take away a large blue drum from the bedroom, from which issued a noxious chemical odour.

In the meantime, the suspect was driven away in the company of Detective Patrick Kennedy and taken to the police station for questioning. This, their first interview, lasted for nearly six hours from 1.30 a.m. until 7.15 a.m., and it would be followed by another two hours later and many more such marathon talks over the next two weeks. The suspect was now not only resigned and co-operative, but anxious to confess, to relieve his soul of its massive

4

burden, to purge himself of intolerable poisonous memories. 'I think in some way I wanted it to end,' he said much later, 'even if it meant my own destruction.' He referred to the confession as 'cleaning out . . . refreshing'.[1] Jeffrey Dahmer proceeded to tell a blinking Detective Kennedy, who was unaware that any crimes had been committed, that he had killed sixteen men in Milwaukee over a period of four years, six of them in the past few weeks; that he had decapitated them, dismembered them, defleshed them and thrown what was left of them into the garbage; that some of the skulls he had retained, and some of the bodies he had placed in acid to liquefy them; that he had started as long ago as 1978 in Ohio, when his first victim had been smashed to pieces with a sledgehammer and scattered in the woods; that three men had been murdered and dissected in his grandmother's house; and – in a flat, bland, monotone voice – that it took about an hour to boil a human head.

Detective Kennedy was understandably reeling from the sudden access of all this information, and emerged from the interview room in a daze of disbelief. He told one of his colleagues that Dahmer must be a fantasist or fruitcake, but Kennedy had yet to learn that, while he had been talking to Dahmer all night, the investigators at Apartment 213 had been assembling evidence which corroborated every word of the confession. Kennedy was made to realise that he had been listening not to a grandiose attention-seeking half-wit, but to the simple truth shorn of emotion or wonder. It was a devastating moment.

It is time to look at precisely what was found in Dahmer's apartment, if only to start with the same parcel of knowledge as confronted the District Attorney, the defence counsel Gerald Boyle, and the seemingly endless parade of psychologists and psychiatrists, as they all grappled with the unpalatable, some in a painful endeavour to understand what had happened and why, others in a barely concealed effort to bend the facts towards a favoured conclusion. But none of them started in ignorance, and neither must we.

The doors of Apartment 213, both inner and outer, were heavily secured with multiple locks and an alarm system. On the walls in the bedroom and hall were framed photographs and posters of male nudes taken in 'artistic' poses and clearly intended to be attractive to a homosexual man. There were some empty beer cans and dirty dishes, and a number of pornographic videos lying around, mostly of the explicit kind commercially made in California. Among the titles which Dahmer possessed were, *Cocktales*, *Chippendale's Tall Dark and Handsome*, *Rock Hard*, *Hard Men II*, *Hard Men III*, *Peep Show*, and *Tropical Heat Wave*. Other non-sexual videos included two that would be referred to several times at the trial, *Exorcist II* and *The Return of the Jedi*. Somewhat incongruously, a lecture on evolution was also found on videotape, and an episode from *The Bill Cosby Show*.

On the kitchen floor were four boxes of muriatic acid. The refrigerator contained, in addition to the man's head already noted, some blood drippings on the bottom, and, in the freezer compartment, three plastic bags. Two of them each contained a heart, and the third some portion of muscle. Against another wall was a floor-standing freezer in which were found three more human heads and a plastic bag containing a human torso. Stuck to the bottom of this freezer was another plastic bag the contents of which appeared to include flesh and various human internal organs; Dahmer subsequently revealed that it had been there for several weeks because he had been unable to wrench it away from the ice. The Medical Examiner decided that this entire freezer should be sealed and removed, with its load, for detailed examination later.

In the hallway stood a closet in which were found, together with bedding, some chemicals (formaldehyde, ether, chloroform), and two bleached skulls on a shelf. On the floor at the back of the closet was a large aluminium kettle containing two human hands, obviously from the same person because they matched, and human genitals including penis, testicles and the pubic hair region. The bedroom was seen to have a single bed with a mattress stained with blood, as well as some blood on the walls and pillow-case. The large knife to which Tracy Edwards had alerted the police officers was still lying beneath the bed, while on top was a polaroid camera. Next to the bed was a metal filing-cabinet. When this was opened it revealed, in the top drawer, three human skulls lying on a black towel. The police officers noted that they had been painted green with black flecks, but the Medical Examiner reported that they were painted and glazed to 'a dark gray marble-like texture', and that the towel upon which they rested was dark blue. The bottom drawer of this cabinet contained a complete human skeleton, and in front of it were two paper bags: one held the dried remains of a human scalp, and the other a second set of genitals, also dried and mummified.

On the floor next to the chest of drawers was a box with a styrofoam lid, in which were two more skulls, and in the far corner was the 57-gallon blue plastic drum with a tight-fitting black lid, removed by a private contractor hired by the Fire Department's Hazardous Materials Unit. This was later discovered to contain three human torsos in various stages of dismemberment and decomposition. In the chest of drawers which Rolf Mueller had found open when he first went into the bedroom were original photographs of a particularly repellent nature. When they were counted, it was found there were seventy-four of them.

The décor of Jeffrey Dahmer's life was labelled, catalogued and carted away with the most painstaking care. A photo album, a black ceramic coffee cup, an empty can of Budweiser beer, an empty bottle of Paramount rum, an empty paper lunch-bag lying on the occasional table by the couch in the living-room – the fragile, dumb debris of ordinary life jostled with the curious and the sinister. A one-gallon jug of Chlorax bleach was no longer as innocent as it might have been, and a bottle of 'Odorsorb' suggested long battles with unnaturally polluted air. Incense sticks had probably served a similar purpose. There were fifty envelopes from Woolworth's, a tube of acne lotion, a shaving kit, an Oral-B toothbrush, the lease form for the rental of Apartment 213, a library card bearing the name of Jeff Dahmer, a pair of men's black nylon shorts. The business card of Lionel Dahmer, Ph.D., was the first indication that the suspect had a family, while various identity cards littered on the kitchen floor, the bedroom floor, and in drawers, poignantly gave names to some of the heads and limbs that had once been people. An identity card in the name of Oliver Lacy, a Wisconsin driver's licence in the name of Tony Hughes, and an Illinois driver's licence in the name of Joseph Bradehoft supplied the initial clues in the investigation, and since Oliver Lacy's I.D. bore a photograph and was the first positive identification, the entire homicide file would be listed under his name. It was Lacy's head which lay in the box in the refrigerator, his heart which was in the bag, his skeleton which was in the freezer.

A few items held significance which would not be revealed until much later. One large hypodermic needle appeared mysterious, and a contact lens cleaning kit quite innocuous, but they had both played a role in the wild distracted turmoil of Dahmer's life. So had two plastic gargoyle figurines recovered from the living-room, and chemical-resistant gloves next to gallons of muriatic acid and six boxes of Soilex cleaner. The purpose of the three-eighth inch drill and one-sixteenth inch drill bits was yet unclear, although the claw hammer and handsaw gave rise to no such doubts. And still, in crazy juxtaposition to this grim inventory were items suggestive of decency and goodness. A King James Version Bible, for example, audio cassettes on Creation Science and the Bible, and other tapes entitled *The Genesis Flood* and *The Bible, Science, and the Age of the Earth*. There were further audio tapes explaining *Numerology and the Divine Tri-*

angle, and a learning kit, in tapes and books, in Latin. Finally, there were four books on the care of fish and aquariums, and a beautifully kept aquarium itself, clean and wholesome, full of living plants and daintily exotic fish.[2]

While all this was being sifted, searched and photographed by police officers, Jeff Dahmer's telephone rang. Detective Michael Dubis answered it. On the line was Jeff's father, Lionel Dahmer, calling from Pittsburgh, Pennsylvania, where he worked. He had been trying to reach his son for a couple of days without success. Was anything wrong? Detective Dubis assured Dr Dahmer that his son was alive and well, and uninjured. He forebore to disclose why he and his colleagues were in the apartment, but said that somebody from the Criminal Investigation Bureau would be in touch with Dr Dahmer later in the day. The father had always feared his son's feeble hold on life and reality might collapse; he had been in trouble with the police before, for indecent exposure and indecent assault on a minor, and Dr Dahmer had pleaded with the authorities to make sure he was treated. So it looked as if something else had happened, Jeff had blown it again! Not in his most disease-induced dreams could the mild and shy industrial chemist have imagined just how much Jeff had 'blown it'.

Nor, indeed, could anyone have suspected that the police had been to Apartment 213 at 924 North 25th Street on three previous occasions, at least once while a dead body had been lying in the adjacent room. Even more alarming, that they had delivered one of the victims into Dahmer's arms. But this is to anticipate. There are more than an ordinary number of coincidences, ironies, and uncomfortable surprises in this astonishing story, and they must await their place. For the moment, it was surprise enough that there appeared to be an enormous gulf which separated Jeff Dahmer the man from the appalling deeds which he was now rapidly and openly admitting. Detective Dennis Murphy took over the major part of listening to

Dahmer's confession on 23 July, and their talks together lasted a total of sixty hours.

Murphy is a solid and reliable man, unexcitable, sensible and decent, and he soon formed a useful rapport with the suspect which enabled them both to relax in the midst of these tales of madness. He liked Dahmer. He appreciated his frankness, his lack of guile, and his shame. They were both private and undemonstrative. Though Dahmer gave no outward show of emotion, though he spoke in a flat monotone which made him seem callously indifferent to the damage he had wrought, Detective Murphy sensed that it was the inability to express emotion rather than the crude denial of it which lay at the root of Dahmer's seemingly offensive blandness. It took him three days to be able to talk without averting his eyes. The detective fell quite naturally into the habit of calling his interlocutor 'Jeff', as did several of the psychiatrists who were later to interview him (and for which one of them was chided in court). As will become clear, it is one of the characteristics of a certain kind of aberrant mental condition that it must smother emotion until it withers. Dennis Nilsen, another murderer convicted of crimes startlingly similar to those with which Dahmer was charged, ruminated on his own fate: 'Nature makes no provision for emotional death,' he wrote.[3]

Over the next two weeks, Dahmer looked at scores of photographs of missing persons in an effort to identify the people who died at his hands. For Detective Murphy, it was an essential job, part of the task for which he had been trained. For Dahmer, it became a frantic personal quest for a scrap of self-esteem. He would not rest, could not sleep, until the last one had his name restored. Why was it so important that he find these people again? It was 'to relieve the minds of the parents', he said. 'I mean, it's a small, very small thing, but I don't know what else I could do. At least I can do that.' He did not want the parents of missing young men to wonder and gnaw at their hearts for years to come, if he could at least tell them what happened, 'because I created this horror and it only makes sense that I do everything to put an end to it, a complete end to it.'[4] Detectives Murphy and Kennedy deliberately included among the photographs some of young men whom they knew to be alive, in an attempt to test Dahmer's veracity. He never once hesitated over the picture of somebody he had never met, and all the identifications were secured with his help. Indeed, some of them would never have been identified without him; apart from dental records matching to the skulls of some, Jeff Dahmer was virtually the investigation's only source.

Jeffrey L. Dahmer killed seventeen people. The first two did not give rise to charges against him, one because he was murdered in Ohio, therefore without the jurisdiction of the State of Wisconsin, the second because there was no evidence – no human remains and no memory of what had occurred, merely an identification from a photograph. On 25 July, 1991, just two days after his arrest, Dahmer was charged with four counts of first-degree intentional homicide, and held on bail of $1 million. On 6 August, he faced eight more murder counts and bail was raised to $5 million. On 22 August, the three last murder charges were brought against him, making a total of fifteen. In the Criminal Complaint they were listed as two counts of first-degree murder and thirteen counts of first-degree intentional homicide, but the distinction is merely one of language; they are the same offence, the Wisconsin Statutes having changed the nomenclature before the date of the third murder.

Here, then, are the bald facts of the indictment:

1. Late at night on 17 January, 1988, Jeff Dahmer met a young man called James Doxtator, and murdered him at his grandmother's house in West Allis. Doxtator's mother reported him missing on 18 January, 1988.

2. About two months later, on 27 March, 1988, Jeff Dahmer encountered Richard Guerrero, aged twenty-

three, and killed him at his grandmother's house. His father, Pablo Guerrero, reported him missing to the Milwaukee Police Department on 29 March and placed announcements in the local press with his son's picture. He heard nothing.

3. A year later, at closing time on 25 March, 1989, Jeff Dahmer met two men outside a bar called La Cage, a white man by the name of Jeffrey Connor, and a twenty-four-year-old black man named Anthony Sears. It was Sears who made the approach. Connor drove them both to the corner of 56th Street and Lincoln, in West Allis, and from there Sears and Dahmer walked to Catherine Dahmer's house, where Dahmer murdered him. His skull, scalp and genitals were discovered in Dahmer's apartment at the time of his arrest over two years later.

4. On 20 May, 1990, Dahmer met a thirty-three-year-old black man called Raymond Smith and drugged and strangled him at his apartment. One of the painted skulls found upon Dahmer's arrest was identified as Smith's.

5. On 24 June, 1990, Dahmer met a twenty-seven-year-old black man, Edward Smith, at the Phoenix Bar. They went to Dahmer's apartment by taxi, had oral sex together, then Smith was drugged and strangled. No remains of Edward Smith were ever found.

6. Outside a homosexual bookstore on North 27th Street at the beginning of September, 1990, Dahmer fell into conversation with a twenty-three-year-old black man from Chicago – Ernest Miller. Miller consented to accompany Dahmer to his apartment, where he was killed. His skull was painted and his entire skeleton kept for future use. Both were discovered on the day of Dahmer's arrest.

7. Three weeks later, Dahmer met David Thomas, a twenty-two-year-old black man, and killed him at his apartment. The following day David Thomas was taken to pieces and photographed in the process. No

remains were ever found. He was reported missing by his girlfriend on 24 September, and identified by his sister from photographs Dahmer had taken during dismemberment.

8. At 4 p.m. on 17 February, 1991, Dahmer met a seventeen-year-old black man, Curtis Straughter, and murdered him by strangulation with a leather strap. He was then dismembered. Dahmer kept his skull, hands and genitals and photographed them. They were in his apartment when he was arrested. Straughter had been reported missing by his grandmother, and his skull was identified from dental records.

9. On 7 April, 1991, a black man not long past his nineteenth birthday, Errol Lindsey, spoke to Jeffrey Dahmer at 27th Street near the homosexual bookstore, and went with him to his apartment. Lindsey was drugged and strangled. Dahmer flayed the body and kept the skin for some weeks. The skull was discovered at the time of his arrest, enabling identification through dental records.

10. Tony Hughes was a year older than Dahmer. He was black, and he was deaf and dumb. They met at the 219 Club on 24 May, and communicated by writing, although Hughes could also lip-read. The mute was drugged, strangled, and left to lie on the bedroom floor for three days. His identity was established by one of the skulls and dental records.

11. Dahmer met Konerak Sinthasomphone, the fourteen-year-old son of Laotian immigrants, outside a shopping centre known as the Grand Avenue Mall on 27 May, and offered him money to go home. Konerak accepted, and posed for two photographs in his underwear, before being drugged and murdered.

12. A month went by before Dahmer murdered again. On 30 June he went to the Gay Pride Parade in Chicago and met a twenty-year-old black man, Matt Turner, at the bus station afterwards. He invited Turner to come to Milwaukee. They travelled by

Greyhound bus, then took a taxi to the apartment, where Dahmer strangled him. Turner's head was found in the freezer, his internal organs were stuck to the freezer floor, and his torso was inside the blue drum in the bedroom.

13. One week later, again in Chicago, Dahmer met Jeremiah Weinberger, a twenty-three-year-old Puerto Rican with Jewish blood, at Carol's Gay Bar. They went by bus to Milwaukee, and then by taxi to the apartment. Weinberger was reported missing the following day, 6 July, but he was still alive and staying with Dahmer. It was not until the third day that Dahmer slew him. The improbable details of their two days together were not revealed until the trial. Weinberger's head was in the freezer, his torso in the big blue drum with Turner's.

14. On 15 July, Dahmer met Oliver Lacy, under whose name the murder investigation was filed, on 27th Street. Lacy was black and twenty-four years old. Dahmer drugged and strangled him. He took various photographs of his victim before and after decapitation. His head and skeleton were found in the freezer, his heart in the refrigerator.

15. It was four days later, on 19 July, that Dahmer encountered a white man called Joseph Bradehoft from Greenville, Illinois. Bradehoft was drugged and strangled. He was left on the bed, covered in a sheet, for two days. When Dahmer was arrested three days later, Bradehoft's head was sitting in the freezer, his torso was lying in the 57-gallon blue drum, along with Turner's and Weinberger's.

The day before Jeff Dahmer jumped off the bus to entice Joseph Bradehoft to his apartment, he had seen and spoken to Tracy Edwards, the man who would bring about his downfall. He saw him again on 20 July, the day following Bradehoft's death. It was two days later that Edwards agreed to go home with Dahmer and thereby unleash the

14

dramatic events which led to the revelations of that night, detailed above. An account of precisely how the meeting took place, why it took place, and what ensued from it, belongs to a later stage in this narrative, as we attempt to understand to what state and condition Jeff Dahmer had by then descended. As his defence counsel was to emphasise, Edwards is a crucial witness, for he alone is able to relate what Dahmer was like as he prepared to kill (although there are others, as we shall see, who spent time with the man and lived). It is for this reason that he was brought to Milwaukee to give evidence, and that he was so brutally cross-examined by counsel for the prosecution.

If the grotesque and deplorable fate of those fifteen men has been reduced to cold summary in the pages above, it is for a reason. There is much more to say about them, and it will be said. There is also much more to tell concerning the cruel indignities to which they were subjected, both before and after death, and it will be told. But these are matters which excite feelings of horror and revulsion, and such feelings are a poor basis on which to found judgement and careful appraisal of the implications. The question of Dahmer's responsibility for what he did rested upon how far he was able to control his behaviour. The prosecution would assert that he was at all times in complete control of himself and his surroundings, that he was, in short, a selfish and callous killer. The defence would agree that he was selfish, but would hold that there was nothing he could do about it, because he was in the grip of a relentless devouring compulsion. There is support for both points of view in the summaries given above. In the first place, it is clear that Dahmer chose his victims carefully and that he planned their destruction with cunning precision – the evidence for deliberation and premeditation. On the other hand, it is equally clear that the incidents multiplied in frequency until they were treading upon one another's heels in a frenzy of unfocused caprice – the evidence for compulsion. To determine which carries the greater weight, the reader must needs persevere with this catalogue of unspeakable deeds, and at the same time strive to think and feel what Dahmer might have been thinking and feeling in order to be driven to such depravity. In other words, behind the monster he must seek the man.

I realise, of course, that this is a dangerous undertaking, and there are many who will take refuge in any manner of evasions rather than face it. Far more comfortable it is to point a finger and declare a devil than to call upon one's own imagination to search into Jeffrey Dahmer's world. This is because one's imagination is a reflection of oneself, and even to admit that one may know Dahmer's world is to acknowledge his *similarity* to ourselves, instead of happily harping upon his *difference*. How else are we to understand except by teasing out these nuggets of recognition? The reader must have something of the therapist who 'draws on his own psychotic possibilities', or he will flounder in the reassuring soup of 'objectivity'.[5] It is fear which lies behind this timidity, the fear of looking at a part of the human condition which is not only frightening, but shared. As Colin Wilson has neatly put it, 'Our interest in murder is a form of stirring in our sleep.'[6]

Man is unique among the species in being sometimes driven by impulses to kill for no social or biological gain, but simply out of passion. Dahmer has frequently used the word 'lust' with reference to his offences. The ethologist Niko Tinbergen ruminated on this ultimate mystery. 'Man is the only species that is a mass murderer,' he wrote, 'the only misfit in his own society. Why should this be so?' This is obviously not a question that can be answered in a court of law, nor is it one, really, which the psychiatrist's definitions can cope with. It is primarily a philosophical question, and, as such, capable of contemplation, if not resolution, by all of us.

Erich Fromm has convincingly listed man's needs as an object of devotion, an ability to relate, a desire for unity and rootedness, the wish to be effective, and the need for stimulation. Every one of these needs may be answered

16

in a positive or a negative way. The object of devotion may be God, love, and truth; or it may be diverted into veneration of perverse idols. The need for relatedness may be satisfied by kindness and altruism; or by dependence and destructiveness. One may find rootedness and unity in brotherly co-operation and mystical experience; or one may find it in drunkenness, drug addiction, and depersonalisation.[7] In each case, Jeffrey Dahmer took the negative route.

Which raises another, perplexing issue which will be explored in its proper place. There is no doubt that Dahmer knew the difference between right and wrong – he was not a moral idiot. Much was made in court of his exercise of choices, of the contention that he had potential alternatives and repeatedly elected to embrace the wrong ones. Moral confusion is one of the salient characteristics of this kind of murderer. If Dahmer were an *amoral* man, his case would not merit investigation, for one cannot learn from a page on which nothing is writ. The fact that he is a *moral* man who has disastrously chosen to do *immoral* things makes him like the rest of us, albeit an extreme example. The difference between him and us is one of degree, not of kind. It is a disconcerting fact that the murderer often has an internal moral system which he is driven to obey; 'his ethical goal is individual, personal, and remains unseen by those around him and by himself also'.[8] Or even more provocatively, in the words of Melanie Klein, 'Love is not absent in the criminal, but it is hidden and buried in such a way that nothing but analysis can bring it to light.'[9] To find the key which unlocks that internal moral system and reveals that mysterious ethical goal is the purpose of an enquiry such as this.

Jeffrey Dahmer's motives and behaviour were certainly bizarre in the extreme, but they are not beyond the reach of comprehension. They are distinguishable from our own motives and behaviour by their severity, by their intensity, by their florid and outrageous expression, not by their essential nature. They represent one of the furthest and most lamentable extensions of human possibility, yet they are still pitifully human. Colin Wilson has devoted a large part of his career to the elucidation of this very point. 'The study of murder,' he writes, 'is not the study of abnormal human nature; it is the study of human nature stained by an act that makes it visible on the microscopic slide.'[10] This concept of *human nature stained* is one which we must strive to keep before us as we walk with Dahmer deeper into his personal hell, for there will be times when his actions stretch belief. Every human being has dark, shameful, nasty impulses – the combined inheritance of the species. They spring from Dionysian* urges of drama,

---

* Apollo and Dionysus represent antitheses in Greek mythology, and hence in human life. Originally the god of agriculture, Apollo had care of the fruits of the earth and the lower animals, then by extension of the higher animal, man himself, with especial regard to the passage of youth into manhood. He was additionally the god of prophecy, which was more often conveyed in song, thus in time the god of music and the arts generally.

Dionysus was the god of vegetation and fruitfulness, and of wine in particular. He is known in Ancient Rome as Bacchus. Dionysian festivals were characterised by orgies and excessive licence, even extending to eating the raw flesh of a just-sacrificed animal.

Hence, though both Apollo and Dionysus may be said to symbolise the fruitfulness of human character, they draw their fruit from opposing sources. Apollo, always depicted as the epitome of physical beauty and moral purity (the finest statue of him is the Apollo Belvedere in the Vatican), represents the best that human endeavour may achieve through control, order, discipline, restraint, the mastery over oneself and the plastic world. Mozart, Bach, Michelangelo, Nash, are typically Apollonian figures. On the other hand, Dionysus shows what human character may do when left to itself, unbridled, unrestrained, spontaneous and free. Raw music and passionate poetry are the province of Dionysus, and the theatre, where emotion is given bold expression, is his home. Apollo is classical undamaged beauty; Dionysus is wild, instinctive, and dangerous.

destruction and anarchy, and they have to be kept in check by the structures of civilisation, including religion and morality. That these savage irrational urges are ever-present is undeniable; so, too, is it obvious that they are mercifully constrained by self-regulation. In Dahmer's case, the constraints failed, the inhibitions collapsed, and Dionysus broke loose.

We abnegate something of our responsibility if we refuse to acknowledge Dionysus when we see him. For it is a refusal to recognise ourselves. Sitting in his cell as he awaited trial in 1983, Dennis Nilsen, who murdered fifteen men, wrote this:

> I am always surprised and truly amazed that any-one can be attracted by the macabre. The popu-lation at large is neither 'ordinary' or 'normal'. They seem to be bound together by a collective ignorance of themselves and what they are. They have, every one of them, got their deep dark thoughts with many a skeleton rattling in their secret cupboards. Their fascination with 'types' (rare types) like myself plagues them with the mystery of why and how a living person can actu-ally do things which may be only those dark images and acts secretly within them. I believe they can identify with these 'dark images and acts' and loathe anything which reminds them of this dark side of themselves. The usual reaction is a flood of popular self-righteous condemnation but a willingness to, with friends and acquaintances, talk over and over again the appropriate bits of the case.[11]

All of which might appear to be no more than the self-serving excuses of a trapped criminal, but he makes none-theless a valid point, and one that Dahmer has unwittingly echoed. Knowing nothing of Nilsen or his case, Dahmer in his confession made frequent reference to the conse-quences of having been in touch with the 'dark side' of himself, and has also commented on his astonishment that his arrest should attract so much unwanted and unthinking attention. Certainly, in Milwaukee in August of 1991 and February of 1992, there was scarcely any other topic of conversation in the coffee rooms and the bars. Most of the conversation was, however, grossly uninformed. The psychological distancing that fell like a suffocating blanket over the whole city was almost palpable. It made the attribution of hideous characteristics so much easier! The less you actually know about Jeff Dahmer, the better able you are to suppose him the unique embodiment of evil.

There was also a reluctance, long before the trial took place, to 'allow' him the refuge of insanity. Because he did not claim to hear voices or have hallucinations, did not fall into convulsions, walk into walls, or pounce upon strangers, because, in fact, he seemed perfectly ordinary, it was assumed that he was perfectly sane also. Dahmer's transparent blandness of manner and evident lack of 'mad' characteristics were undoubted handicaps in the effort made on his behalf to have his life and personality explored. He looked too good to be true. His very normalcy was insulting. Why, he could have been a footballer or a lawyer or an insurance agent! People were not prepared to imagine that insanity might be invisible. R. D. Laing once famously threw the cat among the pigeons by suggesting that the apparently sane were more dangerous than the obviously psychotic. 'When I certify someone insane,' he said, 'I am not equivocating when I write that he is of unsound mind, may be dangerous to himself and others, and requires care and attention in a mental hospital. However, at the same time, I am also aware that, in my opinion, there are other people who are regarded as sane, whose minds are as radically unsound, who may be equally or more dangerous to themselves and others and whom society does not regard as psychotic and fit persons to be in a madhouse.'[12] Something like this idea, that Dahmer, while not psychotic, was clearly mad, would eventually become a central feature of the defence

20

strategy at his trial, and one could almost watch the jury resist it. Even some of the psychiatrists called to give expert testimony steadfastly and stubbornly held to the view that he was sane.

What are the implications of such a view? Jeffrey Dahmer took a shower while there were two dead bodies in the bathtub, and he was sane. He drilled holes in the heads of living people to make them his unresisting companions, and he was sane. He ate a bicep which he had fried in a skillet, tenderised and sprinkled with sauce, and he was sane. For hours he lay with corpses, hugging them, cherishing them, and he was sane. He kept eleven assorted heads and skulls, and two complete skeletons, for eventual use in a home-made temple, and he was sane. The trouble was, in addition to all this, he was polite, diffident, deferential, obliging, just the sort of young man one could imagine weeding his grandmother's garden. That level of imagination is safe; it does not threaten one's equilibrium. To permit the imagination to travel further and visualise the hell in which Jeffrey Dahmer lived was to invite a loathsome infection. And so, despite his examination by detectives, psychologists, forensic psychiatrists, counsel, judge and jury, he was left to dwell in the private, unfathomable world in which he had always been, isolated and untouchable. To him it was genuinely a matter of indifference whether he went to prison or to a mental asylum for the rest of his life. The prison which he had been carrying around with him for years was just as fierce, just as daunting. Apartment 213 had for some years been a prison of vicious memories and visible horrors. He lived surrounded by human debris, slept among it, ate his meals beside it. 'It's just a nightmare, let's put it that way,' he said. 'It's been a nightmare for a long time, even before I was caught . . . for years now, obviously my mind has been filled with gruesome, horrible thoughts and ideas . . . a nightmare.'[13]

Dahmer waived his right to have a lawyer present during his interrogation by the police. He said he wanted to get it all off his chest, to hide nothing. Lionel Dahmer hired Gerald Boyle to represent his son, largely because Boyle already knew him, having represented him on an earlier charge in 1988. Besides, Boyle had a reputation for handling juries on a personal level in the courtroom, contriving to make them feel he was one of them, a simple guy doing a difficult job. His closing arguments were famous for their rhetorical flourish, their emotional gutsy appeal, and their common sense. Opposing him would be the District Attorney, Michael McCann, a kindly, compassionate man who felt the burden of his duty to represent the community and give expression to their outrage. He was thorough in preparation, remorseless in presentation, and only appeared unforgiving. The two men had known each other for many years, having both run for the office of District Attorney in 1968; McCann had held the post ever since.

Boyle immediately asked Dr Kenneth Smail to evaluate Dahmer and give an opinion as to his fitness to plead. Smail declared that he was fit. McCann's team, working with the detectives, set about assembling every possible detail of Dahmer's offences and character. Boyle's team concentrated on his sexual and homicidal history, to construct the portrait of a man thought to be criminally insane. Neither needed to know much about him, beyond and beneath the circumstances of his crimes. Besides which, it was said, there was not much to know. Jeff was a dull man, he had not done much, had achieved less, had little to say. His story, apart from the crimes, was devoid of event. And yet it could not be so. There would have to be some germ of his pathology, some seed out of which this poisonous tree grew. His behaviour with the men he met, and later with the men he killed, was so unusual it would need to be the product of some trauma, perhaps buried out of the reach of his conscious mind. According to one view, our sexual behaviour is the symbolic repetition of our earliest tactile being in the world, 'the ritualistic acting out of vanished realities'.[14] Dahmer's sex was so rich in symbolism and ritual, so distorted by them in

22

fact, that it was simply impossible it should derive from nowhere, that it should emerge or evolve by accident. The 'vanished realities' must be somewhere in his past, perhaps only dimly perceived and faintly graspable, but there.

Jeff Dahmer would not agree. As far as he is concerned, there is nothing to discover but boredom and despair. 'I couldn't find any meaning for my life when I was out there. I'm sure as hell not going to find it in here.' Should his story be told? He could see little point in it. 'This is the grand finale of a life poorly spent and the end result is just overwhelmingly depressing . . . it's just a sick, pathetic, wretched, miserable life story, that's all it is. How it can help anyone, I've no idea.'[15]

Chapter Two

The Child

Shortly after Lionel Herbert Dahmer and Annette Joyce Flint were married on 22 August, 1959, there were indications that this would not be an easy alliance. They began to argue and bicker almost immediately. One evening in the New Year, when the snow lay knee-deep on the ground and the icy winds from Lake Michigan sliced unhindered through the wide streets of Milwaukee, almost cutting off one's ears, Joyce walked out of the marital home, with no boots on, and went four blocks to a park. She sat shivering on a bench until Lionel came to fetch her and thereby demonstrate his love and consideration. Joyce was already pregnant at the time.*

Like many families in the beer capital of America, both Lionel and Joyce had German ancestry. Lionel's father's family had emigrated from Germany in the nineteenth century, but his mother had been born Catherine Hughes, from Wales. Which part of Germany or which part of Wales his forebears inhabited, Lionel no longer knew. Joyce's parentage was Flint and Kundberg, another

* References to Joyce Dahmer's state of mind and character are, for the most part, derived from a deposition in Lionel Dahmer's handwriting, prior to the couple's divorce proceedings in 1978. The author requested an interview with Joyce Dahmer for the purposes of balance, but was refused.

24

German name. Apart from the German blood, the newly-weds had virtually nothing else in common.

Lionel was a quiet, reserved, undemonstrative young man, studious and austere. He was studying for his Bachelor of Science degree in Chemistry at Marquette University, and was twenty-three years old. Joyce (or 'Rocky' as she preferred to be known) was just a few months older, and had been a telephone operator who had recently advanced herself by gaining a position as a teletype machine instructor. In stark contrast with her husband, she was blatantly emotional. Whereas Lionel analysed, pondered and judged, Joyce recognised truth only through feeling, and no amount of reasoned argument could dislodge her from convictions immediately reached. Both were, in different ways, self-centred people – Lionel devoted to his career and his study, with a tendency not to notice emotional fragility, Joyce dedicated to impinging her needs upon the world and having account taken of them. One could hardly imagine a finer recipe for incompatibility.

Joyce had a long training in self-pity, for which she could not be held to blame. She often said how helpless and lonely she had felt as a child, without really understanding why. She knew the emotion of abandonment very early, and only later realised that her father had appeared to be indifferent to her because he was corrupted by his illness. He was a severe alcoholic, a fact which might become significant in the story we have to tell, in so far as alcohol dependence may be hereditary. Mr Flint's drinking deflected his attention from normal family affections; his grandson's drinking would one day so suffocate his inhibitions that he became a murderer.

Joyce was now determined never to suffer neglect, and the only way she knew how was to demand unremitting regard, and to assess others by their level of response. It was as if she might no longer exist if she ceased to be the focus of someone else's eyes and ears. It was a strain for which Lionel was not adequately prepared, nor personally disposed. He, too, had a temper when roused, but he held that it should be kept in check, as a potential enemy, not brought constantly into play as an ally.

, For his part Lionel was so 'married' to his work that he spent more time in laboratories than at home, and could not help but appear neglectful to a vulnerable young wife.

Joyce became pregnant within days of their marriage, and paid a severe price for the burdens which pregnancy brought. She spent almost the whole of February and March 1960 in bed with nausea and was obliged to give up her job. Her muscles tightened so badly that the couple's physician, Dr Dean Spyres, had to give her an injection to make her relax. She complained bitterly about the noise from neighbours – the sound of anyone else's pots and pans was literally intolerable to her. At his wit's end, and naturally anxious, Lionel decided to quit the apartment for the sake of his wife's health, and they moved in with Catherine Dahmer at West Allis in March, when Joyce was seven months into her pregnancy. It is perhaps not fanciful to see in this behaviour some unconscious resentment at having to share attention with an unborn foetus; it is certainly true that Jeffrey Dahmer's mother was rendered ill by having to carry him.

The baby was born at the Evangelical Deaconess Hospital in Milwaukee at 4.34 p.m. on 21 May, 1960. Weighing 6 pounds and 15 ounces, he was 18½ inches long, with auburn hair and luminously blue eyes. (It should be said that both parents were remarkably handsome people.) Lionel and Joyce were entranced by him, their life together momentarily joyous as a result. Joyce began a baby scrap book in which his every twitch and turn were lovingly recorded, remarking that the baby 'scared us by having correctional casts on his legs from birth till four months', but all was fine. He would only need 1⅛ inch lifts on his shoes up to about the age of six. Otherwise, he was absolutely perfect. They named him Jeffrey Lionel.

The child was duly immunised against polio and smallpox (his measles inoculation would wait until he was three), and had his first accident at only a few weeks, when he fell from his spider walker, skinning his hands and cutting his chin. Dr Spyres said he would bear a small scar, thus joining the majority of mankind who bear early souvenirs of wobbly progress. Jeff's first smile was recorded at a few weeks, he first stood up unaided at six and a half months, and by the time he reached eight and a half months he was crawling and showing his first tooth. He was even spanked at nine months ('two pats on bottom') and given his first haircut. A party was given in his honour on his first birthday. All in all, it is the unremarkable advance of a pretty, healthy, normal baby, with every promise of a happy childhood ahead of him. He showed a precocious interest in animals, having a goldfish and pet turtle when only eighteen months old. Jeff was 'so very gentle with the turtle', wrote his mother, as he explored, like many a little boy, his relationship with another living creature. There would be many more to follow the turtle. On 25 November, 1961, it is recorded that Jeff walked alone for the very first time. 'I had to chase him to put him to bed,' wrote Joyce proudly.

Not everything was necessarily as it appeared, however. Joyce did not take well to breast-feeding. Keeping to the demanding schedule made her irritable and nervous, so she gave it up and bound her breasts. She and Lionel argued, and she flounced out of the house. Lionel found her lying in a field of tall grass in her nightgown, and Dr Spyres had to scold her for being so intractable and petulant.

Of course, it is true that thousands of mothers in the Western world decline to feed their offspring at the breast, and one ought not to give the event greater weight than it deserves, but it may be instructive to imagine the effect upon the child of such a sudden withdrawal of sustaining contact. Some children will take it in their stride and be comforted by the bottle. Others may feel the abrupt change in their tactile world as a kind of rejection or distance, which they are, obviously, too young to interpret.

27

Thus do the rejection and distance become incorporated, absorbed, into their view of their own place in the world, and gradually presumed natural and deserved, or just 'right'. The mother, too, may not reflect that by denying her breast to the infant she is placing self before benevolence. Jeff's early emotional development is naturally not recorded, yet it is noticeable how often, as an adult, he has said that he is not good at coping with disappointment.

The young family moved back to Milwaukee when Lionel began reading for his Master's degree in Analytical Chemistry at Marquette University. It was clearly a sensible move to be near campus, but it was Lionel's convenience then, as later, which was addressed. Joyce had to accept it. Her response was to declare the neighbours, once again, irksome. Noise of any intensity distressed her out of all proportion, especially if it was made by other people. She seemed to take it as a personal affront. Lionel was constantly having to speak to other tenants in the building to ask them to keep down their domestic rattle, to protect his wife's health, an approach which they naturally regarded as unwarranted interference. To make up to Lionel for the embarrassment, Joyce was a most fastidious housekeeper, making sure that everything was in place and pleasant. She did expect praise for the effort, however. She needed perpetual reassurance that she was, indeed, loved.

By the time Jeff was two years old he was talking. He called himself 'Jeffy' and held fingers up to indicate his age. He could say 'potty', 'Up pease', and 'TV', and within a few more months had memorised his first prayer. (Lionel was a committed and devout Lutheran.) The words of the prayer were, 'Now lay me down to sleep, I pray the Lord my soul to keep. God bless everyone. Make Jeffy a good boy. Amen.'

In 1962 Lionel gained his M.Sc. degree and was accepted at Iowa State University to do postgraduate work towards a doctorate of philosophy. This involved another upheaval for the family, as they had to move again. They found a small house in Ames, Iowa, and took it. At first, it was almost entirely bare of furniture (the apartment in Milwaukee had been rented furnished), but Jeff didn't seem to mind. He was 'completely content in his bare room with doggie, muggsie, and his bed', wrote Joyce; the references are to soft toys which Aunt Eunice, Lionel's sister, had bought for him. There was also a brand new pet in Jiffy the Squirrel, who came to the window-sill looking for food, and did not run away. Mother and son were photographed pointing at Jiffy; this kind of nature-fun did not happen in urban Milwaukee, and the child was fascinated. Soon he was watching all kinds of small animals and insects to see what they would do.

When Jeff went to nursery school in Ames, he was, says his mother, very shy. This is a word she would have cause to use many times in the future. Because he was called 'new boy' all the time, he imagined that such was his adopted name in this strange surrounding. The teacher gave him a pet grey mouse, but this was insufficient to conquer his timidity, and he did not care for school in the slightest. It seemed he had difficulty relating to other boys, that he did not quite know how to belong; he was awkward, ill at ease. He had trouble getting his boots on and off, and the teacher would not help him. The frustration made him cry.

At the end of 1963, he was treated for an ear infection and mild pneumonia, and his parents were told that an eye would have to be kept on his hernia condition – an operation might become necessary. Meanwhile, there was a lovely Christmas, at which Lionel dressed up as Santa Claus to the intense delight of little Jeff, who touched his beard and tummy wonderingly. A few weeks afterwards, however, it was obvious that the hernia needed treatment, and the little boy was taken to hospital in a state of some apprehension. As it happened, it was necessary to perform a double hernia operation, which would be harsh enough for an adult and was quite terrifying to a four-year-old. Jeffrey remembers being in the hospital with several other

29

children watching a programme called *Bewitched*; this was presumably before the operation. Surgery was performed on 19 March, 1964.

When he recovered from the anaesthetic, all he would be aware of was intense pain in the groin. Twenty-seven years later, he told Dr Judith Becker that the pain was so great he thought his genitals must have been cut off. Indeed, that is precisely how it would feel, and one wonders how much was explained to him. Apparently he asked his mother if he still had his private parts, although we do not know what she replied. In her diary, she noted that Jeff was 'so good in hospital . . . [but] he really disliked the doctor after this ordeal'. Joyce spent as much time as she could with him. At night, he would say to her, 'You can go home now, Mommy, I'll sleep.' The pain lasted for about a week. He never forgot it. One may well wonder, in view of the boy's later disturbance and the florid nature of its manifestation, whether this operation was perhaps disproportionately significant in his life. The deep cut in a sensitive area, the exploration of his inside, the feeling that foreign hands were invading his privacy, would all find uncomfortable echoes at a later date. For a very long time, this would be the most intimate event of his life.

The boy was by no means friendless, but he remained curiously shy. Sometimes it broke Joyce's heart to send him to school, looking so forlorn and frightened – he would sometimes cry. She moved him into Whittier School at the age of five, where he caught the daily school bus with a boy called Kent. After school and at weekends, together with other boys he explored the neighbourhood. It was a low-income area, with a long tunnel under the bridge which they liked to explore because it was dark and spooky. He had one black friend and one white, who lived across the railroad tracks; he had to walk under the tunnel to get to them. The houses were spread out, with large distances between them, and many of them were deserted and derelict, as if nobody wanted to live there any more. The temptation to be naughty with impunity by throwing bricks through the windows of empty houses, and then running for one's life, was too much to resist, and one day the police came to the Dahmers' door to complain that young Jeff was one of a gang of tearabouts. Lionel and Joyce were ashamed. They scolded him, and that was that. He was not thrashed.

'When I was a little kid I was just like anybody else,' he now says.[1] He spent a lot of time playing in apple trees or on piles of coal, would come home filthy, covered in coal dust, and earn another scolding. On the outskirts of Ames, Iowa, was a research centre where all kinds of barnyard animals were kept for study, and Jeff would often spend time in there watching and staring. With hindsight he worked out that it was some kind of radiation testing place, but at the time it was just a magical world of living creatures. The men who worked there wore rubber gloves right up to their armpits, and he once saw a man with his arm right inside a cow's rear end. Then one day he spotted a large, long deserted building, the steps of which were littered with dead mice and rats. Curiosity overcame him. 'I walked up and wanted to see if the door was unlocked. I pushed the door open. I've never seen so many rats and mice running for the corners in my life. The whole floor was complete movement, it was just covered with them. I ran out of there pretty quick. They came out of the door, too.'[2]

In a crack in one of the deserted buildings Jeff found a hornets' nest. He told a little black neighbourhood boy to put his hand in there and see what he found, there might be ladybugs. The boy obliged and was seriously stung, running home to tell his mother he had been bitten by ladybugs. 'It was a rotten thing to do. That was when I was four or five, I think.'[3]

Still, his fascination with animals and insects grew unabated. Snakes, toads, crabs, turtles, fish, wild rabbits, and a kitten called Buff fed his curiosity and imagination. Once he was riding on a bicycle with his father through a parking lot on the research centre when they spotted what looked like a ball of dust. At least that's what Lionel said it was. But Jeff knew better and looked closer – it was a baby nighthawk. They took it home and raised it. 'It was almost like a pet. It would come back when you called it, eat out of your hand and stuff like that. We called him "Dusty".' The bird stayed until it was strong enough to fly, and then, said Joyce, 'it responded to our whistle even after it was gone three days'.

At about the same time, Jeff found some bones under the house, in what is called the 'crawlspace', and thought them altogether astonishing. He called them his 'fiddlesticks', and played with them endlessly. When he held some of his animals, he could feel their 'fiddlesticks' inside, and wondered if they looked the same.

1966 was an important year for the whole family. In the first place, Joyce's hypersensitivity, depression, and need for arguments were increasing. She would make a fuss over trivia in order to earn the pleasure of reconciliation with her husband. She began to take pills to calm herself down, and double the dosage when they failed to give her the peace she desired. There was even an occasion when she may have tried to commit suicide with an overdose of Seconal, but it is just as likely that she threw them down her throat without proper care. She then turned to Equanil three times a day. Joyce was progressively becoming a desperate woman, and her consumption of medicines would increase alarmingly over the next few years. She felt that Lionel was too wrapped up in his studies to notice how difficult life could be, or how nice she made the house for him. Lionel, to be fair, was ridiculously overworked, not only reading for his doctorate, but doing the shopping as well, since Joyce did not have a driving licence. He also did some of the housework when she was laid low with nervous exhaustion and pills. Jeff sometimes saw his father hit his mother when she was screaming and he felt she needed to be calmed, but never brutally and never with malice. The domestic scene was by no means unusual or malignant. Oddly, however, the teacher's report from the school at Ames stated, without giving any evidence, that she thought Jeff felt neglected. Perhaps the rows were so absorbing of energy and concentrated on themselves that a third-party witness, especially a child, may have felt himself to be superfluous.

Joyce then found two solutions to her problems. (One has the impression that Joyce, the more vulnerable and brittle partner, usually had to work her own way out of depression and make decisions to which Lionel mildly assented, yet her personality was hardly sound enough to bear the consequences of decision-making.) First, she discovered the Church of Christ, and had both herself and her husband baptised in that faith. This, said Lionel, made their life together more equable. Second, she told Lionel that she wanted another child. Perhaps he weighed the alternatives, that the strain of extra responsibility might overwhelm her, that on the other hand the joy might replenish her spirit. Whatever the case, it was always easier to acquiesce, and Lionel wanted a quiet life. So they abandoned protection, and Joyce quickly found herself pregnant again.

At the same time, Lionel received his doctorate and began looking for a job. He found an appointment as research chemist with Pittsburgh Plate and Glass Company, but it was in Ohio, and the family would need to get up and go again. For Jeff, this meant giving up his pets, whom he knew he would not see again. The cat Buffy had to be sold. He told neither his mother nor his father what were his feelings about this, nor did he ever talk about them. Jeffrey Dahmer was becoming progressively more withdrawn, remote, private. The combined inheritance of his father's aloofness and his mother's morose sensitivity were beginning to cancel his own personality, to negate it, as it were, before its development was complete. Like his mother, he was dangerously self-centred; like his father, he was unnaturally reticent. He became silent and broody as a result.

For the moment, however, the anticipation of a new brother deflected Jeff's absorption with himself. He was anxious it should be a boy, so that he could play with him, and, wrote Joyce to his grandparents, 'he has very definite ideas about names'. Joyce would hold his head close to her stomach, that he might feel the baby, and Jeff would pat her tummy 'so that the baby will know it has a brother'. Indeed, he appears to have been excited at the prospect of the birth, and thanked her fulsomely for being pregnant!

The Dahmers moved to Doylestown, Ohio, in October 1966, and her second child, a boy, was born on 18 December. It was Jeff, now six years old, who chose the name for his brother – David. Both before and after the birth, Joyce was laid low with depression, which somewhat undermined the joyfulness of the occasion, and Jeff noticed the gloom in the house. He had, however, a new interest in Frisky, a cheerful and playful dog which his parents got for him to compensate for the loss of the pets he left behind. 'That was nice to have a companion like that,' he recalled. 'We'd go out and play in the fields, run around, she was a good dog to have.' He was not jealous of his new brother in the smallest degree. Joyce feared he might be. 'More adjusting for Jeff,' she wrote, 'but he loves Davy and is good to him. Frisky comes first in his heart, though. They really romp and play.'

The sojourn in Doylestown did not last long. Once again, Joyce said she could not stand the noise the neighbours made, and they would have to move. (It was a rural area, so the neighbours would have to be pretty loud to be heard at all.) She begged Lionel to get her more pills when she had run out, clutching his wrists and saying she could not survive without them. Worried and obedient, Lionel found a house for rent in Barberton, Ohio, and the family moved in a few months after having arrived in Doylestown. Fortunately, Jeff did not have to leave Frisky behind. The new neighbours (whom Joyce apparently accepted) built a dog house in the back yard for Frisky.

Jeff did not care for school in Barberton, and was not

good at giving his trust to a whole new set of friends. There did take place, however, an incident which is of interest for several reasons. A number of boys were 'horsing around' and it was suggested, wholly in jest, that they should try and see what it was like to choke one another. This is a common enough game among infants, and offers them an opportunity for intimate tactile contact while avoiding the embarrassment of seeking affection. It is even, in its embryonic way, a sexual experience – the hands on the neck, the closeness of the breath, the feeling of danger and secrecy, the anticipation of rebuke – though never, of course, recognised as such by the infants. One little boy, whom Jeff regarded as friendly, invited him to pretend to strangle him, and promised that he would not tell the teacher. So Jeff put his hands around the boy's neck, and squeezed. The other boy went straight to the teacher and reported him, whereupon Jeff received ten whacks with a paddle on the backside. There is no suggestion, here or anywhere, that young Dahmer derived any more pleasure from the experience than as a schoolboy prank. What matters is the bestowal of trust, which is then rejected as non-serious or unworthy. Dahmer remembers that he felt 'betrayed'.

A salient characteristic of the schizoid personality is the total inability to offer trust to anyone, for fear of its being misprized, scorned, or even received and accepted, for then the donor becomes vulnerable and exposed. It is already clear that the young Dahmer was showing signs which could be interpreted as schizoid. An understanding of trust develops slowly in the child from the first day of life, through trial and error, and enables him to realise his place in the world and his responsibilities towards it. Decline into a totally trust-free, isolated, schizoid state is rare, but its seeds are easily sown, and its crop can be devastating.

There was a teacher at school in Barberton whom Jeff liked. 'I kind of got attached to her, so I thought I'd catch some tadpoles and give them to the teacher as a present.

35

She said thank you and acted like she thought it was a great gift, so that made me happy.' In school a day or two later, he couldn't see them in class. 'I wondered where the tadpoles had gone. She used to keep them on the window-ledge in the school, and then they were gone. I just figured she had taken them home or something.' He then went to see a friend his own age who lived behind the house, and there, in the garage, were the tadpoles, in the very same container. He could hardly believe it. He felt betrayed again, then angry. He poured motor-oil into the container and killed all the tadpoles. 'If she doesn't want them, no one will have them,' he thought. Again, it is not the obvious value of the incident which matters – the two boys were friends again within days and the tactless teacher was ignored – but its cumulative, secret, subterranean effect.

The principal family treat at this time was to go out for a drive on Sundays. Mostly, this was to pacify Joyce, who would otherwise be stuck in the house without respite, but the boys enjoyed it as well. On one such drive they went to Bath, Ohio, and by chance saw a house for sale, which Joyce fell in love with on sight. They had to have it! So Lionel borrowed money from the bank and they bought 4480 West Bath Road and took up residence in 1968. It was their third move in two years, and their sixth address since marriage. Joyce was thrilled. Jeff, too, was delighted, because he could take Frisky with him, and there were woods around and a pond. He thought it was a great place to live. Here, at last, was somewhere they could stay and build a stable future. It was to remain their home for ten years, until the marriage finally foundered and Jeffrey's descent into uncharted waters was under way.

The Bath Road house was enchantment itself after the various makeshift homes the family had recently occupied. It was truly rural, surrounded by nature and air and peace. It was also large, representing a significant step up the social scale for the Dahmers. There was every prospect of happiness and stability in such an idyllic spot. Lionel built a chicken coop so that they could raise chickens and have their own supply of fresh eggs. Jeff participated in this adventure, and also helped raise sheep, rabbits and ducks on the land around the house. Frisky roamed the woods and brought home a dead woodchuck. Joyce went about making the house as pleasant and charming as it could be.

Jeff seemed to take to country life quite eagerly, as long as not much was expected of him. He went to the Lehrs' house nearby to take sled rides with their son Steven, a year younger than himself, and once took over Steve's newspaper delivery round when he went on holiday. He was not interested in applying for a round himself, however. Lionel was becoming anxious that his son appeared rarely to be interested in anything, save solitary pursuits which were secret and inviolate. There were times when Jeff was in a world of his own. Lionel knew that he would have to take the initiative, one day, to shake the boy out of this apparent lethargy. Possibly, he left it too late; he ought to have spent time with him long before.

At Eastview Junior High School Jeff made a number of friends on a superficial level, and played cornet in the school band for a while. He habitually sat at the lunch table with Bill Henry, Greg Rogerson, and David Borsvold, but was regarded by the others as slightly odd, 'a smart kid, but really bizarre', or simply 'nice, quiet, reserved'. He did not fit readily into a gang or group, did not appear to enjoy group activity very much. 'I was never one to go out and voluntarily play football and baseball or anything like that,' he recalled. 'Group sports just didn't interest me.' With David Borsvold, however, he found an interest they could share. Both boys were fascinated with geology and pre-history. They collected rocks and sought out pictures of dinosaurs. Not even Jeff realised, then, that the drawings of dinosaur skeletons and bones answered to something deep in his psyche which other boys could not share and would never suspect. David and Jeff visited often, riding their bikes to each other's houses. They competed in preparing projects for the Science Fair, David concentrating on dinosaurs and Jeff on the various kinds of moulds and fungus he found in the woods on his property. During the Science Fair week, the display case was proudly shown in the hallway.

After a while, Jeff felt he knew David well enough to bring him into part of his private little world. In his solitary moments, which were frequent, he had dreamt up a game involving stick men and spirals. The stick men were spindly figures who would be annihilated if they came too close to one another, as each boy manipulated his little army. The spirals were tightly drawn, intensely imagined symbols of descent, whose ultimate destination was a black hole. He called the game 'Infinity Land'. He was about nine years old at the time, and must not be credited with any major concept, but it is alarming that he should have used such a name for this childish exercise, and with hindsight it is possible to discern signs of which he was entirely unaware. The stick men were fleshless; they were not conceived with the full contours of people, but with the bare essence of bone. Their danger lay in closeness; any contact resulted in oblivion, suggesting that intimacy was the ultimate disaster and the severest risk. The oblivion was represented by the black hole of infinity, an abject, featureless, hopeless nothingness, which, perhaps, the infant already saw when he gazed into himself. Or perhaps he saw it as the danger facing anyone who got near him.

All of which is, of necessity, fanciful, for we cannot know whence the boy dredged this curious game; we can only conjecture, and must do so. The drawings clearly betray an airless personality, suffocating and introverted, positively trapped. Dahmer fantasised about Infinity Land for years, enjoying it by himself, telling nobody. Later, he shared it only with David, who joined innocently in a game which was preparing for the destruction of a personality. David was the first person ever to enter into

Dahmer's fantasy life, albeit merely at the edge. He was also the last to do so voluntarily.

One evening the four Dahmers had chicken for dinner. They usually ate together as a family, whatever tensions may have been hovering in the air. Jeff asked his Dad what would happen if they were to take the chicken bones that were left over and put them in bleach. Lionel Dahmer thought this was commendable scientific curiosity, and it made him happy to see Jeff show initiative. He prepared a pan and placed the chicken bones in bleach, while Jeff watched, silently, unblinking. He was then ten years old.

At around this time, in 1970, Joyce Dahmer's fragile health collapsed. She had been steadily increasing her consumption of drugs, taking eight Equanil per day, as well as laxatives and sleeping pills. Her body began to shake uncontrollably. It was difficult to tell why she should be so unhappy as to want to blot herself out all the time. Lionel was not as attentive as some men, but then neither was he a philanderer. 'It just didn't seem like the parents really liked each other too much,' recalled Jeff. 'It made me feel on edge, unsure of the solidity of the family. I decided early on I wasn't ever going to get married 'cause I never wanted to go through anything like that.'

It was by no means all black. They used to go on hikes together, putting notches on a staff to indicate how many miles they had walked; and they would drive to nurseries to buy plants for the garden. But behind it all was the threat of tension, and the certainty that Joyce would not be able to cope with it. 'When she was on the medication, which seemed like years to me, most of the time she'd be too tired to do anything . . . she just seemed to be in bed most of the time we were in Bath.' David Dahmer confirms that the atmosphere in the house was bad, and that a good deal of shouting and hurling of objects occurred. The children, however, were never attacked. They simply observed and waited. Eventually, Joyce was taken to hospital, where she spent a month in a mental ward. This was followed by twenty-two sessions of psychotherapy over a period of a further month. The ingestion of pills, however, did not significantly abate.

Jeff's response was classic. He blamed himself for his mother's illness. He had known for as long as he could remember that she had been depressed following his birth, and that he had therefore caused the illness. He also must have caused every relapse. He could not articulate his pain, for fear of tipping his mother over the edge again. He had to keep himself to himself, say little and do less, to protect her, to keep a little calm in the house. The more she saw of him the worse it would be for her. His brother David said, '[Jeff] never learned to be open with his feelings of frustration . . . he went out to the forest by himself and cut down trees for firewood.' They could hear him slamming against tree trunks from inside the house. It sounded like vented anger (and would so be interpreted by one of the psychiatrists at Dahmer's trial), but it was more likely the solace of utter isolation. Jeff quite simply felt he did not belong, and that if he were to belong he would only do harm.

This early sense of alienation is a common feature of many men who become compulsive murderers. Joseph Kallinger, whose case was exhaustively studied by Flora Rheta Schreiber in *The Shoemaker*, said, 'I had a lack of feeling that I was a part of anybody – or that anybody was a part of me.'[4] The notorious torturer Leonard Lake, arrested in San Francisco in 1985, similarly felt himself to be outside of life, watching. (He committed suicide while in custody.) So did the boastful 'serial killer' Henry Lee Lucas, arrested in Texas in 1983, whose mother was psychiatrically impaired. They all felt in some way adrift, disconnected from the universe inhabited by everyone else, all those people who *belong* together and who are bonded. They are apart and alone. They live in an emotional no-man's-land. Jeff Dahmer, bashing trees in the forest with only the echo to accompany him, was on his way towards the same dead end.

The strange character of Meursault in Albert Camus' novel *L'Etranger* is a literary echo. This short but compelling story became the almost sacred text of a generation devoted to the notion of the 'absurd' and one's duty to do battle with it, but from our point of view it is the alienation of the central character which illuminates. Meursault kills a man on the beach in Algeria for no particular reason; he is bored, and the man was there. He is indifferent to his arrest and trial, almost like an impartial spectator. He also hardly notices his mother's funeral; it demands as much of his attention as the need for a cigarette. It is not that Meursault is callous and cruel, simply that he does not fit. He cannot respond as other people do, either morally or emotionally, because his moral and emotional development has been blocked. He doesn't care because he *can't* care – he is separate from the world of affection and regard.

To be part of that world, the child must feel that his existence is beneficent, productive of good. If it is not, then he should withdraw. Jeff Dahmer withdrew and soon afterwards began to indulge private fantasies which festered and destroyed both himself and those who came too close to him. It is virtually impossible to exaggerate the dangers of this kind of withdrawal (unless, of course, it promotes the creative isolation of the artist, who is, in this respect, the antithetical twin of the murderer). If the child grows into a man who cannot relate in any obvious way, he will find an aberrant way to relate, through cruelty, or sadism, or control, or ultimately through destruction. Complete isolation, that of having no effect whatever, becomes in the end unbearable.[5]

An anonymous patient articulates the problem in this way: 'I've been sort of dead in a way. I cut myself off from other people and became shut up in myself. And I can see that you become dead in a way when you do this. You have to live in the world *with* other people. If you don't something dies inside.'[6] And this is Dahmer's own reflection: 'I don't even know if I have the capacity for normal emotions or not because I haven't cried for a long time. You just stifle them for so long that maybe you lose them, partially at least. I don't know.'[7]

The fact that Jeff had not been troublesome or demanding as an infant ought not to earn surprise. Most babies are troublesome and demanding – it is their way of finding their impact upon others and the limits to their exploitation of it. It is simply a manifestation of being alive. The child who does not ask for attention, whether or not because he has learnt not to expect it, betrays an inner deadness which can be mistaken for goodness and sweetness of character. Now, Jeffrey Dahmer is adamant that no blame should attach to his parents for what he did, even indirectly. He is fierce in their defence, and has told everyone who has dealt with him that the fault for his crimes lies entirely and solely with him. In a way, he still holds himself responsible for his mother's instability, and wants at all costs to protect her from interference. There is, it is true, no overt instance of ill-treatment in the family history, and it must be said clearly that nobody supposes one to be hidden. But who knows how the young Jeff Dahmer *felt* about his role with a self-absorbed mother and distant, busy father? Certainly not he. The intensity of the inner resistance against full self-knowledge is unfathomable.

Nevertheless, it was becoming increasingly obvious by the time he was eleven or twelve that his withdrawal ought to be reversed. Lionel tried everything to engage his attention, awake his energy. He taught him tennis, and played many a match with him. But Jeff's heart was not in the game, and schoolfriends gained the impression that he was 'pushed' into it. He joined the Scouts for a short period, a reluctant recruit. 'I didn't want to join Boy Scouts, but my folks figured it would be good to get me interested in something,' he said. They sent him off to a ranch, where Scouts go backpacking in the wilderness for two weeks. 'We had to tie up the food between two trees so the bears wouldn't get it.' All of which sounds exciting and enticing, but Jeff behaved for the most part as if he was not there. His apathy extended even to self-expression. 'It was very hard to get anything out of him,' said his brother David, who also remembered Jeff talking in a level monotone from an early age. Lionel had the impression that Jeff was distressed to see the lambs they had reared go off to slaughter, but it could only be an impression. 'Jeff never showed much emotion outside.' The boy had already entered his self-made prison.

Once there, he proceeded gradually to cement the ramparts and make his refuge impregnable. He continued passively to acquiesce in his father's attempts to enliven him, but saw little purpose in them. As for his mother, she appeared to have 'switched off' and was cherishing her own separate refuge in sedatives. Sometimes, when Jeff came home from school at the end of the day, his mother was still in bed, and it looked as if she had not stirred since morning. The threads which bound mother and son, never very strong, had virtually worn away to nothing. They inhabited the same house, ate at the same table, but kept their own counsel. About Joyce, there was an air of desperation, almost panic, in dealing with the manifold little crises of daily life; about Jeff, an awesome air of secretiveness.

As he entered puberty, Jeff Dahmer was not especially curious or anxious about the changes in his emotional responses, probably because they were muted. Whereas most boys would hurl themselves into the expression of these new feelings by way of a passionate friendship or dramatic display of loyalty, Dahmer sat on the edge of the experience, bewildered and untouched. There was no 'best friend' to link arms with, share sniggers, or be proud of being seen with. He was already, perhaps, beyond reach.

With one neighbourhood boy, Eric Tyson, he did have some desultory physical exploration. At ten, Eric was three years younger than Jeff, but somewhat precocious in his appetites. Significantly, it was Eric who took the initiative, and Jeff who merely acquiesced. They had often been together, fishing and hiking, and they had a tree-house or fortress to which they sometimes repaired. It was there that Eric suggested they undress. The two boys touched and kissed and caressed, but went no further. They met here on three or four occasions, until the fear of discovery made them desist. As far as pubescent adventures go, it was a pretty mild one. Dahmer's emotions were never engaged, though he did find that he was interested in seeing Eric's body; it was surely the object, not the person, which caught his enthusiasm.

Everybody noticed a change in him between Junior High School at Eastview, and Senior High at Revere. To begin with, he put on some weight, and it was not immediately evident why this should be so. What was not known until later is that Jeff, from about the age of fourteen according to his brother, had started drinking. Whether he peered into himself and was alarmed by what he saw, it would be idle to speculate now; he certainly does not remember. Or whether it was the creeping isolation which he knew was too profound to be remedied and yet recognised was unusual. Apathy appeared to overwhelm him, and alcohol was its only antidote. Friends in high school noticed that he was not socially accepted. He was one of the 'class clowns' who would make a fool of himself, apparently in an effort to gain attention. One of his pranks was to bleat like a sheep in class and upset the equilibrium of discipline. Or he would fake an epileptic fit, or trip over an invisible object, or spit out his food and pretend to be sick. In a store, he would 'act retarded', knock items off the counter, and generally make an embarrassing scene. This is the kind of behaviour one might expect of an insecure young man in despair over his lack of contact with his fellows, imploring them for some notice and attention. In Dahmer's case it is rather more worrying. He has given up on the idea of contact and already secreted himself from the world. The new character he now displays to the world, that of the unpredictable prankster, is an

invention manufactured the better to conceal and sub-
merge his real self beyond detection.

The friendship with David Borsvold had come to an
abrupt end the previous year on the intervention of Mrs
Borsvold, who thought Jeff to be a dangerous companion
for her son. The excuse given, apparently, was that some
homosexual attachment might evolve, but since there was
little evidence for such a suspicion, it is more likely
Dahmer's oddness and separateness alarmed her. His
friendship with Bill Henry was also superficial rather than
committed. The school librarian and one or two of the
teachers observed his lack of social adhesion, and were
concerned.

At home, in solitude, he discovered the solace of masturbation, and indulged himself on a daily basis. There is
no evidence that it was as yet accompanied by any particular fantasies.

Schoolwork suffered under attacks from apathy, alcohol
and acting the fool, and his grades plummeted. He was
obviously a bright and intelligent boy, which made his
determined failures harder to excuse. Lionel and Joyce
hired a private tutor in an attempt to bring him up to
scratch, but the effort was not rewarded. It seemed that
Jeff was slipping away on his own piece of driftwood.

There was a small hut next to the Bath Road house
where Jeff could be utterly alone. Eric Tyson occasionally
looked for him there and noticed a number of skeletons
of small animals – chipmunks, squirrels, birds – obviously
looked after with care. There was also a moth collection,
and jars of formaldehyde containing preserved insects.
(Some of these jars were kept in Jeff's bedroom.) Beside
the hut was a small graveyard dedicated to the burial of
animals, with small crosses and real animal skulls hanging
from the crosses. David Dahmer knew about the animal
graveyard and thought his brother was 'doing a good service' by burying dead creatures. Once, Jeff wanted to
show him what he was learning in biology and produced
a dead mole. He proceeded to cut the mole open and

45

remove the heart and liver which he then put in formalde-hyde. On another occasion he had helped dissect a baby pig in biology class and prevailed upon the teacher to let him take the head home. Alone in the garage, he removed the skin and flesh and kept the skull of this pig.

Nobody suspected anything sinister in these activities. On the contrary, they appeared at last to indicate a proper interest in something, which could be nurtured and encouraged. Curiosity was a sign of some spark of life in the boy, and there were many others of his age whose curiosity led ultimately to intellectual enquiry. If his future lay in applied biology, that would be no bad thing. Lionel Dahmer was actually grateful that there should be one subject at school which gripped his son, for the boy's grades in everything else were lamentable, and he was beside himself as to how to pressure him into improving his performance. This might be the answer. But Jeff's interest in dead animals was beginning to proceed beyond mere curiosity into a kind of hypnotic fascination. He was starting to look out for 'road-kills', animals which had collided with cars on the wide country highways, and bring them home. He did this several times over the next two years, cutting them open down the front to see what they looked like inside.

Jeffrey Dahmer never killed an animal himself. It is frequently the case that people who grow into multiple murderers have evolved from sadistic children, and cruelty to animals in childhood is a common characteristic shared among them. Dahmer's case is different in this regard as in most others. He displayed no cruelty, and was not interested in watching an animal suffer or react to pain. His experiments were always with corpses. The boy who is cruel towards a living animal is testing his power to hurt and be effective, to relate to another creature, with torture rather than tenderness to be sure, but relate nevertheless. Incipient sadism is therefore relatively easy to spot. Dahmer was not aroused by the infliction of pain upon a *living* creature, but entirely by the cold, mechanical dissection of a *dead* one. Even sadism, though brutal and selfish, is an expression of life, and the sadist looks for response from a sentient being – it is the soul which quickens his interest and which he seeks to hurt. Jeff Dahmer was not excited by the soul or the senses, but by the mechanics – he wanted to see how an animal *works*. He might even, having taken it apart, try to reconstruct it. This obsession with the machine of life in preference to life itself is typical of the necrophile.

The road-kills included dogs, foxes, an opossum. Once he carried home the corpse of a very large dog, something like a St Bernard, left it in the yard or the woods just beyond and waited for the flesh to rot off, then collected the bones and bleached them. He intended to put them together again, but never got around to it. The corpse of another dog was destined to be known all over America many years later. Jeff found it and took it home, then 'I wanted to see what the insides looked like, so I cut it open'.[8] He later stuck the dog's skull on a pole in the woods, as some kind of tentative ritualistic gesture, barely understood, and left it to the elements. Not long afterwards, some neighbours, Jim Klippel with his girlfriend and his little four-year-old brother, were hiking in the woods when they came upon the grisly spectacle. Klippel saw that the dog's body was hanging from the broken branch of a pine tree; it had been completely gutted, its intestines draped around the tree. A little apart was the head impaled on a stick. They were sorely shaken by the sight, as well they might be. But Klippel told his friend, Clark Secard, who went into the woods the next day with a camera and photographed it; this was the picture which would be published in the nation's press when Jeffrey Dahmer was arrested sixteen years afterwards.

Throughout this period of experimentation, he remained loyal to his own dog Frisky, who was now eight years old. It never once occurred to him to harm Frisky, nor indeed to examine the corpse of any dog that he knew personally. There was an occasion when Frisky was playing with the neighbour's dog. 'It stood about as tall as this table, short fur, looked like a Doberman, real friendly dog. My dog was chasing it into the street and this car came by and both dogs were together, right next to each other, and that car slammed into the big dog and just missed mine by that much. Boy, did I feel lucky.'[9] Jeff reported the accident to the neighbours who owned the dog, but he did not yearn to dissect it in any way.

When he was sixteen, Jeff grew even further apart from his colleagues at school. Bill Henry, Greg Rogerson, they all gradually fell by the wayside. It was, of course, Jeff's own fault that this happened. He was more and more morose, sullen, uncommunicative; and more and more drunk. Schoolboys are quite impressed by the occasional display of alcoholic excess as a badge of adulthood, but constant drunkenness, though they would scarcely admit it, frightens them. Jeff Dahmer's frequent stupors made them feel insecure in his presence, and they avoided him. All except one. It was now that he made a new friend in somebody as keen to blot out the present as he was. Jeff Six was also sixteen and was one of Revere High School's suppliers of marijuana. He met Dahmer during the lunch period one day and offered him a smoke. From then on they would drink and smoke together every day, drinking 'until our noses would get numb' as Jeff Six put it, and smoking pot to transport themselves into giggly indifference. This new friendship suited Dahmer well enough, because it involved neither emotional commitment nor contact with the real world. The dope and the alcohol were a passport to unreflective bliss, and the schoolwork came virtually to a halt.

Jeff Six had one habit of which Dahmer did not approve. He loved to drive fast, and 'his big thrill was to find a dog that was walking in the road and speed up real fast and hit it. It just amazed me. In one day he went through four dogs. How many dogs just walked into the road in front of him . . . he'd speed up real fast and just tick them off. The last one was this little puppy that walked into the road and I remember it was horrible, he speeded up real fast and the dog just went flipping over the top of the hood and I looked back and I could see it running off with this terrified look in its face. I don't know how badly hurt it was, but pretty badly. That just sickened me. I told him to take me back and let me out.'[10]

He never forgot the reproachful eyes of that frightened puppy. The eyes are the harbingers of guilt, for they force an impromptu, involuntary recognition of the life they reflect. Dr Hyatt Williams in London once treated a murderer who was haunted by the memory of a wounded turtle-dove that he had drowned to put it out of its misery, but which had looked at him with surprised, uncomprehending eyes before he completed the task.[11] The fact that Jeff Dahmer remembered the eyes of that wounded dog almost permits one to place the last moment when he could have been saved from the collapse of his psyche, for that was the moment when a flicker of responsive sentiment still stirred within him, and was brought to flame by one little tragedy. Thereafter it weakened and dwindled until it was finally extinguished. One of his victims in 1991 died with his eyes open, but then it was far too late for the reproach in them to register; Dahmer merely noted it was peculiar, because all the others had their eyes closed.

The relationship with Jeff Six was entirely restricted to the sharing of drugs. At the age of seventeen, Dahmer was still sexually untried and emotionally barren. His tentative exploration of Eric Tyson's body had been four years earlier, and in the interim he had formed no intimate relationships nor attempted any sexual conquest; nor, for that matter, had anyone shown sexual interest in him. Girls did not appear to notice him, although he was attractive enough, with his shock of blond hair. The affections between his parents were now completely dead, and had been so more or less since Joyce had made Lionel sleep alone in the den. Matters had deteriorated to such an extent that they only responded to each other by verbal abuse. 'Our hearts grew hard to the situation,' said David

Dahmer, then eleven years old. Just how hard his brother's had become he could not have suspected.

There was a school visit to an anatomical museum in Cleveland which may have had an influence upon at least one pupil which far exceeded the intentions of the teachers. Jeff Dahmer gazed at the horizontal sections of the human body, revealing how everything was placed inside, how it all worked, and was transfixed with wonder. It was akin to his own experiments with road-kills, those moments when he had been close, so close to the most secret and personal part of another creature, the inside of him, the source and well of his very being, the engine which made the clock tick. Now he could see those intimate parts of a human's inside as well, there in the museum, visible to all, but only truly seen by him. The rest probably did not realise how important such a moment could be, they did not appreciate it. They had not travelled down this road, so how could they know? Jeff absorbed the sights before him.

At the same time, the frequency of his masturbation had been growing steadily, until it sometimes exceeded three times a day. Such is not remarkable for many a seventeen-year-old, burdened with a greedy libido which must be satisfied somehow. But most have by then found ways to explore the sexual mysteries with another; those who are left to their own devices are a fertile breeding-ground for fantasy. Jeff Dahmer had discovered that there were magazines devoted to the display of naked males, and he managed to procure some. These he used as masturbatory aids, gazing at the pictures which aroused him most, usually photographs of muscular torsos and hairless chests. The chest and the abdomen were the areas whereon he fixed his eyes as he masturbated, and the fantasy of one day holding a chest like that, being with it, possessing it, took shape in his mind. It was not the person to whom the body belonged that mattered – indeed, that might be an intrusion, a complication – but the qualities of the body itself. He did not imagine an intimate relationship with a lover, but an intimate relationship with an admirable and beautiful *thing*. Jeff Dahmer was in fact the pornographer's dream, for he was by this time almost bereft of sentiment.

His fantasy was merely an extension, logical but barren, of a common notion among adolescents unsure of their ability to attract or satisfy a partner. How many boys nurse fantasies of having a girl who would be willing to just lie there and allow him to do what he likes, to explore her body, to touch and investigate, while she does not complain or demand anything further. It is part of the learning process. The fantasy subsides with maturity, as the pleasures of mutual sex are discovered. But it is unlikely to mature if the interest is restricted to the body and is indifferent to the person who inhabits it.

Parallel with this was Jeff Dahmer's other fantasy, of looking into and knowing the interior of a body. The two fantasies had not yet fused; he did not think of the insides of the men whose photographs he contemplated while masturbating. The necrophilic fascination was as yet untied to sexual gratification. But the two objects of his imaginative fancies occurred at the same period of his teenage years, and though they would run separately through his head, not concurrently, the possibility of the one eventually feeding and intensifying the other was already in place. Other memories jostled with his imagination – the recollection of that most intimate moment of his life, when the surgeon's hands had groped inside his bowels to repair the hernia, and the intense ruminative concentration of his Infinity Land fancy, with its promise of absolute inviolate privacy, a secret world all his own.

There had been a jogger who regularly passed in front of the Dahmer residence at 4480 West Bath Road. Jeff eyed him daily. The man had the sort of healthy impressive physique which he wanted to touch, but how on earth could he contrive a meeting? And even if he did, what would he do next? He could hardly invite the man, a stranger, to lie down and let him fondle his body. It would not, could not work. He did not want to have to ask, anyway, he wanted to have the man entirely in his command, an unresisting object for his veneration. He wanted, in fact, to capture him. There was only one way he could think of doing it. He would somehow have to attack the man and knock him unconscious. Then he would drag him into the woods and lie with him there, next to him, on top of him. He would be able to kiss him without the man ever knowing. One day he took a baseball bat and waited at the side of the road for the jogger to pass. He was ready to put the plan into action. Providence worked in favour of the stranger, for on that particular day he did not pass, and the troubled boy returned to the house with his baseball bat and his fantasies. But he did not forget.

Chapter Three

The Fantasies

'I don't know why it started. I don't have any definite answers on that myself. If I knew the true, real reasons why all this started, before it ever did, I wouldn't probably have done any of it.'[1]

The simplest answer is to suppose that the dissolution of Dahmer's personality and the crimes which emerged from the rubble were caused by reckless, selfish indulgence of a fantasy life which ought to have been kept in check. But this is hopelessly to beg the question, for fantasy is not the source of the problem but the instrument by which the problem is tamed, at least for the time being. One is bound to look beyond. Dahmer could not have known what he calls the 'true, real reasons' because they antedated the fantasies which evolved in order to neutralise and contain them. If we follow the evolution of these fantasies into ever more florid and bizarre notions, we must hope that we may peer backwards by degrees and gradually peel away the layers which protect the injured psyche at the centre. There is no quick route; it meanders and buckles and occasionally meets a dead end. But by dint of building up a picture, however incomplete its form and evanescent its focus, the mystery might dissolve.

In the first place, it is important to establish that there is nothing wrong with fantasy *per se*. In the infant, it is a useful prop and nourishment, to be discarded as reality becomes more enticing and rewarding. In the adult, it is the source of imagination and poetry, of artistic creation and outlandish endeavours. There is a celebrated remark by Goya which encapsulates the dilemma at the heart of this book. 'Fantasy abandoned by reason produces impossible monsters,' he wrote. 'United with her, she is the mother of the arts and the origin of their marvels.'[2] In Dahmer's case, it is quite clear that the fantasies did not march with reason, but collided with her. They ultimately became more real, more cherished, more important than reality itself.

Fantasy is the realm of Dionysus, the god of energy, frenzy, freedom and chaos. He liberates the restricted self, allows it to escape from constraint and conformity and to abandon order. That is why he is the god of the drama, of make-believe and pretence. Actors get 'out of themselves' for a living, and fantasists for release, but they are engaged in the same enterprise and are disciples of the same god. Dionysus is also the god of sex and display, of uncontrollable urges and undeclared desires. He transcends the real, and he is very much the god who infected the head of Jeff Dahmer. Dahmer's sexual deviation, already in his mind in mid-adolescence, was a product of Dionysian imagination, born of frustrated discontent and the need to create a better scenario for himself, one in which he would *fit*.

Most fantasies are so peculiar and unfulfillable that they are never admitted, and perish with their hosts in the grave. 'It is well for society,' wrote Wilhelm Stekel, 'that we do not know all the fantasies which accompany, consciously or half-consciously, or unconsciously, every erotic indulgence.'[3] Stekel further pointed out that if we did know them, we would be amazed. It is the tragedy of this story that we do know them and we are amazed. Dahmer's imagination is laid bare for all to see and poke at, and the people with whom he nourished it paid the price with their lives.

Sexual fantasy promotes masturbation and is generally satisfied by it. To that extent, masturbation is not merely forgivable, but blameless. It is a necessary safety-valve without which society might be awash with unspeakable energies suddenly released. As long as the pulse of the energy remains within the fantasy life, it is omnipotent and free; everything will happen as the masturbator wants it to, unfettered and unleashed, without the irritating intrusive contingencies of real life. But because there is omnipotence in fantasy, and restriction in reality, the two must be kept rigorously apart; they must not be allowed to spill over the one into the other. Reality poisons the spring of fantasy, whereas fantasy, when it erupts into the real world, brings destruction in its wake.

There is also a sense in which, by a grim paradox, the freedom inherent in fantasy creates its own prison, for it denies the rich variety of the real world and substitutes the barren, unrealisable narrowness of a single-minded obsession. The man with a secret fantasy life is not to be envied, nor is Dionysus necessarily to be adored. 'The mind is so trapped in frustration that it is like a tiny room with no windows.'⁴ By the time he was seventeen, Jeff Dahmer was securely locked inside this tiny room, and for the safety of all he should have remained there. He was rather like his mother, trapped by the addiction of self-absorption and helpless at coping with the prying demands of reality. There is, after all, something inescapably selfish about fantasy life. It knows nothing of sharing, of mutually exchanging pleasures. Jeff Dahmer did not think about giving the jogger a good time – he thought of the jogger only as furniture in his private drama.

1978 was destined in every way to be a bad year for him. 4480 West Bath Road was stifling with discord and ill-will, and Lionel Dahmer remembered the period as 'a mostly depressing and abnormal existence'. Not long before Christmas, he and Joyce had decided to sue for divorce. In the course of the previous year they had attempted to save the marriage by attending sessions with a professional counsellor, but had failed. The final straw came when Joyce had gone out of state in September to attend her father's funeral and, while there, enjoyed an affair with somebody else. They both then decided on divorce, and told Jeff and David about it, declaring that they wished to keep it an amicable arrangement. But Lionel seems to have changed his mind, doubtless smarting at the humiliation of infidelity, and the acrimony resumed. Joyce received a registered letter from a lawyer telling her she had one week to move out of the house. They fought often, threatened each other in full view of the boys. Lionel told his sons that their mother was crazy, whereupon she fought hard to control herself and remain calm in order to prove him wrong, and this in turn exasperated him to shouting pitch. Finally it was decided that Lionel would be the one to leave the marital home, so he packed a suitcase and moved to the Ohio Motel at 2248 North Cleveland Massillon Road, about ten miles away.

The court decreed that Mrs Dahmer should undergo a psychological evaluation in Akron, Ohio. Lionel sent the psychologist copious notes on her mental condition and the history of her addiction to medication, but he need not have bothered, for she was very agitated when talking with the doctor. He was informed about her nervous attacks and her stay as a mental in-patient, as well as her refusal to share the marital bed (she had told a neighbour that Lionel was 'insatiable'). The psychologist noted that Joyce Dahmer suffered from 'very severe emotional problems. She is constantly angry, frustrated and demanding in her interpersonal relationships. She insists on interpreting the motives of all those around her and seems to deny anyone's right to discuss her own behaviour as it affects others.' He also took note that she had recently 'found' herself by attending a women's group at a Community Mental Health Center, and that, though Mr Dahmer was willing to seek further professional help for their marriage, she was not. Lionel seemed genuinely perplexed that Joyce should be so insistent on a divorce. More importantly, there was much discussion and worry over who, in the event, should have custody of David and where he would live, but no thought was ever given as to what should happen to Jeff, or where he would be expected to live.

He was by now nearly eighteen, and perhaps old enough to look after himself, but it was significant that he was not consulted, and also that the Dahmers were so wrapped up in their squabble that they did not even notice how much their eldest son was now dangerously disconnected. 'Maybe I started shutting down during the divorce proceedings,' he said, disregarding for a moment that he had already withdrawn considerably before then. 'It was my way of shutting out any painful thoughts, just taking an attitude of not caring or pretending not to care, to save myself the pain of what was going on with the divorce. Maybe it started then. That was effective, it worked.'[5]

David was more overtly upset by the whole thing, being younger and less complex or introverted. Jeff's response was characteristically solitary. He drank more and more, and nearly always alone. One of the teachers at Revere High School saw him sitting on the grass outside the parking lot, with a twelve-pack of beer in a brown paper bag. Three of the cans were already empty. The teacher, Mr Smesko, told Jeff that he really ought not to bring alcohol to school and that he would have to report the matter. Jeff told him that he was having 'a lot of problems' and that the guidance counsellor, Mr Kungle, knew all about it. The 'problems' were thought by both teachers to revolve around his parents' divorce. They did not know that he was also struggling with dark thoughts in his head. Mr Smesko could not help noticing, not only that Jeff's eyes were glossy and bloodshot, as one would expect him to observe, but also that the boy was 'solemn and depressed'. It is not often that a teacher in the course of a routine reprimand should notice such a detail of mood.

It is a wonder Jeff graduated at all. Failure, however, is not permitted in the United States if there is an acceptable way to disguise it, and in this case there was the general acknowledgement that he was an under-achiever;

in other words, he would have passed with distinction had he really tried. Jeff was known to be an intelligent boy, capable of understanding propositions which might have been lost on other students – his I.Q. was 117. But equally, his perceptions were blunt and his involvement nil. Though he was capable of a greeting and some desultory small talk, his emotional isolation was impregnable. Thus was he slipped into graduation on very poor grades which ought, legitimately, to have failed him.

The sequel to this was that he would participate in one of America's hallowed traditions, the Senior High School Prom. The culmination of every high school career, the prom is a party, a dance, a celebration, an initiation, and above all a tacit translation into adulthood. Every boy must have a 'date', and every girl longs to be asked by the most exciting or glamorous boy in school, usually a sportsman. Dahmer was not a sportsman to any degree, but he would still have been quite a catch for his good looks, even if they were yet rather boyish. The drawbacks were his failure to make a mark, so that a girl would not have good reason to feel proud to be on his arm, and his well-known drunkenness. Apart from all of which, Jeff himself had never been on a date with a girl anywhere at all, and had never felt the desire to try. He was eighteen in May, and completely without experience. He did not particularly want to go to the prom, but he had to; this was not a tradition which allowed of choice – voluntary absence was unthinkable. It therefore fell to others to find a girl for Jeff Dahmer to invite.

Two class-mates, Mike Costlow and Lynn Soquel, came up with the answer. They approached a sixteen-year-old girl called Bridget Geiger and asked her if she would be willing to be Jeff's date. Bridget did not know him person-ally, but she had heard of his reputation for excessive drinking and was wary. She said she would accept only if he promised not to drink alcohol, and the deal was struck.

When Jeff turned up at her house, he was not wearing a tuxedo (dinner-suit), the *sine qua non* of the ritual, though she had made herself pretty with a long party dress. He was terribly nervous, shaking as he tried to pin a corsage on her dress, almost afraid of touching her skin. In the end, Mrs Geiger had to pin the corsage for her daughter. It was clear to everyone that this shy, blond young man was on his first date. They went to an expensive restaurant for dinner, then proceeded to the prom, held not at Revere High School but in Akron, Ohio. Jeff had been told that he must deliver Bridget home by 1 a.m. at the latest.

The prom was little short of an embarrassing disaster for Bridget because Jeff disappeared shortly after they arrived. She felt stranded, shipwrecked by the boy's bad manners, and very stupid. The truth was, he needed at all costs to escape the expectations and routines of the occasion. He was scared of being found wanting, as he knew he would be, and social graces were never part of his baggage. Bridget, forlornly, began looking for Mike and Lynn to beg a ride home with them, since she had been 'stood up' by her escort, but then Jeff suddenly reappeared, claiming that he had not eaten enough at dinner, had gone looking for a McDonald's where he might find a cheeseburger, and got lost. He had been absent for most of the prom and had clearly been drinking. The four of them left together and stopped in at a bar in Bath before going home. Jeff dropped Bridget at home by 11 p.m., with two hours to spare. He shook her hand and wished her goodnight. If she expected a kiss, she expected in vain.

Throughout this period of activity at Revere – the examinations, the graduation, the prom – preparations for the Dahmer divorce were under way. Jeff professed to be indifferent, shrugging his shoulders in dismissive fashion when Mike Costlow once asked him about it, but the whole business secretly undermined him. The upheaval at home had another, potentially more dangerous consequence. With Dad living in a motel, and Mom frequently running off to see relations in Wisconsin and taking David with her, Jeff was sometimes left to his own devices, and when that happened, his imagination festered. The moment when it might break out and become visible was fast approaching.

On one occasion, the three prom companions – Mike, Lynn and Bridget – together with one or two others, assembled at the Dahmer house for a seance. Jeff claimed that the house was haunted and that the spirit of the previous owner could be summoned by concentration and will. It was all innocent nonsense, if rather spooky with the lights out. The feeling around the table in the dark was too much for Lynn, who screamed when something moved, and Bridget jumped up and said she was leaving. She looked immediately for a house with the lights on, but one of the others came out and drove her home, and that was the last she saw of Jeff Dahmer. The seance was busted soon afterwards when Dr Dahmer showed up unexpectedly and made them all leave.

Another time Jeff Six was in the house and some jewellery went missing. Three rings and a bracelet, valued together at over a thousand dollars, were reported stolen in a police statement given by Lionel, after which Jeff was more or less forbidden to have any guests at all. He went out drinking with Mike and Jeff Six one evening, and when the boys dropped him off at 4480 West Bath Road, Dr Dahmer came out of the house and remonstrated with him. 'I told you not to hang around with those boys,' he said. Later, the same two attempted to make contact with Jeff again, and were rebuffed at the door by Lionel, who told them they were a bad influence on his son and that Jeff did not want them around. Mike said he would rather hear that from Jeff himself, but his request was refused. The irony was that Jeff had been talking with the boys about his interest in the preservation and reconstruction of death by taxidermy, and they had noticed how weirdly intense he became on the subject. If there was any question of an influence being potentially malign, it emanated rather from him than from them.

When Jeff had graduated, his mother invited the Dahmer grandparents for a celebration dinner, and a discussion about the future. It was a decent gesture, and the only time anyone seems to have given any thought to Jeff's ultimate destination. Lionel pointed out that the divorce settlement would so deplete his resources that he could no longer afford to send Jeff to college, whereupon the grandparents offered to pay if Jeff would improve his grades. It was decided he should enrol at Ohio State University to start general courses in September. He was distressingly unenthusiastic.

The divorce was heard in the Court of Common Pleas in July, 1978, and granted on the grounds of Lionel Dahmer's 'gross neglect of duty and extreme cruelty' towards his wife. Joyce was granted custody of David despite Lionel's evidence that she was not fit, an injustice which rankled with him for a long time. It has perhaps passed relatively unnoticed in this account so far that David was the recipient of his father's deepest affection, the very opposite of the kind of disgruntled disappointment which characterised his attitude towards Jeff. The loss of David hurt him at the core. He was given 'reasonable visitation rights', but was subject to a restraining order preventing his showing up at the marital home without prior agreement. In return, the settlement specifically stated that 'wife shall not remove said minor child to a permanent residence outside this Court's jurisdiction without first obtaining permission of Husband or an order of the Court'. Joyce could not simply kidnap David whenever she felt like it.

Lionel would have to pay Joyce, in addition to alimony of $400 a month, the sum of $23,500 for her share in 4480 West Bath Road, upon receipt of which she would vacate the house; otherwise she would stay there. She had the right to the 1968 Oldsmobile (she had eventually learnt to drive three years before), and Lionel would assign to her title in this car. He would keep the 1972 Ford which he drove. There then followed a huge list of furnishings

61

which were to become the sole property of Joyce Dahmer – sofas, chairs, tables, curtains, beds, toaster, ping-pong table, stereo equipment, barbecue, and so on for two pages. The husband would retain the stove and refrigerator, as well as the curtains in the play room. It is a depressing document, of the kind which is drawn up probably hundreds of times a day throughout the Western world, and which purports to measure in objects and belongings the failure of a relationship.

On 24 August Joyce loaded the car and took David with her to Wisconsin, in defiance of the court order. Her sister said she was frightened of Lionel and what he might do. She is also said to have begged Jeff to go with them, but he was paralysed by inertia. So she left, never to return, urging Jeff not to tell his father what she had done.

Jeff was left alone in the house. There was half a gallon of milk in the fridge, but nothing else. Some of the food in the larder was two years old. The house was in a mess. There was no car in the garage. He was isolated, in the literal sense now as well as the emotional. It was some weeks before he was discovered by his father, who had no telephone at his motel and was restrained by order of the Court from visiting the house. He had no idea Joyce had left. As soon as he learnt the facts, he went to 4480 West Bath Road with his new friend, Shari Jordan, whom he had met a few months before at the Springside Racquet Club where she had taken tennis lessons. A big-hearted, big-bosomed lady of confidence and charm, she was devastated by the 'horrible condition' of the house and horrified that anyone could be left unsupervised in such a place. The refrigerator didn't even work. Jeff looked like an orphan, disoriented and vague. He was obviously relieved when they said they would move in right away, and Shari set about tidying the place up.

She had met Jeff and David a few months before, at the Ohio motel. Lionel had wanted to introduce the boys to his new friend. Shari had been struck by the wide disparity in personality between the brothers – while David was 'charismatic' and 'extrovert', Jeff was locked up, introverted, extremely polite and extremely quiet. 'My heart went out to him,' she said.

That was in May. The discovery of his abandonment was in September. A combination of events and circumstances in the intervening period had contrived to place Jeff Dahmer in a vacuum of the most volatile kind. There was no school to attend, and the university term had not yet begun. There was no family life to offer trusted and familiar routines. There were no friends since the very few who wanted to see him had been banished. There were no hobbies, sports, activities of any sort to fill his day. The divorce of his parents was beyond recall – they were effectively separated and it was only a matter of formality for the Court to confirm what had already occurred. Even before she packed her car and left, Joyce absented herself frequently, taking David with her to visit her family in Chippewa Falls, Wisconsin, for a few days. On those occasions Jeff Dahmer was left entirely to himself, without occupation or ambition, and only his fantasies to feed his mind. What he most needed was a firm and solid structure to life, a network of recognition to keep him from wandering into Infinity Land, obligations and duties to hold him down. Even the exercise of going to school was a useful discipline. Now that all structures had evaporated and all ties been severed, his fragile hold on sanity was loosening.

Nobody realised that he was held in the grip of a fantasy of daemonic proportions, or he would surely not have been deserted for a moment. When Lionel and Shari found him aimlessly standing in the middle of an empty house late that summer, they did not know, nor could they have known, that this appalling fantasy had at last exploded into the real world one night in June, and left him marked for life.

Jeff had not forgotten the jogger. Now he had more opportunity than ever to think about him, to dwell upon him, to imagine a successful encounter with him. He masturbated when he thought about it, and after he reached satisfaction the thoughts would recede for a while. But not for long. They became more and more intrusive, more and more insistent. When he had been alone in the house for about a week, and found that these thoughts assailed him several times a day, he looked back to the jogger and beyond, and realised that, ever since he was fifteen years old, his fantasies had fixed upon a man who would lie still and be calm, and even, perhaps, be dead. Did other boys his age think about such things when they masturbated? Probably not; they thought about girls, or naked receptive women. If they thought about boys at all, then they were probably romping about and having sex accidentally, as part of 'horsing around'. Did homosexual boys dream of sexual congress and love? He had no idea. He only knew that his fantasies involved less sex than exploration, less love than ownership. They sometimes even involved the killing of a man in order to keep him. That was absurd; he knew it. It was shameful, impossible, ridiculous. But it was also urgent – it pressed against his ribs and his groin, calling for release. And so he masturbated again, and the thoughts were temporarily sated.

Perhaps it would be a hitch-hiker, he mused. A handsome guy with a nice chest whom he would see on the side of the road, invite back, and, well, who knows? He thought about this hitch-hiker for months, telling himself a story, leading towards a consummation of his choosing. But of course it never happened. It couldn't, because it was just a fantasy. Besides, he didn't have a car, and in that part of rural Ohio he had not once seen such a person walking along the road, not once since these thoughts began. It would be pointless looking for anybody. Things like that didn't occur in reality, they were just day-dreams and reveries. Yet the thoughts continued, they came 'like arrows, shooting into my mind from out of the blue',[6] and he would nurse them and nourish them once more. He had not read anything to instil such imaginings, nor received ideas from movies or books; they came into his head of their own accord, from nowhere, self-generated as far as he could tell. They may even not have come *into* his head at all, but been born there.

It was a warm summer's day in mid-June when Jeff decided to get out of the house for a while. He asked his father if he could borrow the blue Ford so that he could go to the cinema; he would drop Lionel off at the Ohio motel and return the car next day. Lionel agreed and Jeff left the motel in mid-afternoon.

Driving along the highway at about five o'clock, he saw him. There, coming towards him on the opposite side of the road, was a hitch-hiker. He looked about nineteen years old, more or less coeval with Jeff himself, who had just turned eighteen the previous month. He wore jeans and tennis-shoes, but because of the heat he had left his shirt off. That was the most important, the most enticing detail. The boy's chest was exposed, visible, perhaps touchable. He had shoulder-length brown hair and looked quite nice. His thumb was out, but nobody much passed on that stretch of the road. Jeff drove on, thinking. The fantasies reared up before him and inside him. Should he perhaps try? It all seemed to be orchestrated for him, set up. He had not seen a hitch-hiker before; he might not have noticed this one were his shirt covering him; the house was empty, so he could not be disturbed; he had a car for once; everything fell into place. It was obvious! The hitch-hiker had in a mysterious way been *sent* to him! The circumstances were too perfect for him to resist their message. Yet he felt very nervous.

Jeff turned back and caught up with the hitch-hiker. He told him he wasn't going anywhere much, but he was welcome to come back to the house and have a few beers and a joint. His folks were away, so they would be left alone. The young man accepted, and hopped in the car. He introduced himself as Steven Hicks, from Illinois. Sure, he would come back for a while. Jeff was thinking what he would do, playing through his mind the voyeuristic *frisson* of looking at this man's body and caressing it –

he was like a picture in one of those books, yet he was for real! The idea of conquest or seduction did not enter into his makeshift plans; that was not an idea which formed part of Jeff Dahmer's imaginative furniture. It would have been better for all if it had, for conquest and seduction are relatively normal ambitions, achievable by most people without harmful effect. There then passed through his mind, once more, the drama of death and sole possession. This he tried to set aside, to banish, but it was a constant struggle.

They drove to 4480 West Bath Road. Frisky was there to welcome Jeff home. The dog was quickly placated, and the boys went to Jeff's room. He had some marijuana left over from a supply which Jeff Six had obtained, but Steven wasn't too keen. He would have a beer, though. Jeff wanted to make a pass, but did not know how to. It soon became clear that Steven was not homosexual, and would resist any approach with a sexual motive. Steven said he had just celebrated his nineteenth birthday and was going to visit his girlfriend. That was blatant enough. Jeff wanted to ask him to undress, but didn't dare. It was the first time he had ever had the chance to indulge his homosexual fancies, but he just could not do it. He was scared. He would be certain to be rejected, and then left with those dreadful, clinging thoughts, all by himself.

All this talk of girlfriends and moving on and the future worked upon Dahmer like a creaking vice, edging upwards towards explosion and calamity. He had no future; he was moving on nowhere; he was doomed to sit in that house and poison himself with thinking. He needed to stop this, urgently, to grab hold of events and shape them to his will, to exercise some control for once and *be himself*, whatever that self was. He liked Steve's company and lusted after Steve's body; why should he be forever denied?

After a couple of hours' drinking and talking, Steven Hicks thanked Jeff and said he ought to be getting along before it got dark. The swell of frustration within Jeff Dahmer rose until it filled his nostrils and pressed at his temples. He was not going to leave. He couldn't leave. He wouldn't let him leave.

He went to the cellar and got an eight-inch-long barbell, without the weights on the end. When he came back upstairs, Steven was still sitting in the chair, with his back to the door. With a sudden surge of strength, Dahmer struck him on the head with the barbell. Steven responded, astonished. There was a quick scuffle, and Dahmer hit him a second time. Then Steven fell unconscious. Dahmer was swamped by a mixture of panic and excitement, fright and anticipation, his actions driven by a surge of feeling no longer accessible to reason. With the barbell, he strangled the limp body of Steven Hicks until no breath stirred.

Once he had stopped panting, Dahmer carefully removed Steven's clothing to reveal the beauty which had disturbed him. He ran his hands over the chest, caressed it, kissed it, then lay down beside the body. Finally, he stood above Steven's corpse and masturbated on to it.

Then it was that reality rushed in upon him. 'I was out of my mind with fear that night,' he said. 'I didn't know what to do. I had gone to such an extreme.'[7] When darkness fell, he dragged the body outside and to the front yard, then into the crawlspace beneath the house, left it there, and went back indoors. He didn't sleep. His heart pounded with panic at what he had done, and how he could undo it. He would have to cover up somehow. This kind of thing was impossible; people had bad dreams about murder and unwanted bodies and responsibility and discovery – anxiety dreams in other words – but this was for real. Nothing would suffice less than the total obliteration of evidence; the rest would wait.

The next day he went out and bought a large knife. When he returned, he went straight to Steven's body beneath the house. The so-called 'crawlspace' is almost exactly what the name implies, an area of unused space beneath the house, into which one may crawl. It is as if the house were on stilts and the space were between the stilts, and of course it is most common when the house has been built on sloping land. At 4480 West Bath Road, a man could stand upright in the open end of the crawlspace, which became lower as one went further in until the ground and the floor of the house met. There it was that Dahmer set about the dismemberment and disposal of Steven Hicks. He first cut off the arms and the legs, and then the head. In a cruel, pitiful echo of the experiments with road-kills, he slit open the belly to see what it looked like inside. (Only very much later would the true purpose and function of this operation be revealed as more than mere curiosity.) There was a great deal of blood, which soaked naturally into the earth. The various parts were then put into three triple-lined garbage bags, while the identity card and clothes belonging to Steven Hicks were burnt in the trash barrel behind the cliff, about fifty yards from the house. The garbage bags remained for the time being in the crawlspace.

Dahmer spent the whole of the next day pondering. He felt frantic at what he had got himself into and terror at the thought of discovery. Shame was slow in coming. At length he decided that he would dump the remains in a ravine about ten miles away, late at night, when no one would see him. After a few beers to work up the courage, he put the bags on the back seat of the car and drove off. It was the middle of the night.

At 3 a.m. a police car came up behind him and signalled him to stop. There was only one officer – he and Jeff were alone together on an empty country road. The officer called for 'back-up' and another car arrived on the scene shortly afterwards. Dahmer was told that he had been observed driving left of centre, in other words slightly to the wrong side of the road. Would he please get out? Jeff did as he was told, and was walked round behind the car to take some tests. He was asked to place his finger on his nose and to walk in a straight line, both of which tasks he accomplished to the officers' satisfaction. (This was before the days of breathalysers.) The ordeal was not quite over yet, however. One of the policemen shone his flash-light on to the back seat of the car to reveal the large plastic bags. 'What's that smell?' he asked. Jeff explained that it was household trash that he was taking to the city dump. Why so late? Because his parents were in the throes of a divorce and he could not sleep; he thought the drive would get things off his mind.

The officers were prepared to accept this and did not investigate further. Had they done so, of course, the Dahmer odyssey would never have occurred, and there would have simply been one more murder case in the local press to shake one's head over. Even so, as he himself has pointed out, it would have been too late for the family of that young hitch-hiker. Nobody reflected more upon this than the policeman who flagged Dahmer down; thirteen years later, it was, by coincidence, the same man who was sent by the Ohio Police Department to Mil-waukee to interview Dahmer. Police Officer Richard Munsey was now Lieutenant Munsey, and he was in deep shock when he looked up the record of that late-night offence and found that he was the one who had stopped Dahmer on the highway.

Jeff was given a ticket for erratic driving and allowed to go home, having spent a total of about half an hour with the police officers. What he then did was disturbing and bizarre. He placed the bags back under the crawl-space, then opened them to find the head. He took it out and carried it upstairs to his bedroom. He placed the head on the floor and proceeded to masturbate in front of it, looking at it. It was *his* now, his companion and solace – this severed head – his fantasy become real, his own private stimulant, and as he stood there, moving his hand towards the artificial restoration of peace, a boy of eighteen in a solitary house in the quiet Ohio countryside took his first step towards madness.

The following night Dahmer dragged out the bags contain-ing the torso and limbs of Steven Hicks and stuffed them down a wide, deep drainage pipe in the back yard, covering them with earth. He could not think what else to do with them, and did not pause to wonder whether they would have to be retrieved one day, or whether their very existence was evidence of his crime. He could not think straight at all. He kept the head a little longer, but then that, too, badly decomposing, had to be shoved down, out of sight. If only he could push the whole ghastly episode out of mind as well, as effectively as this, he would. He drove to the Cuyahoga River and threw Steven's necklace into the water, together with the knife he had used to cut him up. But he could not throw the memories into the water, could not discard the images in his head, could not throw away the fear which beset him all day long. He knew he was doomed. 'That night in Ohio,' he recalled, 'that one impulsive night. Nothing's been normal since then. It taints your whole life. After it happened I thought that I'd just try to live as normally as possible and bury it, but things like that don't stay buried. I didn't think it would, but it does, it taints your whole life.'[8]

It is hardly to be wondered at that his struggle to erase the memory of what he had done, and to soften the shock he felt, was eventually defeated. It was to endure for another nine years, the image of Hicks surging before him at any moment, without warning, to be only partially assuaged by large doses of alcohol. In some measure there were two victims of that first incident, one of whom did not die. The memory of it retained the capacity to cause Jeff Dahmer distress long after his normal human responses to the death and destruction he caused had atrophied. He wept over it in the coming years, as he wept over none of the others. Remembering it with a psychiatrist in 1991, his voice faltered and silence fell. The doctor felt the need to remind him that 'I won't let you fall back into a hole' as he watched the man recede into intolerable introspection. The most Dahmer managed to say, as he emerged from it, was so inadequate as to verge on bathos, and yet it was simple: 'I'd rather be talking about anything else in the world than this,' he said.[9]

Retaining the religious habits of childhood, he occasionally prayed for forgiveness, and at the same time knew he was beyond such a gift. He recognised that his 'perverted lust' had caused the death of Hicks, and that this lust had grown on the fertile ground of moral inertia – 'not caring about other people, not caring about myself'.

In July of 1978, the day after his parents' divorce became absolute and the day after his mother had finally fled to Wisconsin, Jeff Dahmer was fined $20 by the Traffic Court at Akron, Ohio, for having driven left of centre on 25 June at three in the morning. The last day Steven Hicks was seen alive (other than by his killer) was 18 June. His remains were not found for thirteen years.

After Lionel and Shari had found Jeff in a state of confusion, living by himself with a dog and an empty refrigerator, they set about deciding his future. They tried to talk to him, to see what he wanted, but he was completely devoid of any ideas or ambitions. He seemed to have renounced life, which was, they thought, unutterably sad in one so young. All he wanted to do was drink. Every liquor bottle in the house had emptied to within an inch of the bottom, and Shari came home early from work one afternoon to find Jeff passed out on his bed, blind drunk after having consumed a whole fifth of Jack Daniels whiskey. He begged Shari not to tell his dad, and said he only drank because he was bored and had nothing to do. Lionel insisted Jeff should go to university, but he wasn't very keen, so Shari made up her mind to take the bull by the horns and enrol him anyway. She was more dynamic than Lionel, more resolute, and she could see that this dreadful situation might simply drag on aimlessly with no positive outcome in sight. She took him shopping, bought him clothes, and within a couple of weeks she had him ready for college. She and Lionel drove him to Ohio State University.

Jeff was installed in Ross House dormitory, Room 541, sharing with three room-mates – Craig Chweiger, Michael

Prochaska and Jeffrey Gerderick. They all thought Dahmer was pretty weird, and he gave them good cause to form such an impression. In the first place, he spent most of his time lying on his back in the top bunk playing a Beatles album over and over again, and singing along with it, especially the track 'I am the Walrus'. For no discernible reason (for he was apolitical then as now), he pinned a photograph of Vice-President Walter Mondale to the wall. More than anything, however, they were unnerved by his unremitting intake of hard liquor, such as to make his attendance at classes impossible. He simply could not get up in the morning. He would tape the lectures and then listen to them while he got drunk, getting through a couple of bottles of whiskey a day. He could not finance his alcohol dependency entirely out of the allowance sent by his father, which was naturally modest, so he found a way to supplement his funds by donating blood twice weekly at the university plasma centres. His fingernails had finally to be marked to prevent his giving blood more than once a week.

His behaviour was erratic and unpredictable. The other three room-mates went out for a drink one evening, leaving Jeff behind as usual – he had no friends or even acquaintances of any kind while he was at Ohio State but appeared to live in limbo. When they returned they found all the furniture stacked up in one corner and pizza thrown all over the walls. No explanation was offered. Another time he had kicked the tiled wall of the bathroom and damaged it, for no apparent reason. He lost his keys, had his rented bicycle stolen, and finally was suspected of stealing a watch, a radio and $120 cash from the boys while they were at lectures, and of spending the money on drink and pawning the objects; in his notebook was written the address of a local pawnshop.

Chweiger, Prochaska and Gerderick determined that they had had enough of Dahmer; he was a negative influence, caused nothing but trouble and cut himself off from them in every conceivable way. They petitioned to have him thrown out of their room, but were told that nothing could be done until the end of term, and they would have to put up with him. As it happened, the problem was solved for them, because Jeff's grades for that first semester were so poor that everybody concerned – himself, the university and his father – agreed that the continuation of his college career would be fruitless. Despite having paid in advance for the second term, he would drop out at Christmas.

With hindsight, it is not difficult to discern a fairly standard pattern of retreat from reality in this sorry few weeks at college. The dangerously escalating alcohol intake points to a desperate attempt to blot out thought, ever more frantic as it repeatedly fails to achieve its purpose. The inability to form a convivial relationship indicates disgust with oneself and distrust of one's place in regard to other people – a confirmation, in other words, of the basic schizoid dilemma and its solution in total alienation from the rest. The expression of rage against a bathroom wall (which recalls Dahmer's earlier primitive smashing of logs against tree trunks), though obviously insignificant in isolation, shows Dahmer in crisis as he fights to banish memory and guilt. As for the inexplicable behaviour of piling furniture in a corner, it is symptomatic, in the light of what we now know, of a terrible inner need to drive out self-knowledge by *any* displacement activity which might occupy the mind; it is a form of lying to oneself. But none of it could work, and it is scarcely a surprise to find that during these weeks, when left alone with his drunken stupor in Room 541, Jeffrey Dahmer broke down and cried.

Back in Bath, Ohio, he sought his oblivion again in marijuana and was frequently in the company of Jeff Six; the two of them were cautioned for driving over somebody's front lawn. Once he borrowed his father's car without permission and then proceeded to lose it – or couldn't remember where he had left it. Lionel and Shari had to go out and hunt for their own car.

There was only one solution to Jeff's problems, it

seemed – he would have to enlist in the army. His father took him to the recruiting office in Akron, Ohio, and he was accepted for a three-year enlistment with an initial posting to the Military Police School at Fort McClellin, Alabama.

A couple of weeks later, on Christmas Eve, Lionel and Shari were married. Jeff did not attend the wedding. On 29 December, he left for Alabama.

During the first four weeks of basic training no alcohol at all was permitted. This was precisely the sort of unarguable discipline that the Dahmers thought their errant boy needed. He was also overweight and placed on a strict diet for fast remedy – five hard-boiled eggs per day and a five-mile walk – which brought immediate results. Having the day packed with duties and activities allowed no time for cogitation, but when drinking was again permitted Jeff rushed into refuge with the bottle. He was regularly reprimanded for drunkenness, and once succeeded, to his chagrin, in getting the whole platoon punished for his insubordination, whereupon several of the men turned on him and gave him a severe beating. He was bloodied and his ear-drum was broken, causing him to suffer periodic attacks of ear-ache even ten years later. He was never popular or liked, and kept himself rigorously apart, but following the beating he took greater care not to be caught in a state of alcoholic paralysis.

It was also during this period of basic training that he received word his dog Frisky had died of a stroke in the house. 'She was twelve years old,' he recollected. 'No, I didn't cry. I loved her, she was a great dog, but no, I didn't have any strong emotions.' He hadn't cried since 'I was in college that day, thinking about Hicks. I was drinking and in a weepy sort of mood, and I cried about that.'[10]

On 11 May, 1979, Dahmer was sent to the Army Hospital School in San Antonio, Texas, where he followed a six-week course in medicine and emerged a qualified medic. It was entirely fitting that his bent should be towards the scientific discipline, his father being a chemist by profession, and it was the first time in his life he had succeeded in settling down to a sustained course of study and seeing it through. Unfortunately, he learnt much at medical school which he was to use in years to come for purposes other than the preservation of life.

His training complete, Dahmer was assigned to Number 2/68 Armour Division, Second Battalion, stationed in Baumholder, West Germany, and when he arrived there in June, 1979, he duly joined the squad at the Battalion Aid Station.

Considering that he was to spend nearly two years in Germany, it is remarkable that so little is known about his life there or the impression he made. Perhaps the very paucity of information is itself evidence of his almost total withdrawal from the society of his fellows. He naturally saw people every day, ate at base with them, went to restaurants with them, chatted with them in a desultory way, but he made no effort to know anyone, still less be known by anyone, and so his privacy was respected. He is remembered, once again, as a loner, very quiet and moody, evidently sunk in perpetual depression. It also became obvious very soon that he was sexually innocent.

Some of the men, taken aback by the absence of a girlfriend back home and astonished by his admission that he had never kissed a girl, determined that they would assist him in losing his virginity. So a whole group of them took him to Annabella's House, a well-known brothel in Vogelway, and two soldiers who were Dahmer's own age dragged him into the brothel and introduced him to a girl there. They then split up and lost sight of one another. It later transpired that Dahmer had sneaked out of the house without doing anything, which they ascribed to shyness until he told them that he had never wanted to go there in the first place and did not 'need' any girl. One of the older men privately thought he might be homosexual, not because of the brothel incident, nor any overt feminine attributes, but because 'he always seemed like he was hiding something'. It was an astute observation, and a telling one.

Dahmer had no sexual adventures of any kind while he was in Germany. He claims an older sergeant propositioned him, and he declined. One of his colleagues remarked that he 'looked like a little kid in a man's body'. He discovered the homosexual bookshops which abound in Frankfurt, and bought some pornography to serve as aids to masturbation. He did feel frustrated, as he came to realise how most men of his age had experienced some kind of full sexual congress, but since it was other men who excited him, and he knew this to be an inadmissible vice, he vented his frustrations in solitary onanism. Only he knew to what dangerous extremes his sexual urges might lead if they involved anyone else. For the time being at least, Dahmer condemned himself to further isolation because it was the only safe course.

Some of his other pleasures were likewise pursued alone. He liked to walk in the countryside and see what he might come across. 'I remember seeing a family of wild boars going down a hillside a long distance away. They were so big at first I thought they were boulders rolling down the hill. It was snowy out, it was white, but it was a family of wild boars. They get four to six hundred pounds, solid muscle, covered with dark brown hair. Very ill-tempered, they'll tear you apart, but boy, can they run. They can run up to thirty miles an hour.'[11]

He enjoyed shooting, too, and at one point considered turning it into a hobby when he eventually left the army. Target practice was something to look forward to, and he soon found he had accumulated a lot of useful knowledge about different types of gun. 'I fired M-60s in the army, those are the guns that sit on top of the tanks. Those things will go through three inches of solid steel. And I fired 45s.'

Nevertheless, it was the availability of cheap liquor which provided Jeff with his most lasting hobby – getting drunk. Soldiers were able to obtain liquor at half-price, a convenience of which Dahmer took full advantage. On at least one occasion, the liquor either summoned up memories of Steven Hicks, or failed to subdue them, and he gave way to a fit of sobbing. It is important to stop and imagine what he was crying for, however. Remorse for what had happened to Hicks had by now utterly given way to self-pity for the burden he had inflicted upon himself by the murder.

For Thanksgiving in November, 1979, Carlos Cruz and his wife invited some of the younger soldiers to share the traditional celebration dinner at their home. (Cruz was serving in the same squad at the Battalion Aid Station.) Among them was Dahmer and a soldier named Preston Davis. While they were having dinner, the snow began to fall heavily outside, and Cruz suggested that it would be wiser for them all to stay the night. For some reason or other, Dahmer and Davis fell into an argument, and Davis told him to get the hell back to Baumholder. Jeff decided that was exactly what he would do, and he quietly walked out of the door into the snow at 10.30 p.m. Baumholder was about eight miles distant, around a mountain, and it was freezing cold. When Cruz realised what had occurred he went out to search for about fifteen minutes, but was driven indoors by the cold to get heavier clothes. He went outside and looked for another half an hour before he finally gave up, assuming Jeff had found a taxi to take him to Baumholder.

Four hours later Jeff was back at the door. Davis called out 'Here's the orphan!', and they all welcomed him back inside. He appeared confused, vague, his mind elsewhere. He had also lost his glasses. His jacket was not especially cold to the touch, as they might have expected, nor was he as affected as a man who had been four hours in sub-zero temperatures ought to be. Cruz took him to the kitchen, where he washed his hands energetically. Cruz thought he noticed signs of blood on his clothing. Jeff then sat down and stared at the kitchen table. He told Cruz that he could not remember where he had been nor what he had been doing, but he assumed it must have been 'something bad'. Could he have tried to damage himself with his own spectacles? He was considered 'weird' enough to be a suicide case, that much is certain. More likely, he had found a hole somewhere and just sat there, thinking. Thoughts would not leave him alone, they would permit no peace; they continued to oppress, relentlessly. A few days later Cruz invited Jeff to say what was bothering him, but he could not articulate it, or would not. He did, however, make an interesting and pertinent remark. 'You know,' he said, 'sometimes the best thing for the soul is to confess.'

Instead of confessing, Dahmer went on smothering the self within him to keep it under control, or drowning it in alcohol. At such times, he seemed stupid and vacuous; it was only, said his colleagues, when you engaged him in conversation that you realised how intelligent he really was, but then few attempted this, and those who did were not rewarded. Eventually, the alcohol got the better of him, and he found himself drinking on duty as well as off. After several reprimands, punishments and disciplinary reports, and when it became obvious that his abuse interfered with his ability and desire to obey orders, Jeffrey Dahmer was dismissed from the service six months before his expected release date. It was an honourable discharge, but a premature one nonetheless.

On 24 March, 1981, Dahmer was sent to Fort Jackson, South Carolina, for debriefing, and given a voucher to travel to any destination of his choosing in the United States. He did not relish returning to the cold climate of Ohio, so he flew direct to Florida, where he imagined the permanent sun and warmth would be a cheerful influence, and the proximity of the ocean a calming one. His parents did not know he had left the army until one day his trunk and personal effects, including correspondence from the government, arrived at 4480 West Bath Road. It was in this trunk, much later, that David Dahmer found the German pornographic magazines which gave him the first clue as to his brother's sexuality. Jeff had put them in the trunk and sent them off to Ohio, rather than take them with him to Florida, in an attempt to start out on a fresh road. From this point in his life we see an increasingly urgent need to escape the past and take a new direction, any direction, so long as it is away from himself.

At Miami Beach he took a room at a motel and found a job at the Sunshine Subs, a local sandwich bar half a mile down the road. Here he worked seven days a week and spent all his earnings on drink. Florida did not turn out to be the panacea he had hoped for; it was a struggle making ends meet, and the job was hardly very challenging or diverting. He made no attempt to find the homosexual areas of town, nor to meet anyone for sexual purposes. Even casual friendships eluded him, except for one unlikely instance. During the six months that he spent in Miami, Dahmer struck up an acquaintance with another worker at the Sunshine Subs, an English girl called Julie. It was the only female friend he was ever to have, until after his arrest in 1991. Julie was working illegally, since she had only a visitor's visa to the United States, and she wanted very much to legitimise her position. She and Jeff talked about the problem, and she went so far as to ask him if he would marry her to make her a U.S. citizen. He was not keen on the idea, to say the least, and though he liked Julie, he discouraged her interest in him.

When he ran out of money and could no longer afford the motel room, Dahmer took his few belongings and camped out on the beach. He would go there straight from work and fall asleep beneath the stars. It was not an ideal situation, and he soon reached the conclusion that life like this would lead nowhere. He had been reduced to homelessness and penury in a very short time, all as part of his plan to escape from himself, and even that had not worked. The thoughts were still insistently there; they haunted him, tormented him when he least expected them. There was, he thought, only one way finally to conquer them, and that was to rid them of their nourishment. There must be *nothing left to think about*.

He telephoned his father, who sent him the fare from Florida to Ohio, and in September he arrived back home to the house he had known since the age of eight. It was a house of memories – of one in particular that had to be exorcised. While his father and Shari were at work, he dug down in the drainage pipe where he had stuffed the bags containing the remains of Steven Hicks three years before and uncovered them. He hauled the bags into the woods beyond, atop a small cliff, and opened them. The flesh had rotted off, but the bones were there, permanent timeless reminders of what he once called 'a horrid mistake' and now referred to as his 'sin'. He took them out and smashed them, one after the other, with a large rock, until they had been reduced to splinters. The skull he smashed too, pulverising it; 'I had to,' he said, edging towards apology. He had to demolish not only the evidence, but the images which buffeted and bruised inside his head, taunting him. With his bare hands, he picked up the fragments of bone which had been Steven Hicks' head, and scattered them wide in the woods.

Chapter Four

The Struggle

The prodigal son was not entirely welcome in Bath, Ohio. Lionel had grown accustomed to the equable style of his second marriage. Shari had a job of her own to go to, instead of being confined to the house as Joyce had been, and they looked forward to meeting each other in the evenings. It was a peaceful, unmolested life. There had, it is true, been a lodger for a brief period – a young man whom Shari wanted to help and who returned the favour by keeping the yard clean – but otherwise the domestic scene was firmly *à deux*. A lumbering, unemployed and uncommunicative twenty-one-year-old was not the ideal house-mate.

This is not to say that the Dahmers did not worry about Jeff and try to help him think about his next step in life. They were sure, however, that whatever that step was, it should be away from the nest. Lionel was disappointed that his son seemed to lurch from one spoilt opportunity to another and was beginning to wonder what on earth could be done with him; if even the army had failed to contain him, or fire him with enthusiasm, it was unlikely anything else could. Jeff was the very picture of accidie – indolent and torpid if left to himself, passive and acquiescent to the suggestions of others.

He recognised his failings and tried to correct them. He was, after all, pleased to be home, and asked his father to give him things to do so he could keep himself busy.

81

For instance, he insulated the crawlspace underneath the house. Julie, the English girl, telephoned from Miami a few times to see how he was getting on.

Only two weeks after his arrival, Jeff was arrested at the Ramada Inn for being drunk and abusive. He had been asked to leave the Maxwell lounge of the hotel because he was drinking straight from a bottle of vodka. He had refused and been escorted outside, where he continued to drink at the front door. Two employees told him that it was illegal to drink even there, and when he again declined to move, the police were called and he was taken to Akron Correctional Facility and incarcerated. He would not answer questions and swore at the officers. The charge against him was disorderly conduct and resisting arrest, but it went no further than a municipal citation. Still, it did not bode well for life in Bath. Eventually, Lionel and Shari decided he should go and stay with his grandmother in West Allis, Wisconsin, for a while, to sort out his future. Catherine Dahmer was getting old and feeling lonely and she could do with some company as well as help in the garden. In return for the performance of some household chores, Jeff would have room and board. As usual, it was not an idea to excite him, but Lionel and Shari insisted that he take the chance. Thus it was that in December he moved to West Allis, to the house where Lionel himself had grown up and lived until his first marriage.

It did not take Jeff long to realise that he liked the arrangement and he elected to stay. There then followed six years of apparent stability and concealed turmoil. 2357 South 57th Street was a cosy little house, with the advantage of a quiet neighbourhood, yet within easy reach of downtown Milwaukee. Jeff was very fond of his grandmother. Characteristically, when asked directly if he loved her, he replied, 'Yup, she's lived in that house a long time,' which is a rather bold evasion. The response epitomises the difficulty he experiences in making emotional contact. He knew perfectly well that his grandmother was *lovable*, and said so, but could not bring himself to say that he loved her, because he did not think himself capable of love; to use the word subjectively would be presumptuous, even insulting. So he avoided it.

This is what he says about Catherine Dahmer: 'I guess she's what you could call a perfect grandmother, very kind, goes to church every Sunday, easy to get along with, very supportive, loving, just a very sweet lady.'[1] She took the old-fashioned view that people will behave decently if you treat them decently, and her religious principles sustained her goodness of heart. Mrs Dahmer could have been a splendid example to and influence upon Jeff, had he been able to share life with her much earlier, but now it was too late. He appreciated her qualities well enough, and was beyond imbibing them.

Their days together were marked with simplicity. 'I'd shovel the walks and mow the lawn, help her with the flowerbed, and she'd cook the meals, so we helped each other out a lot.' After eating, they would watch television together. There was only one prohibition she enforced. In the army Jeff had become seriously addicted to cigarettes, and was now smoking a pack a day. 'I'd always have to smoke outside,' he said. 'She couldn't stand cigarette smoke in the house. I didn't blame her at all so I did my smoking outside.'

Dahmer was hired by the Milwaukee Blood Plasma Center as a phlebotomist soon after his move to Wisconsin. The job involved drawing blood from volunteers, at which he was adept enough, having learnt the technique as part of his work in the army medical aid station. But he did not care for it, and regarded it merely as a way to earn a simple penny. Before that, he had been relying on his grandmother's generosity.

In January, he bought a gun from a Milwaukee store, a .357 snubbed-nose Magnum with a black rubber-grip handle and a silver body, weighing about a pound and a half. It was a very powerful gun, but he used it only for target practice, another habit bequeathed by the army. 'Once my dad and grandma got wind that I had that, they didn't think it was a good idea, so my dad took it away and ended up selling it down in Ohio.' In fact, there was a large family conference to decide what to do about the wretched gun; it made his grandmother nervous to think it was in the house at all, so they confronted Jeff with the situation, and he consented with no hesitation to hand it over to his father. He had kept it for about six months.

There were other things he was doing secretly which Grandma might also have deemed 'not a good idea'. He had secured a copy of Anton LaVey's *Satanic Bible* which he pored over in his room while she said her prayers to a more benign God. Even more peculiar was an experiment he conducted at work. Taking so much blood from people in the course of his job, he found himself wondering what it might taste like and what effect it might have upon him. He concealed a vial of blood in his pocket and took it to the roof of the Plasma Center, where he proceeded to drink it. He did not like it and spat it out. Why, one must ask, try in the first place? Dahmer contends that it was mere curiosity which impelled him, but, in the light of what subsequently occurred, perhaps other streams of unconscious desire were motivating his conduct.

These were the first stirrings of an interest in what Dahmer mistakenly referred to as Satanism: it was to develop progressively over the years and work towards a startling *dénouement*. It was a personal quest, a diffuse and stumbling attempt to establish contact with those turbulent, dark and unanswerable exigencies of primitive Nature, recognised by the pagans before civilisation tamed them by denying them. But they are never entirely denied, and they display themselves in disguised form throughout history, for they pre-date history and infuse the acts and thoughts of men with involuntary notions they barely apprehend. Art and law and society seek to keep them under control; religions unwittingly perpetuate their power. The essence of these elemental forces is their necessity and irresistibility; they are not contingent, but constant and immutable. They cannot change, or be fought against, for they represent the endless cycle of the earth and its doings, its infinite progression and regression, surge and swell, movement towards no other end than self-regeneration.

I do not suggest that Dahmer made any intellectual enquiry into such matters, but that he, unknowingly, was fumbling for an understanding of them. Since he could not perceive himself within the accepted norms, categories and assimilations of civilisation, perhaps he might find some glimmer of recognition and explanation in the chaos of primitive night. He was searching for his daemons,* that is his personal guardians, through the unlit world of urge and response. The tight spirals he had drawn as a child were summonses to that remorseless swirling and circling of inescapable Infinity, where, dimly, he felt he belonged. The wish to look upon Satan was a demand for identity, the hope that a mirror might be thrust before him. The drinking of blood was an unconscious initiation into that world of the earth and its deep, prehuman spirituality. He did not like it. He spat it out. It was not his way. But he would find other ways in the future, and gradually grope towards an expression of coupling with the underworld which was all his own.

Dahmer was fired after ten months for poor performance. As he did not like the work and it was poorly paid, he hardly minded losing the job. With his grandmother, he went to Bath, Ohio, to spend Thanksgiving of 1982 with Lionel and Shari. It was a happy time, and the start of a new resolve on Jeff's part, the desire to 'walk the straight and narrow', as he put it, with the help of his saintly grandmother. A couple of months before he was fired from the Milwaukee Plasma Center he had once

* Christianity misuses the word demon to indicate a dweller of Hell, an evil spirit. The Greek *daemons* were spirits from a nether world, both good and evil, who helped one to understand and interpret the mysterious. Socrates talked of his daemon as his 'guardian' spirit.

more fallen into trouble with the police. At the Wisconsin State Fair on 7 August, 1982, he was arrested and charged with Disorderly Conduct. The offence was more precisely that of urinating in public, but the police officer who made the arrest did not mention urination. He 'observed the defendant with his pants pulled down and his penis exposed leaning against the planter on the south side of the Coliseum in which 25 people were present including women and children'.[2] He was convicted on 19 August and fined. This was the first instance of Dahmer's exhibitionism to be recorded; the frequency of such behaviour would escalate at a later point, and its meaning become clearer. For the moment, Jeff was conscious of the shame he threatened to bring upon his grandmother (he had instead given the address in Bath, Ohio, as his residence when he was arrested), and he determined to turn over a new leaf.

As soon as they returned to West Allis, Mrs Dahmer and her grandson began spending more time together. They went to church together and read the Bible. Jeff immersed himself in the Bible while he was alone, too, in a conscious attempt to wrestle with the blackness within him and purge it. For a long period he appeared to succeed, which was all the more remarkable for his being out of work, subsisting on unemployment benefit. These were precisely the loose unstructured conditions which had proved his undoing in the past. This time, however, with the example of his grandmother and the support of the Church, he gradually came to terms with a placid life uncontaminated by his primal urges. 'I was reading the Bible then, trying to get my life straightened around, and I'd give some money to the street people sometimes, or send it in to different missionaries.'[3] By being charitable and kind, he hoped to eradicate his sinfulness or at least smother it. The memory of Steven Hicks faded and no longer lunged tormentingly at him in the middle of the day. He also managed to control his habits of masturbation and limit himself to one time per week. He felt it was wrong and had to be reduced; by rubbing himself against the bed instead of using his hand, he was able to convince himself that he was not really indulging in self-abuse. He also felt guilty about the imaginings in his head which accompanied this pseudo-masturbation, because they were always homosexual and the Bible taught that homosexuality was sinful. He succeeded in repressing them and was pleased with himself.

This 'good' period of about two years, unsullied by any incidents or longings, would be cited by both sides in the murder trial of 1992 as evidence in support of their case. It proved either that Jeff Dahmer was able to control his conduct when he wanted to, and was therefore in charge of his life; or that he was engaged in an almighty struggle which he eventually lost to powers greater than himself. Both points of view have merit, and the conflict between them which was manufactured by legal and psychiatric semantics was largely contrived – they are not mutually exclusive. One way to measure a man's morality is by the degree of effort he invests in the struggle against immorality; the repeated sinner may well have repeatedly tried to resist sin.

It was also during these years that Jeff visited his mother for the last time, spending Christmas of 1983 with her and David. He had not seen her since the divorce of 1978, and would not speak to her again until the year before his arrest on murder charges.

On 14 January, 1985, Dahmer started work as a mixer at the Ambrosia Chocolate Factory in Milwaukee. It was a humble position requiring no great skill that could not be learnt in a day, but it was something at last, and it enabled him to be more responsible and give his grandmother a reasonable rent – $300 a month. He worked the third shift, from 11 p.m. until 7 a.m. six nights a week from Sunday to Friday. Life was pretty dull and empty, but at least it was not stalked by ghosts. Until one hapless, ordinary day when everything suddenly went wrong.

Jeff Dahmer was sitting in the West Allis Public Library

reading a book when a stranger passed and dropped a note in his lap. He unfolded and read the note. It said, 'Meet me in the second-level bathroom. I'll give you a blow job.' He could scarcely believe it. There was no build-up, no preparation, he was completely taken by surprise. Though he was now twenty-five years old, he was still sexually untried, totally without experience except for the one surrogate occasion with the corpse of Steven Hicks. He thought he had at last rid himself of that terrible memory, and with it the fantasies and urges for homosexual activity. He felt he was cleaner, redeemed. Now, in that single moment in the library, the insidious thoughts clawed back into his mind again. He re-read the note. He had never been propositioned before. He did not obey the command to go to the bathroom and never saw the man. 'It's going to take more than that to make me stumble,' he said to himself. Yet the incident made him think that he was being manoeuvred, 'set up', and his resistance began gradually to erode.

He found himself giving way to masturbation more and more frequently, as the fantasies he summoned were less and less effective. As Stekel pointed out, fantasies do not have the desired effect the second time round, because the true goal has been replaced by a fictitious one; gratification is therefore only possible through exhaustion. 'Most of these cases go to excess in masturbation and often succumb to onanism twelve times a day,' he wrote.[4] Dahmer's daily average was about four times. He told psychiatrists that his urges became stronger and stronger until, some two months after the library incident, his control broke down.

It was now that he knew he had to find someone, a man he could lie with. But he did not know how to start. He was so naive that he was afraid to approach anyone and still more apprehensive about the sexual or emotional demands which might be made of him if he did. He did not want to get 'involved', hoped only that he might find a sexual partner for a casual encounter. His attendance at church slackened, much to his grandmother's chagrin, and he started drinking again.

The first step was to discover where to go. In a gay newspaper he found the addresses of bookshops which specialised in homosexual pornography, and sought them out. He bought a great deal of material, but still felt furtive and guilty about it. Then he found that there was a manner in which he could make anonymous contact without risk or threat to his privacy. A number of these stores, in Europe as well as America, have coin-operated video booths where a man may watch a few minutes of a sex film until the money runs out, and prolong his enjoyment of it by putting in more coins. They are meant to be used by one person at a time, but it does happen in some, where security is lax, that the door to the booth is left ajar. There are also sometimes so-called 'back rooms', where a group of men may assemble in total secrecy. They are pitch-black or very gloomy, enabling contact only by touch, and thereby permitting the release of sexual urges in an utterly anonymous setting. No word is spoken. Eye-contact is impossible, and personality therefore does not intrude. The concepts of love and friendship are entirely banished from such a place. It was in this environment that Dahmer had his first tentative experience.

He also took once more to exposing himself in public places on about six occasions when he was not apprehended. Krafft-Ebing was of the opinion that this kind of activity is at root sadistic, because it seeks to offend other people's sense of modesty by forcing them to witness something they have not chosen to witness, which is a form of cruelty.[5] In Dahmer's case it is more likely to have been the result of timidity, of the conflict between desire for sexual relief and fear of emotional commitment. Exhibitionism was, for him at least, a fruitless and arid kind of being with somebody at a safe remove. He did not consider the feelings or susceptibilities of the people who were made props in this experiment; to him they were already as objects. Before long, this would involve him in his first court appearance, and the second opportunity of stopping him before his deviance again became dangerous.

Another activity he indulged on at least one occasion was *frotteurism*, the pressing of one's groin against an unsuspecting and unconsenting partner in a crowded place. This, too, derives from a wish for sensuality without involvement, and is an expression more of fear than temerity; it can always be explained away as an accident. It may also be felt by the perpetrator to be, like rubbing oneself against the bed, less 'dirty' than real sex, because it is tentative, 'only pretending', does not imply overt complicity of the mind. Frotteurism is a manifestation of guilty feeling, indicating in Dahmer's case that the guidance of the Church still lingered. He would shortly find a way of doing this without having to explain anything at all.

It is possible already to spot the development of Jeff Dahmer's obsession. I have already pointed out that many a pubescent boy desires, first and foremost, a partner who will lie still and allow herself to be touched and fondled, and that the fantasy is eventually superseded by a maturer desire for mutuality; it comes as confidence grows. With Jeffrey Dahmer, it never did come; he was stuck in the early adolescent phase of seeing sex as nothing more than self-gratification, and the object of sexual desire as, *ergo*, an object. He did not want to be with a person who would move, be energetic, express desires of his own, perhaps surprise him and demand too much of him. His ideal was a person who would lie down and permit himself to be stroked and admired, and finally used *merely as an aid to masturbation*. Such people are not easy to find.

His first step on this road occurred one day in 1984 when he was walking through Southridge and his eye fell upon a male mannequin in the shop window of the Boston Store. It immediately struck him that he would like to have the model at home. One evening he concealed himself in the store until after closing time. 'At about eleven o'clock at night, when everyone was gone and the store was locked up from the outside, I went out and undressed the mannequin and I had a big sleeping-bag cover. I put it in that, zipped it up and carried it out of the store, which was a pretty dangerous thing to do. I never thought of them maybe having security cameras or being locked in the store, but I walked out with it and took it back home. I ended up getting a taxi and brought it back and kept it with me a couple of weeks. I just went through various sexual fantasies with it, pretending it was a real person, pretending that I was having sex with it, masturbating, and undressing it.'[6] The behaviour seems less odd when one considers how many shops devoted to sexual aids sell a great number of inflatable dolls which men use to extend onanistic activity; nor the number of times men in art museums, thinking themselves alone, are seen by hidden cameras to run their hands over the bodies of statues. But it is no less pathetic for that.

Dahmer's idea of 'having sex' with the mannequin did not, of course, involve simulated penetration. That was not his purpose. But it was still unsatisfactory and barren. When his grandmother questioned him about the model, he made some excuse about having bought it, then got rid of it when he saw that she was anxious. He smashed it up and threw it in the trash. 'It would have been better if I'd just stuck to the mannequins,' he said. 'Much, much better.'

The same year, his brother David came to visit with his grandmother and stayed two nights. He was now eighteen, and Jeff twenty-four. They were obliged to share a bed. Jeff, as he put it, 'felt the urges and everything to be with someone', and there, next to him, was the very thing, a prostrate body, asleep, unconscious, available for exploration. Jeff attempted to touch his brother. 'He didn't go for that at all, that's for sure. He told me so in the morning,' he said. Jeff made a suitable apology, and the incident was never repeated. He felt both embarrassed and disappointed, and also, obscurely, that his brother had rejected something that was an essential part of him. But it would be wrong to imply that this bothered him unduly. It had been another experiment with passivity, no more.

Later, in 1985, he discovered the bathhouses, and a more satisfactory method to ensure passivity. The homosexual bathhouses were a cultural phenomenon of the 1960s and 1970s, superseding the more discreet Turkish baths which existed before. They were usually clubs, with coffee-bars and television lounge, sauna bath and pool, and later, jacuzzis and whirlpools. The hub of the place, however, was upstairs, where lines of cubicles containing a simple bed and a shelf or bedside table allowed people to parade themselves for sex and make sudden assignations by entering a cubicle and closing the door. Some of these clubs were rudimentary and sordid, but others were bright, cheerful and popular. Early in her career Bette Midler performed in one such establishment in New York, singing to gentlemen with towels girding their loins as they rested from their labours.

Dahmer found the bathhouse to be a relaxing place, and sometimes a strange one. It attracted people with the most unusual fetishes, for the virtue of anonymity in an environment which accepts deviance is the freedom to express peculiar desires without fear of inviting shock. There was one man whom he encountered there who liked nothing better than to suck people's feet. He apparently had no teeth: Dahmer lay back and enjoyed it.

For the most part, however, the men he met required more strenuous exercise to satisfy their needs, and he was put off by all that energy. Twice he was subjected to anal intercourse, which he did not like, and sometimes he would play the active part in the sexual act, which he liked rather better. But what he most wanted was for the man to keep still.

'I trained myself to view people as objects of potential pleasure instead of people,' he said, 'instead of seeing them as complete human beings. Sounds callous and it is, but that's what I did.'[7] To which one ought to add, so did the other members of the club. It is the function of such a place to encourage sex for its own sake, and the bath-houses are therefore lamentable breeding-grounds for selfishness, just as brothels encourage the insensitive trait in heterosexual men. Visited but seldom, they can serve a purpose; frequented at the expense of all other sexual activity, they must damage the soul. 'I looked at it as an experience of taking,' said Dahmer. 'There wasn't any mutual giving, not in my mind anyway. I was always quite selfish.'

The earliest record of a prescription issued to Jeffrey Dahmer for sleeping pills is 6 June, 1986. The doctor was Rodolfo Suaverdez of West Lincoln Avenue, Milwaukee, and he was to issue two further prescriptions in the following month before his patient moved over to Dr Carroll Ollson of South 90th Street. To both medics Dahmer told the same story: he needed help in getting to sleep as he was working night shift and could not adjust his body to such unnatural hours. Both times he was lying. The sleeping pills were his latest experiment. He took them with him to the bathhouses together with liquor which he smuggled in, to give to his temporary partner in the privacy of their cubicle. The man would pass out within half an hour and subsequently oblige Dahmer by lying in an unconscious condition for up to eight hours, leaving him free to exploit his fancies. If he woke up too soon, Jeff would increase the dosage next time, until he reached an average of five pills per 'partner'. A number of young men were subjected to this treatment without any harm coming to them, a fact we know not just from Dahmer's own account, but from testimony of people who remember being with him.

Nineteen-year-old Richard Burger who was up from Texas when he met Dahmer at the bathclub on Wisconsin Avenue at 7th Street was drugged by him. He made no complaint. Kevin Byrne had sexual contact with Dahmer three times at the club, and in subsequent months saw him frequently at bars, when they would greet each other. Byrne said he was a very quiet man, and remembered hearing him once say that he shaved his body because he liked a smooth hairless chest. About eight other men were drugged, and made mild complaint to the management, but no action was taken until an oriental man went into such a deep sleep that he had to be taken to hospital and did not revive for two days. It was said that he spent over a week in the hospital. At this point the management decided enough was enough and revoked Jeff's membership. They did not, however, inform the police. Naturally, it was important to the owner that such an establishment should be as little noticed by the authorities as possible.

Quite so. But it might have been helpful had he and his colleagues realised just how potentially sinister was this man who drugged people in order to have them stay with him. There can be little more obvious clue to a necrophilic character than this, the comatose state being only at one remove from the dead state. On the other hand, most people would be more likely to dismiss such a connective leap as preposterous.

Having lost the benefit of the bathhouse, Jeff substituted a cheap room at the Ambassador Hotel, and on another six occasions took men back there and drugged them. The crucial circumstance, both at the bathhouse and at the hotel, is not so much that he drugged his partners, as how he behaved to them afterwards. Having robbed them of the opportunity for 'heavy' sex, he would then lie next to them and imagine that they belonged to him. Whereas he had difficulty in achieving an erection while they were awake, once they slept his capacity for tumescence was totally restored, and he would masturbate three or four times during the long encounter. At other times he would fondle them and enjoy their proximity. He was in control, with nothing to disturb him and no necessity to rush or feel pressure to perform. After a few hours, he, too, would fall asleep next to the prostrate body, sometimes holding it. Most peculiar of all, he would spend a great deal of time lying with his head on the man's chest, listening to his heart-beat, or on the man's stomach, listening to the sounds of his body. If he could fall asleep in that position, he was at his most content, for the man's insides, his internal organs, the most secret parts of him, would belong to him too.

A young man named William Blair came perilously close to Jeff Dahmer's dream-world during the summer of 1986. They knew each other from the bathhouse, where they had had sex on three or four occasions. There had been no arrangement to meet, they had merely bumped into each other by chance and spent some time together. There was no affection between them – their tenderness was functional, invented for the occasion. One day Blair saw Dahmer on the corner of 7th and Wisconsin and they exchanged greetings. Jeff told him that he occasionally rented a room at the Ambassador for a night, and he was just going there now; would Blair join him? The young man accepted, and they went to the hotel together. Blair took a room himself, whether for propriety or comfort it is hard to say, but first went to Dahmer's room for a drink. He has no memory of what happened next, for he woke up the following morning, lying naked on the bed in his own room, having lost several hours of his life. Jeff told him that he had carried him to his own room in the middle of the night, but he told him nothing more. How he might have used Blair's sleeping body to furnish the décor of his own disturbed vision was not revealed. William Blair subsequently saw Dahmer a number of times at Milwaukee's gay bars and saluted him in a friendly manner, but never spent time alone with him again.

The bars were Jeff's new haunt. There are several in town within walking distance of one another, three virtually adjacent on South 2nd Street. The 219 Club is a bright, cheerful, good-natured place, 'gay' in the proper sense of the word and therefore potentially as attractive to heterosexual men and women who enjoy night-clubs as to homosexual men seeking to congregate in a convivial enemy-free atmosphere. The large dance-floor is lit by colourful laser-beams and the music is loud. At weekends the 219 is packed, 'wall-to-wall people' in Dahmer's words, and the overspill might go next door to 'C'est La Vie' or to the corner bar, the Phoenix, where there is no dance-floor and conversation is rather easier. None of them is squalid in any degree, but rather pleasant and agreeable. Jeff was a regular customer at the Phoenix and the 219. He enjoyed 'the excitement of being around people that I didn't know and the chance of meeting some nice-looking guy, the same thing that led me to the bath-clubs, the excitement and anticipation of meeting a stranger in the night . . .' And yet, he did not appear to make any effort to socialise. At the Phoenix, he always took the same stool at the bar, drank and smoked alone, did not respond in a lively fashion when the barman tried to engage him in conversation. He was polite and very well-mannered, and somehow distant. He did occasionally fall into conversation with black customers, it was noted, but otherwise kept himself to himself. He rarely smiled.

Apart from the odd night at the Ambassador he was still living with his grandmother in West Allis, and adjusting himself to the revolution in his habits since he abandoned the guidance of religious teaching. Catherine Dahmer did not like her grandson to come home so late; it was not, in her view, seemly in a Christian to appear so nonchalant about the decencies of life. Jeff was beyond fighting with her on this; he was twenty-six and thirsty for experience. His formerly repressed libido was now given some expression, and hypersexuality took the place of self-discipline. He bought more and more pornography and masturbated to excess. In this he resembled many another man whose personality does not disintegrate into murderousness. For Dahmer was straining with tensions which could not be satisfied owing to their fantastical nature. He was still trying to keep the lid on, to find ways of dealing with his needs which were acceptable, and he thought he was succeeding. He did not realise that he was doing so only at the price of mental equilibrium.

As his fantasies grew ever more elaborate, commensurate with their dwindling power to arouse, so his desire to turn people into objects intensified. To objectify is to control, to demystify, to possess, to drain the living juice from a person and render him malleable. Certainly Jeffrey Dahmer's imagination was encouraged by the pornographic images with which he fed it. The images were themselves objects, flat things on a page; the mannequin was an object, a three-dimensional thing on the floor; the bodies of drugged companions were objects, breathing things of heart-beat and intestinal music. There was but one step to progress to the richest thing of all, a depersonalised person.

Dahmer's hypnotic fixation was an androgynous creature of muscular physique and power combined with feminine passivity and hairlessness, mother and father, wife and husband, earth and ocean, the unrealisable perfect friend as possession and plaything. This creature was to be his own avenue to Eros, his own piece of porn. 'Sex is the point of contact between man and nature, where morality and good intentions fall to primitive urges.'[8] Dahmer's urges were primitive indeed, too primitive to fathom save perhaps in retrospect. They dwelt in the depths of Freudian murk, and were the very antidote to the kind of Rousseauesque optimism which believed man's essential nature was bathed in the good.

One day he conceived the idea of finding for himself a fresh corpse, and scanned the obituary columns in search of a suitable candidate. An eighteen-year-old boy took his fancy, so he attended the funeral and watched where the body was buried. Later that night, he went to the cemetery with the intention of digging up the corpse and taking it home, but the ground was frozen and would not yield, besides which a dog barked and an owl hooted to frighten him off. Dahmer told this story to all the psychiatrists who examined him, and was consistent in the details, but none of them asked him whether he took a spade, nor whence he might have obtained it. This is not to say the story is untrue, only that it is imaginary – the fruit of fantasy. Dahmer would not have been the first to dream up such a solution: Sergeant Bertrand in France during the mid-nineteenth century was almost a legendary figure who would swim through icy rivers in order to get to a cemetery, dig up a corpse and ravish it, and there have been many since. The police are full of stories of men arrested for lurking in graveyards, but they rarely reach the press due to readers' resistance. That Dahmer did not actually get a ready-made corpse is immaterial; the thought that he might was in his head.

He rented a video called *Faces of Death*. This is not on a pornographic subject which has to be sold surreptitiously, but a commercially available depiction of grisly reality, an examination of the way in which various cultures deal with death. It includes the scene of a detailed autopsy on a young man killed in war, with the skull cut open to remove the brain. Jeff rewound the film more than once to watch this scene, and claimed that he did not understand why he was so intrigued by it.

Meanwhile, there were additional signs of volatility in his social behaviour. On 18 August, 1985, he was cautioned for making obscene gestures to police officers at the corner of Wells Street and 7th Street (he had 'given them the finger'). On 7 April there had been a more serious incident, at 3.15 in the morning at a bar in South 2nd Street. Dahmer was drunk and abusive. The bartender, Miss Kluczynski, refused to serve him, whereupon he threw tokens across the bar at her and demanded he be served or he would shoot her. She called the police and Dahmer became even more furious. Four police officers were required to hold him down and take him into custody. He remained at the police station until 1 p.m. that day, released on his own recognisance against charges of Disorderly Conduct, Threat to Injure, and City Hindering. The charges were never brought to court.

On 8 September, 1986, two twelve-year-old boys, Richard Kohn and John Ostland, were standing by the bridge on the Kinnickinnic River Parkway in Milwaukee when they saw a man by the river, with his pants around his thighs and his shirt pulled up. The man appeared to be masturbating. Richard, who was old enough to know what 'jacking off' amounted to, shouted out, 'Are you having fun?' to which the man replied, 'Yeah, I'm having a great time.' The boys reported this incident to the police and gave an accurate description of the man, which was then broadcast to all squad cars. Police Officer Richard Menzel spotted a man who fitted the description at West Jackson Park Drive and stopped him. It was Jeff Dahmer. He was brought back to Kinnickinnic River and positively identified by the two boys, at which point he was arrested and charged with Lewd and Lascivious Behaviour and Indecent Exposure.

Dahmer's defence was that he was urinating and had no idea he was being watched, but in fact his exhibitionism was always latent, and he had indulged it before in public parks. Now, for the first time, he attracted the attention of the courts and his personality would be subject to scrutiny and analysis. Light might at last be shed upon his weird private imaginings by doctors who would know what to look for. The charge against Dahmer was reduced to one of Disorderly Conduct and he was duly convicted by Judge Arlene Connors on 10 March, 1987. The sentence was suitably mild – one year's probation – but a condition of his bail was that he undergo psychological counselling for sexual deviance and impulse control, and the court referred him to clinical psychologist Dr Evelyn Rosen.

First of all, Dahmer was given two written tests designed to alert the doctors to likely problems and disorders of the personality. They both have impossible titles (the Millon Clinical Multiaxial Inventory and the Forer Structured Sentence Completion Test), but their purpose is to permit the subconscious to speak through the conscious use of signal words. In the first (Millon), the patient is invited to read a number of self-descriptive statements and to indicate, merely by colouring in a circle, whether he regards the statement as true or false in his own case. Dahmer indicated that most of the statements did not apply to him, but some of those he marked as 'true' are interesting in the light of what we so far know about his character:

'Lately, I've begun to feel lonely and empty.'
'Ideas keep turning over and over in my mind and they won't go away.'
'I've become quite discouraged and sad about life recently.'
'Looking back on my life, I know I have made others suffer as much as I have suffered.'
'I keep having strange thoughts I wish I could get rid of.'

The doctors drew attention to some of these by again circling them, but there is no evidence that anyone questioned Dahmer closely about these 'strange thoughts' and 'ideas', nor about the reasons for his emptiness. Since he was hugely uncooperative, it may well be that opportunities for searching enquiry did not arise. One other statement he thought was true is more alarming than the rest, because insidious: 'I know I'm a superior person, so I don't care what people think.'

The second test (Forer) consisted of completing sentences which had been left open-ended. Dahmer's showed, on the whole, that he did not take the test very seriously, but it was illuminating, nonetheless, to see how many times he made reference to his father, and always saw him as a man working rather than loving or being with him. (The italicised words are in Dahmer's handwriting.)

'My father always *worked hard*.'
'My earliest memory of my father is *when he went to work*.'
'When my father came home *I was happy*.'
'When my mother came home, *I was watching TV*.'

Other characteristics which stand out are a distrust of marriage, a tired cynicism, and a reluctance to be made to fit into any established pattern. The only glimmer of affection is in the sentence, 'He felt blue when *his dog died*.'

The cumulative effect, in both tests, is of a man seemingly self-doomed to isolation and disconnectedness. Despite the reference above to superiority (or perhaps because it is a postulated ideal and not a perceived reality), he is a man who feels powerless to cope with the world of the living, where people do and say things without reference to him. Secondly, he is trapped by the trivial and utterly devoid of grand design or purposeful energies. His self-image is extremely weak; he feels that he counts for nothing and is worthless. He needs to be something more than he is, something greater; he needs to grow and expand, but feels smothered. 'The man who is able to assert himself in a socially acceptable fashion is seldom vicious; it is the weak who are most likely to stab one in the back.'[9]

The truth of this remark of Storr's needs to be emphasised. It is a paradox, and one of which we must take firm notice if we are to spot murderers in advance, that the worst and most hideous crimes are committed not by monsters of power and magnetism, but by individuals who feel impotent and inadequate. The man whose will reigns over his life and environment does not need to nourish it on destruction; it is satisfied already. But if one's will to achieve is blocked, either by oneself or by outside influences, the resulting dam of frustration is extremely dangerous. Jeffrey Dahmer had no self-image to validate his life or justify his existence. He was a waste. He felt reduced to an inconsequential object, a piece of flotsam bobbing on the surface of life. Just as he objectified his sexual partners, because he knew no other way, so he was in turn objectified and rendered useless by the cruel sweep of circumstance. Or so he felt.

The man who walks alone, outside society and untouched by its norms, is a volcano waiting to erupt. Nothing simmers with greater threat than the thwarted will. Dahmer's will was crushed by apathy and by the most appalling self-knowledge. He did not think himself 'superior' because he had, nine years earlier, killed a man without anyone ever finding out. On the contrary, he knew that he was diminished by this, and tied, trammelled, by the need to prevent its ever happening again. If he were to assert himself, to allow the real 'Jeff' to break free, the expression of his will might be devastating. Only he knew how dangerous he was. The few occasions on which he had shown anger (against a tree trunk or against arresting officers) were as nothing compared to the force which lay in ambush. He saw himself as flawed, and self-imprisoned by the need to restrain this aberrant trait. He *had to* smother his will-drive, because he knew where it might lead, and the result was severe psychological impairment.

The philosopher Abraham Maslow once famously put forward a theory about the 'hierarchy of needs', which had a crucial influence upon the generation to reach maturity in the 1960s.[10] According to Maslow, the first human need is for security and food; it is only when this is satisfied that the need for sex comes forward to demand satisfaction; when sexual needs are met, then the desire for acceptance by one's fellows is paramount, and this is the most important – the need for self-esteem. Above this occurs the intellectual and creative level which finally craves to be fulfilled, and which inspired some young thinkers of the sixties to recommend 'doing your own thing'. Maslow postulated that to snap off one rung of the ladder in this hierarchy was to invite danger; if there is a blockage, a hindrance to advancement, then the will which works its way through these progressive needs cannot go forward and becomes redundant or supine. This, he says, leads inevitably to mental sickness. The only route to psychological health is an uninterrupted journey from the need for food to the need for creativity.

The need for self-esteem comes after that for sex, and is usually more difficult to satisfy. In Jeff Dahmer's case,

he had hardly moved forward from the most basic requirement and was living like an automaton, working to earn
enough money to live until the next day when he could
work again. Satisfactory sexual or emotional commitments
were unknown to him, and pride in achievement un-
imaginable. At bottom, he would still have liked to do
something which would please his father and make him
feel that he had not let him down by being so useless, but
he could not even contemplate this until the lower need
was fulfilled. Thus was he completely unable to make himself worthy, *while at the same time* he knew that worthiness
was laudable. It would have been easier had he been
stupid. As it was, his lack of self-esteem was an endless
frustration.

It is for this reason that he resented the requirement
that he should confide in Dr Rosen, and was frequently so
uncooperative as to turn his back on her (a fact repeatedly
asserted by the prosecution in court four years later). Dr
Rosen's notes present a vivid picture of a difficult patient,
silently turbulent and sullen. She noticed how reluctant
he was to talk about himself, how he became more and
more monosyllabic as the session continued. The next
time they met he was again 'unresponsive', complaining
about the length of the journey to her office; surprisingly,
she did not notice the significance of this irritability, which
is a disguised way of looking for approval for having made
the journey at all. She told him that if he had a car then
he would not have such problems getting around, which
is not what he wanted to hear; after that he 'became stubbornly mute'. He also resisted any discussion about his
family.

Jeff's next complaint addressed the issue of money.
Why should he have to pay for these sessions, which he
didn't want anyway, if they were ordered by the court?
Surely the court should be responsible. Then he regressed
into gloom again, leading Dr Rosen to the plaintive
reflection, 'Talking to him was like pulling teeth.' She
invited him to choose a topic, and he refused. He wanted

her to give up. She noticed that his anger was brittle and that he had to take hold of himself to control it. He was 'a tightly-wound individual who maintains rigid control'. Gradually, Jeff was a little more ready to speak about the past, and through this Dr Rosen learnt what a traumatic event the divorce had been. She did not know, of course, why it was so traumatic – being so closely associated in time and place with the death of Steven Hicks; Dahmer's response when his parents' divorce was mentioned often collided with his hidden response to the reminder of Steven, whose fate was contemporaneous with it.

Dr Rosen tried to talk about the indecent exposure which had brought Jeff to her desk, and he became very angry with her, accusing her of collusion with the legal system. 'When angry he becomes almost delusional in his paranoid beliefs,' she wrote, adding, 'These seemed genuine.' On the other hand, she remarked several times that he was always nicely dressed, clean and neat, which may well have been signals of a subconscious effort to please her. Not unnaturally, she preferred to note his utter refusal to discuss anything probing or private. He would give nothing of himself, and the therapy grew more and more pointless. She wondered why he maintained such an unskilled job at the chocolate factory when he was clearly above average intelligence and could have stretched himself towards a greater endeavour, but her annoyance at his infectious morosity prevented her from seeking an explanation without his assistance.

It was at this point that Dahmer began the behaviour which was referred to in court. He kept appointments in obedience to the court order, but refused to speak for the whole fifty-minute session, turning his chair away from the therapist. 'He continues to show [up] conscientiously but I don't know why,' she wrote. His capacity to avoid contact was clearly exasperating. At a session before Christmas, however, he did talk about the presents he had bought for his grandmother, then clammed up again when Dr Rosen sought to probe the relationship. He told her he would rather spend time in jail than in psychotherapy, especially with her! Nor would he discuss his problems with alcohol.

The sessions came to an end without any worthwhile insights being achieved. If any conclusion was possible, it was that the patient regarded introspection as such a threat that he would go to any length to avoid it; why it should be that he was so terrified of revelation was not a question that was directly addressed.

In addition to the therapy, Dahmer was sent for a psychological evaluation at the Clinical Psychology Department of the University of Wisconsin, the first of several evaluations which were to bestride the last few years of his career. He was more forthcoming with the clinician, Kathy Boese, than with the therapist, although he did tell her some straightforward lies, such as that he had had a girlfriend in high school, had slept with a prostitute in Germany and had resorted to the services of prostitutes since then. About his father Lionel he revealed something of his assessment, though not of his feelings; these could only be conjectured. He said that his father was always too busy to spend much time with him and that he was autocratic to the point of being bossy. He did not keep in touch with the family on a regular basis because he did not like writing letters and anyway, 'there's not a whole lot to tell'. It was perfectly clear to the clinician that Dahmer had no friends at all and was, furthermore, destitute of interests or hobbies. She noticed that his patience was short, in so far as he shuffled his feet a lot and tapped his fingers on the table; only a constant supply of cigarettes kept his irritation in check.

In the tests to which he was subjected, his tolerance of frustration was evidently low and his concentration brief. Despite this, his 'exceptional performance in the use of language and abstractions' indicated that he was potentially far more capable and intelligent than his lethargic display suggested. Dahmer was introverted and isolated. The test which was designed to illustrate underlying

105

emotions drew from him 'exceptionally slow' responses 'extraordinarily few in number and abnormally restricted in regard to affect'. His attitude towards the offence for which he had been referred to the clinic was angry. 'He resents being told what to do by others and is easily disappointed and hurt.' Most interesting was the unexplained reference to his fantasies: 'His own goals for himself in this world, for what he hopes to achieve, are not congruent with reality.'[11]

It is somewhat unnerving now to realise that the therapy sessions with Dr Rosen embraced the period when Dahmer's struggle with himself finally exploded. One of their meetings took place on 16 November, 1987. Four days later Jeffrey Dahmer met Steven Tuomi.

Steven came from Ontonagan, a little town in Michigan, and was working at Schuster's Family Restaurant on East Wells Street, just behind the Milwaukee Athletic Club. An unpretentious place serving hamburgers and hot dogs, in England it would be called a working-man's café and in the United States it is a diner. I frequently had a quick snack there myself. In 1987 it was called George Webb's Restaurant, and Steven had taken a job there as cook in September working third shift, from 10 p.m. to 6 a.m. On his job application sheet, in answer to the question how long did he intend to keep the job, he had written, 'I have no limitation'. On 21 November he had a night off and went to the South 2nd Street bars.

At closing time men crowded the pavement outside the 219 Club, making assignations or just getting a ride home. Jeff Dahmer was among them. He spotted the sandy-haired Steven, twenty-five years old but youthful and engaging, and fell into conversation with him. Steven had no plans and nowhere much to go, so he willingly accepted Jeff's invitation to accompany him to his room at the Ambassador Hotel. Indeed, he was keen, for he rather liked the strong, masculine look of Dahmer and his air of nonchalance; he did not need persuading. Had Steven been aware of the opinions of both Dr Rosen and the

Clinical Psychology Department of the University of Wisconsin, he would not have gone anywhere with Jeff Dahmer, whatever the enticement.

For Kathy Boese had concluded her report with a startling prediction. Dahmer, she said, 'could become a psychopathic deviate (sociopath) with schizoid tendencies. His deviant behaviour will at least continue in some form if not be exacerbated . . . Without some type of intervention which is supportive, his defences will probably be inadequate and he could gravitate toward further substance abuse with possible subsequent increased masochism or sadistic tendencies and behaviours.'

Evelyn Rosen's prognosis was more colloquial and consequently even more alarming. With her own emphasis, she wrote in her notes, '[There is] no doubt at this time that he is a Schizoid Personality Disorder who may show marked paranoid tendencies. He is definitely *SPOOKY*!'

Jeff and Steven took a taxi to the Ambassador Hotel in the early hours of the morning.

Chapter Five

The Collapse

When Jeff Dahmer woke up the following morning, he was lying on top of Steven Tuomi. He immediately saw that the man was dead. His head hung over the edge of the bed and there was blood coming from the corner of his mouth. Worse than that, Dahmer could feel the man's ribs beneath him, as if he was holding the bones. Tuomi's chest had been beaten in, was severely bruised and partly exposed. He then looked at his own arms and hands; they, too, were black and blue with bruises. He realised that, once again, they were the arms and hands of a murderer.

'I felt complete shock,' he recalls. 'Just couldn't believe it. Shock, horror, panic, I just couldn't believe it happened again after all those years when I'd done nothing like this.' He had a terrible hangover, but fought himself to his feet to ponder what could have occurred. First, he dragged the body to the closet and shut it in, out of sight. Then he spent the next five hours pacing up and down the hotel room, smoking cigarettes non-stop, 'wondering what to do, how to handle the situation'.

Try as he might, he could remember nothing of the death. He knew that they had gone up to the room the night before, had drunk lots of rum and coke. He also knew that he had doctored Steven's drink with the sleeping pills he had prepared in advance, in case he met someone at the 219 Club who might come back with him. But he was sure he had had no intention of harming anyone.

108

They had undressed and gone to bed, masturbated each other, kissed and cuddled with mutual consent before the sleeping pills worked. After Steven passed out, he had continued to stroke and enjoy his body. At some point he had fallen asleep as well. His mind recorded nothing more until the awesome sight which greeted him that morning.

'It's almost like I temporarily lost control of myself,' he said. 'I don't know what was going through my mind. I have no memory of it. I tried to dredge it up, but I have no memory of it whatsoever.' They had been drinking rum, but where was the bottle? It was missing. That might mean that he had taken it out and left the door open, that somebody might have peered inside, it might mean anything. He searched everywhere for the bottle. Had he thrown it out of the window? 'I looked down, went down to the sidewalk under the window, I don't know what I did with it. Sometime during the night I must have taken the bottle and put it somewhere. I never did find out what happened to it. That scared the hell out of me, haunted me for a long time.'

If he could not remember *when* he killed Steven, it was evident from the bruises *how* he had done it. But *why*? It was put to him years later that to beat a man to death suggested an access of rage. 'You're right, you're right,' he said. 'I can't side-step that. That shocked me in the morning. Where that rage came from or why that happened, I don't know. I was not conscious of it. Why I had the rage, why I took it out on him, I don't know. I must have pounded awful hard, because the rib-cage had broken, I could feel the bone. Everything went blank on me.'[1]

There is another possibility, less obvious than rage but, in this case perhaps, more persuasive. It is also more demonic. We already know that Dahmer was hypnotised by the heart-beat and body sounds, that his fascination was with the chest, upon which he liked to lay his head. Is it conceivable that, blinded by alcohol and madness, he dug his fists into the sleeping man's breast in order to get inside him, to achieve that which, in his deranged mind, was the ultimate intimacy? There are easier ways to kill a man through anger than to attempt to tear his heart out.

At about 1 p.m. he went out to the Grand Avenue Mall and bought a large suitcase at Woolworth's. It was more like a trunk, with wheels, the largest he could find. When he returned to the hotel, he booked the room for another night and went upstairs with the case. Late that night, he stuffed Steven's body into it, secured it, and lugged it down to street-level where he called a cab. The taxi-driver helped him put the suitcase in the boot, and then drove him to his grandmother's house at West Allis. His grandmother was asleep. Dahmer placed the suitcase in the fruit-cellar and went to bed.

The family was due to congregate at Catherine Dahmer's for Thanksgiving five days later, thus obliging Jeff to leave Tuomi's body in the fruit-cellar for a week. How it was possible for him to join in the festivities, to get through a normal day, and to go to Ambrosia Chocolate at night, it is difficult to imagine. He took sick leave from work on Monday and Tuesday, but reported for duty as usual on Wednesday, Thursday and Friday.

By the weekend his relations had left the house and he addressed himself to the task of disposal. 'I hated to have to do it at all,' he said. Dismemberment was unpleasant and messy, but it was the only practical option open to him. The weekend was 'anxiety-ridden', as he put it. With a knife which he had bought for the purpose, he removed the head and slit open the belly, then cut the flesh from the body into pieces small enough to handle, dropping them into plastic garbage-bags. On the floor of the fruit-cellar he lay an old sheet and wrapped the bones in it before smashing them with a sledge-hammer; the sheet was used to prevent splinters and fragments from flying all over the basement. The entire undertaking took about two hours to complete. Early on Monday morning he placed the bags with their burden into the trash for collection.

Meanwhile, Dahmer kept the head for a further two weeks, hidden in a blanket on the top shelf of his closet. He boiled it in Soilex and bleach in order to retain the skull, which he then looked at when masturbating. But the bleach had rendered the skull too brittle, so it, too, was eventually smashed and thrown away. No charges were ever brought against him for the murder of Steven Tuomi; nothing of him remained, and there was insufficient evidence to support an indictment.

Notice for eviction was served on Steven by his landlords, alleging non-payment of one month's rent in the amount of $240. The letter was delivered the day after he was last seen alive.

The Ambassador Hotel was the point of no return for Jeffrey Dahmer. Until then, he had succeeded in suppressing what he knew to be unholy thoughts and desires and limiting himself to enjoying the pseudo-death of a drugged partner. But now, after a murder which was neither intended nor recalled, he felt powerless to resist, as if the floodgates had finally burst open. He gave up the struggle. From now on he would not fight the urge, but embrace it, go along with it, accept it as a friend.

The notions of compulsion, addiction, obsession, begin to shape his view of himself as compliant collaborator with an evil force. 'One thing I know for sure,' he said. 'It was a definite compulsion because I couldn't quit. I tried, but after the Ambassador, I couldn't quit. It would be nice if someone could give me an answer on a silver platter as to why I did all this and what caused it, because I can't come up with an answer.'[2] The hunt for the perfect prop, the fantastical become real, would henceforth pervade his every thought and grip him with such intensity as to banish all interfering concepts of morality or safety. 'By that time my moral conscience was so shot, so totally corrupted, that that was my main focus of life. These were my fantasies. That's what happens when you think you don't have to be accountable to anyone. You think you can hide your activities, and never have to account for them. It can lead to anything then, which it did.'[3]

Bewilderment on the one hand, acceptance of personal responsibility on the other, the two quotations above would eventually be the twin pivots upon which Dahmer's trial would swing. It is essential to our understanding of the case that they should not be seen as contradictory, for a man can retain a perfectly clear idea of what is right and good and still be compelled to do what is wrong and bad. It is the nature and the source of that compulsion, as well as its depth, which need to be examined, and it does not help simply to deny it. Psychiatrists talk about a 'personality disorder', which supposes a pre-existing order that has been sent off course; doctors refer to a 'chemical imbalance', which likewise postulates a balance knocked awry. Coming from a religious family, and having spent two years wrestling with the evil that he saw within him, it was natural that Dahmer's understanding of his dilemma should express itself in terms of diabolic possession. The Devil is seen as the *agent* of the imbalance or disorder, the creator of chaos and moral anarchy. 'Am I just an extremely evil person or is it some sort of satanic influence, or what?' he wondered. 'I have no idea. I have no idea at all. Do you? Is it possible to be influenced by spirit beings? I know that sounds like an easy way to cop out and say that I couldn't help myself, but from all that the Bible says, there are forces that have a direct or indirect influence on people's behaviour.'[4]

From this moment, Dahmer began to welcome the intrusive thoughts, no matter where they came from. 'The Bible calls him Satan. I suppose it's possible because it sure seems like some of the thoughts aren't my own, they just come blasting into my head.' They grew stronger and more urgent, and steadily gained momentum; it was as if his life were being *guided* by malignancy. 'These thoughts are very powerful, very destructive, and they do not leave. They're not the kind of thoughts you can just shake your head and they're gone. They do not leave.' The episode at the Ambassador Hotel unleashed forces which could no longer be contained. 'After the fear and the terror of what I'd done had left, which took about a month or two, I started it all over again. From then on it was a craving, a hunger, I don't know how to describe it, a compulsion, and I just kept doing it, doing it and doing it, whenever the opportunity presented itself.'[5]

Dahmer had earlier referred to his 'dark side', and it was this part of himself which henceforth dominated. The concept of a dark component in human nature ascends almost to the beginning of thought, when mankind first contemplated his capacity for wrongdoing and ruminated on its source. Unwilling to see themselves as inherently bad, men have consistently sought to lay the blame for badness outside their own volition, and the notion of possession by evil spirits is pre-Christian in origin. Examples abound in early Jewish history as related in the Old Testament as well as in many primitive peoples, and the idea enjoyed notorious resurgence in the Middle Ages. In 1484, Pope Innocent III declared as unassailable fact the existence of lecherous demons. Even today, mischievous spirits are held to account for headaches or bad temper in some peasant societies.

It has already been noted that the idea of the demon was originally a tutelary spirit who accompanied one through life, watching over mortals with sage advice, since they were not capable of understanding the spirit world by themselves. (The modern 'guru' is a variation on the theme.) These beings were not exclusively evil at all, but influential for both good and bad. It is only with the advent of Christianity that the idea of a supernatural being devoted to promoting the bad gets established. The unitary origin of good and bad influences is supported even etymologically, the words 'God' and 'Devil' being ultimately from the same source. When the ideas became separated, the Devil was initially the obedient servant of God, who happened to be allotted the less agreeable duties among the angels. Christianity effected the complete division of the two concepts, making the Devil responsible only for evil influence, while God was credited with the healthier aspects of human nature.

So deeply-rooted is the conviction of diabolic power that it crops up unwittingly in ordinary conversation, as with the person whose conduct is so out of character that he exclaims in bewilderment, 'I don't know what possessed me', the implication being that a malevolent force should take responsibility. And the common appellation for an unpleasant dream, a 'nightmare', is evidence of its persistence, the second syllable being derived from a word meaning 'spirit' or 'elf' (the second syllable of the French *cauchemar* is from the same source). Even the word 'epilepsy', from the Greek, shows how historically the victim of an attack was thought to be possessed, or 'seized' by the Devil. It is not therefore unusual that Jeffrey Dahmer should have attributed his attacks of murderousness, haltingly, to the work of a malevolent presence. The late Dr Brittain, in his pioneering study of 1970, showed how many murderers of this type speak of two opposing forces battling within them for possession of their soul, and there have been many since to confirm his observations.[6]

There are two other extensions of this idea which will need to be addressed. In the first place, it is by now clear that Dahmer was an acutely depressive man, and one of the many signs of depressive illness is the tendency to identify demons as consuming the patient and stealing his will. The depressive often feels himself to be rubbed out, erased, cancelled. 'In depressive disorders,' writes Herschel Prins, 'feelings of being controlled or influenced by evil or Satanic forces are not uncommon.'[7] Furthermore, excessive alcohol intake may complicate a depressive illness and induce states of 'possession'. It would have been enlightening, perhaps, had Dahmer's trial lawyers investigated the potency of his depression, for which there was ample evidence, instead of concentrating on an illness which nobody could define.

The other point, already touched upon, is the universality of the belief that sexual behaviour is especially the province of demonic influence, a belief tacitly shared even by those who point to the sexual appetite as beneficent. The declared aim of sexual enjoyment, 'ecstasy', is itself a Greek word meaning to stop being oneself, to go outside oneself and experience a change of personality. Thus the purpose of sex is to release that other, hidden, unfettered self which lurks within and craves expression. The sexual imagination is nearly always demonic, a fact amply attested by the wild, Dionysian images of pornography. It was only Dahmer's sexual urges which 'possessed' him, while the rest of his behaviour, when not driven by this compulsion, remained innocuous. One of the most well known of American multiple murderers, Theodore Bundy, was a perfectly pleasant and reasonable man except when he felt himself slipping under exigent influences which consumed him and prevented him from 'being himself'; at such times, he said, he was 'despicable and inhuman'.[8]

When Bundy was sentenced to death, he said something very strange to the court. 'I cannot accept the sentence,' he said, 'because it is not a sentence to me . . . it is a sentence to someone else who is not standing here today.'[9] He did not mean to imply that they had got the wrong man, but that the murderer was not in him *at that moment*, that the disruption he caused to Bundy's personality was episodic. It would be difficult to find a more graphic depiction of the *feeling* of momentary diabolic possession than this, for the *idea* of it is merely an intellectual construction. St Augustine himself believed that evil was a separate power which operated independently of the man whose conduct it infected: 'It is not we ourselves that sin, but some other nature (what, I know not) sins in us.'[10] To live with the feeling that evilness is natural to the human species is a possibility that most people, and all religions, find intolerable.

There are many murderers whose language and behaviour fit the pattern of momentary possession.

Edward Paisnel was known as Uncle Ted by dozens of children on the Isle of Jersey and was a very popular Santa Claus. At the same time, he terrorised the islanders by a vicious series of murders until he was caught in 1971. Ed Gein in Wisconsin, whose murders were utterly conscienceless and brutal, was a likeable and reliable babysitter. Mack Edwards gave himself up in 1970 saying that the demon had left him; before that, he had been killing children for seventeen years. In these cases, and others, it is striking how often a seemingly kind and gentle man may suddenly be inhabited by an alien character, who lets chaos rip. One of the young men who escaped from Dennis Nilsen in 1982, because he was lucky enough to survive until Nilsen's murderous phase had passed, said that before and after the attack the killer had been a 'saint'.[11] A similar incident occurred with Jeff Dahmer, as we shall see, when he refrained from killing Luis Pinet, and did not understand why. In the Tracy Edwards incident, hours before his arrest, we have a picture of Dahmer actually on the threshold of an alteration in personality, about to be 'possessed' if you like, as Edwards saw him on the edge of the bed 'rocking and chanting'; the prosecution was understandably anxious to discredit this piece of evidence.

Dr Hyatt Williams makes the point very clearly. 'The most cruel and destructive behaviour,' he writes, 'can be perpetrated by a person at one time, while almost immediately before or after such conduct he can be kind and compassionate.'[12] It seems that some kind of internal short circuit may occur to release that mode of behaviour which the individual finds uncontrollable, and therefore not really coming from him. Frederic Wertham called it a 'catathymic crisis',[13] but we are at liberty to call it possession if we wish; it is only a difference in nomenclature, and the language of myth is more accessible than the language of doctors.

The language of literature is also rather more vivid. Dualistic characters exist throughout world literature, and are particularly abundant in the work of Dostoievsky, witness Raskolnikov in *Crime and Punishment* or Versilov in *A Raw Youth*, who says, 'I am split mentally and horribly afraid of it. It is as if you have your own double standing next to you.' James Hogg wrote an entire book on this precise theme, entitled *The Private Memoirs and Confessions of a Justified Sinner*, in which the protagonist, Robert Wringhim, meets a stranger under whose influence he commits a number of murders. He resembles him in feature and manner. It is only gradually that the reader comes to realise that the stranger may not be another person, but a personification of that part of Wringhim's own self which cannot be acknowledged. It does not matter whether you call the stranger Dionysus, or the Devil, or Wringhim devoid of conscience, or Wringhim's 'dark side', and the novel is so beautifully ambiguous that all four are simultaneously possible. Now, Jeff Dahmer has not claimed to have a 'double', but his words and evident bewilderment point to a similar conclusion. He cannot believe that the whole story is 'real', that he did all those things, although he knows he did and can describe his acts in detail and with chilling objectivity. The British so-called 'Moors Murderer', Ian Brady, is on record as believing that he was watching his mind and feeling detached from it at the same time.

This division between the self that is wicked and murderous and the self which can catch a bus, eat a meal, do a job of work, would cause great travail in the courtroom when the question of Dahmer's sanity was addressed. Suffice it to say for the moment that a murderer may be able to tell time accurately and draw inferences from the information, but he cannot fathom the springs of his deviant behaviour; if he could, then he would take charge of it. 'I doubt if there's any good in me,' Dahmer once said.[14] He drew Dr Judith Becker's attention to a passage in St Paul's Letter to the Romans, Book V: 'What I do is not what I want to do, but what I detest . . . it is no longer I who perform the action, but sin that lodges in me. For

117

I know that nothing good lodges in me . . . The good which I want to do, I fail to do; but what I do is the wrong which is against my will; and if what I do is against my will, clearly it is no longer I who am the agent, but sin that has its lodging in me.' This is what should be understood by Dahmer's frequent allusion to his 'compulsion'.

In the weeks following the death of Steven Tuomi, Dahmer continued to honour his appointments with Dr Rosen, while refusing to co-operate in any but the most perfunctory manner. His panic subsided when nobody seemed to notice that Steven was gone, or to connect his disappearance with the Ambassador Hotel (where Dahmer had registered in his own name). The desires, correspondingly, mounted. In January of 1988 he took a twenty-three-year-old black man, Bobby Simpson, back to the house in West Allis. In the basement he drugged him and masturbated four times with him. But he went no further. Simpson had no idea just how fortunate he was.

It was one in the morning on 17 January, 1988, when Dahmer left the 219 Club. At the bus-stop he noticed a young man in faded burgundy jeans with suspenders hanging loose, a sweater and a golfer's cap. He was James Doxtator, a Native American, who had several times threatened to run away from home because he did not get along with his step-father, and who lusted after a Jaguar car which a neighbour promised to give him when he turned eighteen. He told his mother Debra that if he ever did leave home, he would keep in touch with her, but he did not say that he was going to the gay bars of South 2nd Street and enjoying male company. The man who approached him that night was very pleasant. Dahmer offered him $50 to come home and spend the night with him, which Jamie gladly accepted, and they took the bus out to West Allis, alighting at 57th and National. Dahmer says he was looking for 'companionship' and found the boy attractive; 'he appealed to me'. The chances are, Jamie

118

Doxtator was also looking for companionship, but of a different order.

Mrs Dahmer was fast asleep upstairs. She never stirred during the night. The two men started in the sitting-room, undressed each other, kissed and felt each other's bodies. This went on for well over an hour, with Dahmer performing fellatio upon his willing partner. Then they went down to the basement; it is not clear why they should need to do this, unless Dahmer had already formed the intention of harming him. The possibility was hovering in his mind because he was enjoying Jamie's body and wanted the pleasure to continue. At about 4 a.m. Jamie let slip that he would not be able to stay too late in the morning but would need to get back home. The threat of departure. The promise to abandon. The fact of leaving. Dahmer mixed a drink.

The drink was a cocktail of Irish cream, coffee, and crushed sleeping pills. As the drug began to work, which took about half an hour, they kissed frequently. Then, in a tableau of painful poignancy, Jamie fell asleep on Dahmer's lap, secure in the arms of his new friend. Dahmer held him for a long while, stroking his skin. His body was comforting and warm. Then he stretched him out on a sheet on the cellar floor. In his own bland and icy words, 'I knew my grandma would be waking up and I still wanted him to stay with me so I strangled him.'[15]

Jamie knew nothing of what was happening, as he had been deeply unconscious. Dahmer lay holding him a little longer until day was about to break; it was time to conceal the body in the fruit-closet. He went and had breakfast with his grandmother and waited for her to go off to church (it was Sunday morning). Then he went downstairs again to fetch the body. 'I brought him up to the bedroom and pretended he was still alive.' He kissed and caressed the body, and proceeded to penetrate it anally.

Doxtator was returned to the cellar where he remained for another week. Dahmer was at work all that week, during the course of which he went down three times to lie with the corpse. After four or five days an odour began to drift up to the house, causing Mrs Dahmer to remark upon it. Jeff told her that the cat litter was smelling and he would see to it. The following Sunday, he disposed of the body in the same way that he had done with Tuomi, cutting off the head and flesh and breaking the bones with a sledge-hammer, and taking care to put newspaper at the little cellar window so as not to be observed. The blood was easily hosed down the drains. All except the head was placed in the trash for collection on Monday morning. Dahmer took sick leave from work that Monday, but kept his appointment with Dr Rosen. He boiled the head and bleached the skull, as before, and kept it for a further two weeks, imagining that, each time he took the skull out of the closet, he was still with the young man whose spirit had inhabited it.

Dahmer intended to keep this skull indefinitely, for he had by now conceived the notion, albeit only in tentative form, that he would create some kind of temple at which the skull would be on show for his private, secret worship. By his own admission, the 'compulsion' was now 'in full swing' and he no longer had any thought of containing it. He would struggle only to find a way forward – to indulge, replenish and perpetuate the fantasy which had taken him over. But the skull again became too brittle and had to be destroyed. All trace of Jamie Doxtator disappeared, hostage to the febrile fantasies of a lost mind.

Doxtator was a tall boy, at just under six feet almost the same height as Dahmer. He had a small moustache and looked sixteen or seventeen years old. In fact, he was only fourteen.

Dahmer claimed he did not know where the pressure which drove him came from. Asked to describe it, he said it was 'an incessant and never-ending desire to have someone at whatever cost, someone good looking, really nice looking, and it just filled my thoughts all day long, increasing in intensity throughout the years when I was living with Grandma. Very overpowering, just relent-less.'[16]

The next to fall victim to this suffocating greed, barely two months after Doxtator, was Richard Guerrero, aged twenty-three. The pattern was established. They met out-side the Phoenix Bar at 2 a.m. on the morning of 27 March, 1988. Dahmer offered Richard $50 to spend the rest of the night with him, to which he agreed. They took a taxi to the Mai Kai Tavern and walked the two blocks from there to Grandma's house. She was asleep. This time they went upstairs to Jeff's bedroom and had 'light sex' together – the usual body-rubbing, kissing, and mastur-bation. About two hours later the decision to kill was made and the potion prepared. At this point another Dantesque image, at once hellish and pathetic, thrusts itself before our contemplation, for Dahmer strangled the sleeping Guerrero with his bare hands as he lay naked next to him, looking at him, and when the deed was done, threw his arms around the corpse and embraced it. From now on, this would be a constant theme, the act of killing as a grotesque distortion of the act of love. He did not enjoy the killing, but had to kill in order to love, in order to indulge the hideous parody of intimacy and cherishing which was the only kind of 'love' he knew how to show. He now had Richard all to himself for another few hours, and performed oral sex upon his corpse.

Dahmer left it in bed while he had breakfast with Grandma, and took it to the basement when she went to church. Sunday being the only convenient day when he could dismember, and as he did not want to leave the body for a whole week, he was obliged to take Richard to pieces there and then, and place his remains in the garbage for collection Monday morning. He kept the skull for several months, having found a way to prevent its crumbling by diluting the bleach which he used.

The following weekend brought Easter and another encounter for Jeff Dahmer which did not end tragically; it does, however, afford us a further glimpse into his mode of behaviour during the hours preceding an attack. Ronald Flowers, a handsome, broad black man of twenty-five, went to the 219 Club two or three times a week from his home in Racine, Wisconsin, an hour away. Friends had invited him down that Saturday, but he had declined as he was awaiting delivery of a water-bed. When the water-bed did not arrive, he drove himself to Milwaukee and met his friends (two men and a woman) inside the club. They all four left at the same time, the other three driving off in their own car. Flowers walked over to his 1978 Oldsmobile Regency, parked opposite, and could not start it. After three attempts, the battery went dead and he realised he was stranded. Outside the 219 Club is a much-used pay phone, generally with a queue of people waiting for it. Flowers tried some calls to get someone to rescue him, with no luck, and was about to surrender the cause as lost. It was then that Jeff Dahmer approached him.

When the problem was explained to him, Dahmer invited Flowers to share a cab home with him, where they could retrieve Dahmer's car, bring it back, and jump-start the faulty car. Jeff Dahmer, of course, had no car. Flowers had only drunk one rum and coke, as he had intended to drive back to Racine, so his wits were about him. In the taxi he found it difficult to make easy conversation with his Good Samaritan; Dahmer averted his eye constantly, and spoke in gloomy negatives, about how he hated his work, how he did not get along with his family, and so on. Flowers quickly formed the impression he was a depressive and depressing character, even boring. Still, he did need to get his car working, and was not interested in sharing any other activity with this man.

They alighted two blocks away from the house. Dahmer explained that this was to avoid waking his grandmother with headlights or slamming doors. Flowers noticed that there was no sign of a car outside the house, and grew suspicious. As they went in, a voice from upstairs said, 'Is that you, Jeff?' 'Yes, Grandma,' Dahmer said, 'I'm just going to make myself a cup of coffee.' The reply implied he was alone.

Flowers' anxiety was heightened by Dahmer's demeanour and conduct in the kitchen. They sat at the kitchen table to have their coffee, but Dahmer was so nervous he was visibly shaking. Flowers was thinking how soon he would be able to get out of the house, and how to get back to his car, when he began to feel dizzy and sleepy and passed out. He woke up two days later in hospital, where he was told that he had been found unconscious in a field and brought to town by ambulance. There was no sign of drugs in his body, nor of any sexual assault, but his necklace, bracelet and $200 were missing. His brother collected him and he was discharged.

Back home, Ronald Flowers noticed two things: there were strange bruise marks either side of his neck, about two inches round, and his underpants were inside out.

He made complaint that Dahmer had drugged him and stolen his property, and police officers interviewed the suspect on 5 April after Flowers had shown them the house. Dahmer denied the allegations, claiming that Flowers had drunk too much and that he had helped him get to the bus-stop the next morning. There was no proving either way, and charges were never brought. But it is interesting to speculate what might have happened. Catherine Dahmer stated that her grandson had made a bed up for his friend in the basement and that she had seen them leave the house together on Sunday. It may well be that Flowers was put on a bus, got off somewhere and wandered into a field, still under the effect of the crushed tablets he had been made to swallow. More crucially, why did Dahmer not kill him?

Various reasons were adduced at the trial, all of which pointed convincingly to the murderer's cunning and calculation. Ronald Flowers was too strong, too masculine, to have been summarily despatched; there might have been a struggle, some noise, Grandma might have woken up. Even if she hadn't, she was already a witness, for she had heard them come in and divined that Jeff's guest was to stay the night. And yet, there were the marks on Flowers' neck, indicating that Dahmer had probably attempted to go through the motions of strangling him. Is it possible that he 'snapped out' of his murderousness in time to prevent himself going through with the kill? Probably not. One is bound to admit that it is much more likely he realised the risks and desisted. The marks on Flowers' neck conjure an image of Dahmer wishing he could keep Flowers and holding his hands on him, knowing he couldn't, struggling to control the surging desire, and succeeding. It would be one of the most potent images against him at his trial.

He doubtless was able to keep Ronald Flowers long enough to explore his body, which would account for his underwear being put on the wrong way round.

Three months later, Flowers was again in the 219 Club, where he recognised Jeff Dahmer by his singularly grubby Hush Puppy shoes. He went up to him and asked if he remembered him. Dahmer said he did not, but invited him to come for a coffee anyway. 'You know who the fuck I am,' shouted Flowers, who was about to attack him until his companions dissuaded him. Outside the club, he again saw Dahmer getting into a taxi with another black man about to join him. 'Don't go with him,' screamed Flowers, 'he's fucking crazy.' On hearing this, the stranger withdrew and, presumably, is unaware how close he might have come to a brush with madness.

It was largely the result of the incident with Ronald Flowers that the family decided it was time for Jeff to move out of his grandmother's and find a place of his own. The old lady was tired of his drinking and uneasy about his 'guests'. 'There was pressure from my grandma and dad and my aunt Eunice. I guess you could say I was sort of eased out.' A family conference was held, bringing Eunice, Lionel's sister, up from Greendale some ten miles from Milwaukee. 'Word had gotten around about my late-night activities, drinking, going to the bars, and so they thought it would be better to finally just move out.'[17] Another decision reached that day was that Jeff should seek some help for his excessive drinking. Accordingly, Lionel took his son to the Family Services on West Highland Avenue on 26 April and presented him to Dr Michael Bleadorn to be treated for alcoholism. Unfortunately, the course only lasted four sessions, and it had anyway to compete for influence with a new obsession of Jeff's which evolved at the same time. He had bought a video of the movie *Return of the Jedi*, in which the emperor is all-powerful and possesses ultimate control over mortals. He was watching it several times a week, and became so entranced by it, so identified with the character of the emperor, that he bought yellow-tinted contact lenses in the vain hope that they might lend him some of that power, and wore them when he went to the bars. It might ordinarily have been a mild eccentricity, but with Dahmer it was a further sinister indication of his descent into unreason.

To match this development, in the summer of 1988 he bought a long black table and two statues of griffins. He still nurtured the idea of his own temple, and these were steps towards its realisation: the black table would be the altar, and the griffins, mythological creatures with the head and wings of an eagle and the body of a lion, would be its protection.

In June, Dahmer took the lease of a small apartment at 808 North 24th Street, and stocked up on his supply of sleeping pills, still regularly prescribed by Dr Carroll Ollson. He took the skull of Richard Guerrero with him to the new apartment.

Dahmer's surface existence continued to be unremarkable and utterly undisturbed by these subterranean fissures. His work at the Ambrosia Chocolate Factory was satisfactory, if not intellectually demanding. As a mixer he was required to measure out powdered sugar into four giant drums, each with a capacity of eleven thousand pounds, and operate machinery to start the mixture working. He would then cut open the cocoa-bags and add the contents of these manually into the mixers, pour in the soybean treacle ('It looks like maple syrup but tastes like motor-oil'), and finally add vegetable oil. The whole lot coalesced into a thick paste, at which point he would turn the mixer off and signal to workers on the floor below, who opened a hole in the bottom of the mixer and the paste would drop out in big blobs; this went on through other processes to become powder, thinner paste, and finally chocolate. 'A lot of heavy lifting there, a lot of bags to cut open, but it wasn't a bad job.'[18] Soon after he had started, he experienced pain in his knees and various other joints, which the rheumatologist ascribed to lifting heavy weights, but it passed quite quickly.

For the first four years, Dahmer gave no cause for complaint. Not only was he commended for the quality of his work, but he was found to be 'resourceful, alert to opportunities for improvement', which comes as something of a surprise, 'always congenial and co-operative', 'neat and clean'. His report at the end of 1986 was lyrical: 'Jeff is consistently improving and is proving to be an asset to the mixing department.' The following year he was 'willing to learn', was 'rarely absent and rarely tardy', though it was observed that he required motivation and guidance; his concentration was beginning to wane. It was not until the last year that chronic absenteeism proved his undoing. But by then his sanity had irrevocably cracked.

He was always quiet and unsociable, normal and pleasant when spoken to, but unlikely to seek the company of his fellow-workers. Another mixer thought he appeared to be under stress at times, while Timothy Mills noticed he had a tendency to fall asleep on the job. He was always reading books about animals and fish when not actually mixing. Tim McNamer corroborated the impression that Dahmer would fall asleep on occasions, and Dahmer himself admits that he never did get the sleep he needed, because there were often things to be done during the day when he should have been resting. The night shift is a punishing routine in any job.

There was only one man he spoke to regularly in the mornings, before punching out and going home, a man whom he bumped into at one of the bars by chance, whereupon they both realised they shared an interest in the homosexual scene. Otherwise, nobody at Ambrosia knew that Dahmer was homosexual, nor would have suspected it, because he was so intensely private.

His professional life, such as it was, went on thus placidly until September of 1988, when he found himself suddenly placed under arrest.

It was 3.30 in the afternoon on Monday, 26 September. A student at the Milwaukee School of the Arts, Somsack Sinthasomphone, felt the presence of a man walking behind him on North 25th Street. The son of a large Laotian family, refugees from political turmoil in South-East Asia eight years before, Somsack had been rapidly Americanised and, unlike his father, spoke English fluently. The man stopped Somsack and initiated a conversation. He said he had just acquired a new camera and wanted to try it out. He had been asking other people in the street if they would pose for him for $50 an hour, but nobody had taken him up on the offer, which he thought was odd; you'd think someone would want to make an easy $50 just to help him out! Would he like to try? It wouldn't take long.

Somsack was wily enough to ask if he would need to strip or pose with his clothes on. Dahmer said it really didn't matter. Was it for a company or for himself? Just a new hobby, said Dahmer. So the boy said he would come. 'I thought he was nice and just wanted to try out his new camera,' he later said. They walked the one block to 24th Street.

Once in the apartment, Dahmer produced a polaroid camera and began to prepare his poses. He told Somsack to take his shirt off, but the boy resisted, whereupon he assured him it would make a better picture and pulled the shirt up over his head, revealing his chest, clean, beautifully shaped and disastrously appealing to Jeff Dahmer. 'You have a nice body,' he said. 'Lie on the bed with your hands behind your head.' The boy obliged and was photographed. They went to the kitchen where Dahmer made a cup of coffee which they shared, Somsack drinking most of it at Dahmer's instigation, while he gingerly sipped. Back in the living-room, Somsack pulled his shirt up again, and the photographer suggested he open the top button of his trousers and pull the zipper down. He did this, but pulled the zipper down only halfway, whereupon Dahmer pulled it right down, lowered his underpants and attempted to handle him. Somsack stopped this. The whole thing was getting out of hand and he felt this man to be strangely threatening, intense. 'You know I want more from you than a picture,' the man said.

At this point Somsack declared that it was time for him to go. 'Do me a favour before you leave,' said Dahmer. 'Come and sit beside me.' That seemed innocuous enough, so the boy sat beside him for a few minutes. Dahmer then made a weird and worrying request. 'I want to hear your stomach,' he said, and, placing his head on the boy's abdomen, he began to kiss and lick him from the navel to the groin. 'I really felt scared and sick,' the boy related. He jumped up, grabbed his school satchel and made for the door. 'Wait! Don't forget your $50,' said Dahmer, 'and don't tell anyone, O.K.?' Somsack fled the apartment and went straight home, but started to feel oddly tired and disoriented along the way. By the time he got to the house, he could barely stand. Two hours later, his father was unable to wake him and immediately realised there was something seriously wrong. He took him to the Good Samaritan Hospital, where he was diagnosed as suffering from the effects of a drug overdose. The police were summoned.

Somsack Sinthasomphone was detained at the hospital for about three hours, from 7.30 to 10.30 p.m., and told the police officers who came to interview him exactly what had happened. He took them to 24th Street and pointed out the apartment. It did not take long for them to identify the tenant and his place of work, and they went straight to Ambrosia Chocolate to confront the suspect and make an arrest for Second Degree Sexual Assault and Enticing a Child for Immoral Purposes. Handcuffs were placed on him there and then. Dahmer was more horrified by the embarrassment of public exposure than by the nature of the charges; his privacy was now irretrievably compromised, and everyone at work would know that he was homosexual.

Jeff Dahmer was taken to jail, where he spent the next six days in a fever of anxiety. The police searched his apartment and carefully removed the polaroid camera, the bottle of Bailey's Irish Cream, two photographs of Somsack, some male nude magazines and some sleeping pills. What they did not find, and what drove Dahmer into much terrorised apprehension, was the skull of Richard Guerrero.

Thus passed the second occasion on which the police might have discovered Dahmer's crimes before they escalated into demented catastrophe, the first being when flashlights were shone upon the bags containing Steven Hicks in the back of his car in 1978. One must not chastise the police for this; we would soon complain if they always assumed the worst and behaved without any sensitivity at all. It is nonetheless worthy of remark, as there will be several other moments of uncanny propinquity or nearmisses before Dahmer's course is finally stopped. He was so preoccupied by the skull that he forgot to tell his employers that he was in jail, and lost several days' leave in consequence.

Another result of the affair was a visit from Lionel, who was confronted for the first time with the fact of his son's homosexuality. Jeff recalls the meeting in his characteristically anodyne manner: 'He asked me if I was gay and I told him yes, and he accepted it fairly well. He didn't get upset or anything about it. He just acted surprised and wondered why I'd never told him before and I said I didn't tell him because I was embarrassed.'[19] There was probably a little more to it than that, as Lionel was not disposed to be tolerant on such a matter and still felt that perversity was condemned by God. There was no doubt that he thought Jeff should be helped, and that he would do what he could to promote that help, but there can equally have been no doubt that Jeff felt the undercurrent of paternal disapproval.

The sequence of psychological evaluations which then followed, before Dahmer's appearance in court, are little short of astonishing in their prescience and the urgency of their warning. When taken in conjunction with the reports of 1986, they constitute the plainest possible signal of alarm. With Dr Charles Lodl, Dahmer was unusually frank, telling him that he was in 'significant psychological distress', that he was 'anxious, tense and depressed', and that he harboured 'deep feelings of alienation'. I hope it is not too fanciful to see in these words a request for further exploration – the much-derided 'cry for help'. There were very few occasions when Dahmer's iron self-protection could be pierced, but this meeting with Dr Lodl was, I think, one of them. He certainly did not have the courage to turn himself in entirely of his own accord.

Lodl opined that the patient was a 'very psychologically problemed man', and darkly concluded, 'There is no question that Mr Dahmer is in need of long-term psychological treatment.'

This is the first time that we meet Attorney Gerald Boyle, hired by Lionel Dahmer to defend his son against the pending charges. It was Boyle who sought the opinion of Dr Lodl, which he then forwarded to Probation Officer Gloria Anderson. She in turn commissioned a second opinion from Dr Norman Goldfarb, whose report is, if anything, even more cautionary. The interview took place two months after that with Dr Lodl, and in the interim Dahmer had sloughed off that tentative hint of co-operation he had shown before. Now he was 'resistant and evasive', showing irritation, anger, agitation, and answering in monosyllables. Despite this, his voice was utterly devoid of emotional shading or life, and Goldfarb noted that he was 'suspicious of the motives of others' – a classic schizoid trait. He thought Dahmer was impulsive, unlikely to tolerate frustration or delay of self-gratification, dismayed by his lack of accomplishment, manipulative and self-centred. It was curious that there was not a single person whom he could call a friend.

It was clear that Dahmer was able to function without arousing suspicion, but he 'would not show others the depth, severity or extent of his pathology', and in consequence 'others may not take his behaviours as seriously as they should'. In conclusion, Dr Goldfarb declared Dahmer to be 'a seriously disturbed young man' with a mixed personality disorder; 'the pressure he perceives seems to be increasing' and 'he must be considered impulsive and dangerous'.

Gloria Anderson appended her own recommendations for the court's attention, pointing to the mental problems which Joyce Dahmer had suffered and the alcoholism of her father. She continued: 'There has been much emotional instability in this family and . . . much confusion and isolation among family members. Jeff grew up in an atmosphere clouded by turmoil, mental health problems, unhappiness, confusion, and rejection, which had led to a breakdown in the family structure.' She further quoted Dr Evelyn Rosen's view that Dahmer had a 'schizoid personality with paranoid features', and added a dire prognostication: 'Jeff is not psychotic, but not much is needed to push him, and alcohol serves this purpose.'

Jeffrey Dahmer appeared before Judge William Gardner at the Safety Building in Milwaukee on 30 January, 1989, and pleaded no contest to the charge of Second Degree Sexual Assault. He claimed the administration of the drug was accidental, that he had not noticed a residue in the cup he had himself used earlier. He also said he was shocked to discover the plaintiff was only thirteen years old. A verdict of guilty was returned, the judge reserving sentencing until a later date to allow himself time to consider the psychological reports. Three months later, Dahmer was given one year in the House of Correction, and, consecutively, five years' probation. Upon application from Attorney Boyle, Judge Gardner subsequently signed an order for work release, permitting Dahmer to continue with his job at Ambrosia Chocolate six days a week and report back to the House of Correction for his accommodation.

Two important letters were written as a sequel to this episode in Dahmer's life. The first was from Jeff himself, some time into his sentence, writing to Judge Gardner. 'Sir, I have always believed that a man should be willing to assume responsibility for the mistakes that he makes in life. What I did was deplorable. The world has enough misery in it without my adding more to it.' He requested a modification of sentence.

Knowing what he knew, this display of contrition is either monumentally cynical, or pathologically disconnected from reality. He now says he did not write the letter anyway. It was written by another prisoner who was keen on helping people, a man of about forty-five or fifty who Jeff thought was serving time for armed robbery. It was 'basically his letter with my signature on it. No, I didn't write a word of that.'[20] He did, however, copy it out in his own hand.[21]

The second letter, also to Judge Gardner, is from Dr Lionel Dahmer, expressing his concern that the court had ordered no follow-up treatment for his son. He had only discovered about the therapy with Dr Rosen, he said, after the sessions were well advanced, and was dismayed to be told that she was not a specialist in treating alcohol-related problems. Every time his son had been in trouble, it had been due to alcohol. In the circumstances, wrote Lionel, 'I have tremendous reservations regarding Jeff's chances when he hits the streets.' He concluded with the request that Jeff not be told he had written, presumably because he did not want him to realise he was urging more psychotherapy, and a touching imprecation: 'I sincerely hope that you might intervene in some way to help my son whom I love very much and for whom I want a better life . . . This may be,' he said, 'our last chance.'[22]

The most pathetic postscript to the case was given by the victim himself, Somsack Sinthasomphone, and his father. The boy said that after he came out of the House of Correction Dahmer should be watched everywhere he went. The father told Somsack that if he had not been healthy and athletic he might have passed out in Dahmer's apartment 'or', reflected the boy, 'maybe he would have killed me'. What makes this sage and loving advice so unbearable is that, by the most cruel, capricious coincidence, Somsack's brother met Jeff Dahmer two years later and died at his hands.

By this time, no amount of advice to individuals or warnings from psychologists appeared able to stop Dahmer when in the grip of his 'compulsion'. It is scarcely credible, but true, that in the intervening weeks between his conviction for sexual assault and the passing of sentence upon him, Dahmer had killed for the fifth time.

Chapter Six

The Nightmare

Depressed by his conviction and convinced that his life was hardly worth living, Dahmer sank further into lassitude. He began to think of suicide, at the same time fully aware that he lacked the courage to do more than talk about it. He could see no way to correct an empty and destructive life. All he had was the ceaseless compulsion to be with somebody, some *body*, and alleviate his isolation for a few hours; he described the compulsion to Dr Becker as 'painful'.

On 20 March, 1989, he took a ten-day vacation from work which would stretch over the approaching Easter period. He moved out of his little apartment in preparation for his pending incarceration at the Work Release Center, and returned to his grandmother's house at West Allis. Five days later, on Easter Saturday, the urge to prowl and capture a companion was once more upon him, so he went to his usual source, Richard's Pharmacy, and replenished his supply of sleeping tablets. He regularly bought thirty tablets at a time, usually prescribed by Dr Carroll Ollson. This was his fourteenth such prescription.

That evening Dahmer went out drinking at the bars. He barely spoke to anyone at all, and gave up any hope of a meeting. The yearning seemed to have worn off; he was resigned, even a little relieved. The final stop was a bar called La Cage (inspired by the uproarious French film *La Cage aux Folles*) on 2nd and National. Just before closing time, 'I was walking towards the entrance, I wasn't planning on meeting anyone or going out with anyone, and this nice-looking black guy starts talking to me, just out of the blue.' This is the first occasion on which Dahmer has not picked up a victim, but has himself been picked up by one. It was to be a fateful initiative on the part of twenty-four-year-old Anthony Sears.

Tony was indeed an attractive man, extrovert and friendly. He wore a V-neck sweater with a white T-shirt underneath, old faded blue jeans with holes at the knees, white tennis shoes, and drew his hair back in a small ponytail. He was not alone, but his white friend Jeff Connor was chatting to somebody else when Tony made his approach to the reserved and quiet stranger. Connor overheard him ask the man if he had any coke, to which he replied that he had some rum as well. 'No,' said Tony Sears, 'I mean cocaine!' Tony had recently fallen into the cocaine habit rather badly. Dahmer invited him to spend the night, and Tony eagerly agreed. He was, it must be said, very keen. Jeff Connor saw what was happening and volunteered to drive them wherever they needed to go. He heard Dahmer say that he was from Chicago and was on a visit to his grandmother in Milwaukee. They all three walked to the parking-lot and found Connor's car; Connor got into the driving-seat, Dahmer and Sears sat behind.

Dahmer asked him to drop them off at the corner of 57th and Lincoln and they would walk the rest of the way. On the journey, Sears unzipped Dahmer's trousers and performed oral sex (fellatio) upon him, 'which was a surprise. I didn't think he was that anxious.' Jeff Connor knew what was going on and did not want to interfere, but he nonetheless felt rather uneasy. He had what he called 'bad vibrations' about this person. When they arrived in West Allis, Dahmer got out first and waited across the street. This gave Connor an opportunity to express his misgivings to Tony and extract from him a promise that he would telephone as soon as he was ready, say in a couple of hours, so that Connor could return to collect him. It was already 3 a.m. when he drove away.

The two men sat in the kitchen at 2357 South 57th Street for a while, then went up to bed. They kissed and lay one on top of the other in mutual enjoyment, Dahmer fellating Sears this time. He then asked him how long he could stay, could he stay tomorrow, could he come back? Tony, fatally, said he would have to leave soon and probably would not return. Dahmer went down to the kitchen and put together his concoction of coffee, Bailey's Irish Cream and seven sleeping pills, and brought it to Tony Sears. Half an hour later, Sears was fast asleep. Dahmer again kissed him and lay as close as possible to him. And there, in the bed, he strangled him.

Grandma woke up and prepared breakfast. This being Easter Sunday, she would be at church longer than usual, possibly four hours, and Jeff could be alone with his 'friend' without fear of disturbance. As soon as she left, he went upstairs again and got into bed, kissed him, felt him, and entered him. He did not have the leisure to stay all day like this, however, and soon began to think about disposal. He dragged the corpse into the upstairs bathroom and hauled it into the bathtub, thinking that the blood might drain more easily in the tub than in the cellar.

What happened next is acutely distressing. Indeed, as this story unfolds it becomes ever more hard to bear and upsetting to think upon. Dahmer decapitated Anthony Sears and attempted to flay him. Then he stripped the flesh in the usual way, and cut off the genitals, which he placed in a separate bag with the head. He did this *because 'him I like especially well'*, as an expression of affection, as a salute to the good time they had had together. He did not want to lose him, and, if he kept the genitals as well as the head, perhaps he wouldn't! The bones were smashed and disposed of, but the keepsakes had to be carefully looked after. The next day, Dahmer called a taxidermist and asked advice on how to preserve animal remains in such a way as to keep the flesh as well as the skeleton. He was told to use acetone.

At Ace Hardware he bought a 10-gallon plastic bucket with a tight-fitting lid, filled it with acetone, and left the head and genitals in this for one week on the floor of his bedroom closet. He also bought base make-up and painted the genitals with this in order to make them look more 'real'. After a week the head was dry but still very life-like; on four occasions Jeff held it in one hand while he masturbated with the other, and could even mimic the action of having oral sex with it. In time, he would scalp it and use the pony-tailed scalp both for stimulation and as a remembrance. That Anthony Sears should have his life stolen at so young an age and to no purpose is in itself vicious and pitiful; that his remains should be thus used further offends one's sense of respect; but that Dahmer's mind should be so deranged as to find solace and comfort in such acts stuns comprehension.

Jeff Connor was very concerned when Tony did not telephone early on Sunday morning. He suspected he might be in trouble and drove back to West Allis to look for him. He did not know, however, which house to enquire at. Another friend, Karolee Lodahl, reported Tony missing when she went to his apartment and found his pets had not been fed. She told the police that she suspected foul play because his life-style might expose him to danger. Other friends were interviewed, and Jeff Connor gave a detailed description of the man last seen with Tony. This was the first time in the course of Dahmer's criminal progress that the police had a full account of a missing person and a suspected felony. With his accurate description on police files, it ought not to have been long before the person identified as 'Jeff from Chicago' was spotted somewhere. But Connor never saw him again, and the file lay dormant.

Meanwhile, Dahmer was disappointed that the head which had kept so well for a week was beginning to shrivel and look mummified. He had taken it out of the acetone and placed it in a small metal trunk which he kept double-locked. When the time came for him to report to the

137

House of Correction to serve his sentence, he realised that it would not be safe to leave all this at the house. And yet he could not bear to lose 'Tony' altogether. His solution was odd; he bought an oval Samsonite cosmetic case, put the head and genitals in this, and deposited it in his locker at the Ambrosia Chocolate Factory. The cosmetic case and its contents remained undiscovered in Dahmer's locker for the next nine months while he was resident at the House of Correction.

For Thanksgiving he was allowed a ten-hour pass to spend with his family. He could not face going to West Allis in view of his predicament and the embarrassment his conviction had caused, to himself as well as to the family, so he wandered the streets instead. None of the shopping malls were open, as would be expected, but the bars were. He drank first some beers, then went on to a very strong liquor called Yukon Jack, and ended up late at night talking to a white man, older than himself, at the 219 Club. The next thing he remembered was waking to find himself strung up above a bed in the stranger's house, 'hog-tied' he called it, being spanked and violated with a candle. 'I made enough noise, I was yelling loud enough, that he took me down.'[1] Dahmer, for once the victimised, dressed and left as quickly as possible and was five hours' late returning to the House of Correction. It was not until the next day that he was able to evacuate the candle.

On 2 March, 1990, Dahmer was released from the prison three months prematurely, probably as a result of the letter he had written to Judge Gardner, mentioned earlier. It is also possible that Gary Parker, the agent from the Department of Health and Social Services with whom he had had several meetings, recommended curtailment of the sentence. Immediately his five years' probation began, and he was assigned to Probation Officer Miss Donna Chester. At their very first interview, he told her that his problem was with drinking and that, as he had no friends at all, he drank alone. Within a month of his release he had consulted Dr Ollson and received a prescription for thirty sleeping tablets, to be augmented two weeks later by a further supply of sixty tablets. He had also been to his locker at Ambrosia Chocolate.

The cosmetic case was intact. He took it home to his grandmother's, where he was again living until he could find an apartment for himself, and opened it. The painted genitals had preserved fairly well, but the head had grown an unattractive mould, so he decided to boil it and deflesh it. First, however, 'I took a knife and cut the scalp part off and peeled the flesh off the bone and kept the skull and the scalp.' At least he would have the best part of Tony to remember him by. He would one day tell Dr Dietz, 'If I could have kept him longer, all of him, I would have.'[2]

Dahmer decided he must get an apartment of his own again, and devoted a whole day to the task of looking for one. He wanted a single bedroom, at low rent, close to work, close to the buslines, and by chance he stumbled upon the Oxford Apartments on North 25th Street. No. 213 was available at $300 a month, including everything except electricity, so he took it despite its location. 'I was willing to take my chances in that neighbourhood,' he said. 'It was generally quiet, there wasn't a lot of distraction or noise, a lot of privacy. It was nice enough for the price.' The apartment came furnished with a bed, a dresser, a lounge chair, some endtables and lamps, a kitchen table and fridge. 'It was big enough for me, the bathroom was clean, it had air conditioning, so it was good and liveable.' He moved in on 14 May, 1990, taking among his personal luggage the skull, scalp and genitals.

What he left unsaid was that North 25th Street was in one of the most insalubrious and dangerous parts of Milwaukee. The streets are faded and threatening, and sunk in hopelessness. Drug-related crime is there an almost daily event.

Dahmer was almost the only white person in the block. That did not bother him, as he did not intend to have much to do with the neighbours. Most of his contact with them was restricted to a casual greeting. 'One time the guy and his wife who lived across from me, they came over and asked to borrow $25 because he said they had some emergency, they had to get a bus to visit some sick relative, so I loaned him some money. Never got the money back, of course.'[3] In consequence, they invited him in for a chat as a neighbourly thing to do, but the hospitality was not repeated or returned.

The move to North 25th Street was the final step in Jeff Dahmer's decline. It is not an exaggeration to say that the freedom which total privacy and easy accessibility afforded him was his passport to disintegration. At first he was discreet enough, turning up regularly for work and, for recreation, joining the Unicorn Bath Club in Chicago, which he is on record as having visited on ten separate occasions. No word was ever whispered of his having drugged anyone at this bathhouse, whereas at the previous establishment in Milwaukee he had become known as the guy who slipped mickeys into people's drinks. Secretly at his apartment he spray-painted Sears' skull with a granite paint he bought at a famous art store and placed it on show – another stage towards the acquisition of his 'shrine'. His restraint, however, was fragile. His sixth victim died only five weeks after he moved into Apartment No. 213, and in the fourteen months that he lived there until his arrest in July, 1991, a total of twelve people were to fall prey to his fevered imagination. He was about to descend with frightening rapidity down one of his own spirals into Infinity Land.

On 20 May, Dahmer 'ran into' Raymond Smith, a thirty-two-year-old black man also known as Ricky Beeks. Smith was, by his own admission, a hustler who engaged in sexual activity with men for money, although he was not himself homosexual. The reputation was sufficiently well known for him to have a nickname in addition to the two names he already bore – 'Cash D' – tattooed on his chest. He was three years older than Dahmer, but short,

well-built, muscular. Dahmer spotted him wandering
around at the 219 Tavern, offered him $50 to come home
for sex, and they left by taxi. The taxi stopped on Wisconsin Avenue, Dahmer went to an all-night gas station
for a couple of packets of cigarettes, and they got to the
apartment by 3 a.m.

Cash D made it pretty clear that he wasn't going to be
around long for $50. Dahmer asked him to stay the night,
and was sharply told that that would cost a lot more. He
said he would pay the extra in the morning, but instead
went to the kitchen and prepared a drink with seven pills
which he gave to Cash D. Within half an hour he was
asleep and Dahmer strangled him on the floor.

For the first time, he had a victim and an altar at once.
Cash D was the first with whom Dahmer could experiment
on the newly-acquired black table. He placed the corpse
on the table in various positions which he found attractive,
always posing it to look good, and rushed out the next
day to buy a polaroid camera at Black's Photo on 125 West
Wisconsin Avenue. He was, in a way, virtually creating his
own pornography, as if the *picture* of beauty was more
alluring than beauty itself. This is tantamount to saying
that fantasy – solid, sculpted, manageable, unthreatening
– has finally become more deeply important than reality.
It is also more stimulating; whereas Dahmer had found it
impossible to reach orgasm with the partners he met at
the Unicorn Bathhouse in Chicago, he was able to stand
over the dead body of Cash D and masturbate to ejaculation. The camera translated reality into fantasy, and the
orgasm celebrated it. From this point, photography will
assume an ever more significant role in Dahmer's pathology, and we shall see how this aspect of his behaviour will
gradually render him more clinically definable.

There was very little tactile sex on this occasion, and
no invasion of the body.

Disposal, on the other hand, was necessarily more gruesome in a second-floor apartment than in a suburban
house. He could not use a sledge-hammer or have free

exclusive access to a trash container. The dissection took place in the bathroom, separating legs from pelvis at the joints, and boiling them in an eighty-gallon steel kettle in a solution of water and Soilex. Soilex is generally used by painters and decorators to remove wallpaper. The boiling went on for an hour, after which he poured off the water and rinsed the bones by hand in the kitchen sink, removing what flesh remained. He intended to keep the skeleton (and bought a freezer in Southridge the following day for this purpose), but without connecting tissue it simply fell apart. To dispose of this, he bought a large trash container with a tight-fitting lid secured by handles which rise up from either side. In this he placed the bones of Cash D and some potent acid, and sealed it. 'I waited a week or two and they had all turned to slush at that time, which I scooped out with a smaller trash thing and poured it into the toilet and flushed it down. It was just all slush, black slush.'[4] He saved the skull of Cash D, spray-painted it and placed it alongside Tony Sears'.

At the trial two years later it was suggested by Dr Dietz that this murder introduced a fresh motive. Dahmer killed Cash D because he was annoyed by his greed and felt threatened by him. I do not agree, and suspect that it is fruitless to look for rational motives in order to explain an irrational act. Most people, to be sure, would respond in this entirely explicable way, but it must by now be clear that Jeff Dahmer was not like most people and cannot be understood by the application of most people's rules. He did not kill because Cash D wanted more money, but because he was transfixed by Cash D's physique and wanted to keep him to himself. Madness has its own logic.

A week or so later, Dahmer made a mistake which inadvertently saved a life. He brought a man back to Apartment 213 and prepared his customary drinks in two coffee cups. For some reason, perhaps because the man was wiser than his predecessors, the coffee cups were mixed up and Dahmer drank the drugged one, leaving the harmless one for his guest. When Dahmer woke up the next day he discovered that he was poorer by $300, some clothes and a watch. The man, not unnaturally, has never come forward, but Dahmer told his probation officer Donna Chester about it on 29 May and she noticed that he was 'unkempt and upset'. Any temptation one may feel to see the funny side of this must be dispelled by the knowledge, as related to Dr Becker on 3 January, 1992, that Dahmer would certainly have strangled this individual had he not drunk the wrong cup of coffee.

Dahmer was not only attending regular meetings with Donna Chester; he was also required by the terms of his probation to participate in group therapy sessions at De Paul Hospital. It will hardly surprise the reader to learn that he was a recalcitrant patient, entirely unable to respond to the kind of treatment which involves blatant and unselfconscious revelation to a group of people one has never met. His counsellor, Patti Antony, was beside herself with frustration at his lack of involvement. The orientation session was due to take place on 22 May, barely thirty-six hours after he had killed Cash D. He telephoned to delay his initiation by one day. 'He introduced himself to the group and was attentive,' reported Miss Antony. 'He did not share any personal issues.' The next month 'he appeared very uncomfortable in talking about his mother', and in July, 'Patient needs to get in touch with his feelings involving the sexual assault and is resistant in talking about the incident.' Miss Antony would not know that Jeff Dahmer had not been 'in touch' with his feelings for many years.

It was also observed as the months went by that he was less and less concerned about personal hygiene. The man whose neatness had made an impression in 1986 was slipping into lethargy: 'He admits he just doesn't feel the energy to clean himself or his clothes.' A Dr Krembs was asked to make yet another psychological evaluation. Having noticed that Dahmer was 'very isolated, no friends, hobbies, interests, whole life is dull, sterile, monomaniacally directed, which is excellent breeding ground for depression', the doctor diagnosed a 'mixed personality disorder associated with depressed mood'. He was further of the opinion that a 'major relapse is just a matter of time'.

When Dahmer was discharged at the beginning of December, Patti Antony summarised his lack of progress. He had not studied his sobriety plan booklet, nor written to his father in fulfilment of an assignment given to him. He had told her that he did not intend to go to Alcoholics Anonymous or attend a Serenity Club 'because he felt there was no purpose in any of these and did not see any purpose in socialising either'. Her conclusion was that he suffered from 'alcohol dependency syndrome, continuous'. In fact, during these eight months of hopeless therapy at De Paul Hospital, Dahmer's secret life had been expanding into yet more bizarre experiments.

On Saturday, 23 June, four weeks after the death of Cash D, there took place in Milwaukee a Gay Pride Parade which was especially well attended and lighthearted. It was a fine summer's day to lift morale, and the mood was aptly defiant in view of the residual intolerance which ever rumbled beneath the surface in that town. One who would never miss such an occasion was Eddie Smith, a twenty-seven-year-old black man with ambitions for the stage and a yearning desire to shine, to break out and be something. The only gay member of a large family (with nine brothers and four sisters), Eddie knew he was different in more than just his sexuality. A graduate of Brookfield Central High School, he had learnt to compensate for dyslexia by quick verbal responses, wit and a rich vocabulary. He was also very amusing.

Eddie stood out from the crowd in two distinctive ways: he wore an Arab headband to disguise his premature baldness, from which he earned the nickname 'The Sheik'; and nearly all his many friends were white. He lived with a white man for several months, and would sometimes travel to the east coast of America with the crowd. Still, he had no place of his own. When at a loss for shelter, he would sometimes curl up on his sister's sofa. The members of this large brood were close, and constantly in touch.

Unfortunately, Eddie's talents fell short of his ambitions. He had wanted to join the Milwaukee Ballet (and sometimes told people he was an ex-dancer), but did not make it. He tried his luck as a female impersonator on the night-club scene, but that, too, was not a distinguished success. He continued to wear light facial make-up and mascara. Eddie had mentioned during that summer that he had met a movie producer who was going to promote him. Whether this was invention on his part, or he had imagined that Jeff Dahmer could be such a person, it is not entirely clear.

Eddie's friend Ted Frankforth saw him talking to Dahmer at the 219 Club in May, went over to join them and was introduced. They shook hands, and in the confusion of social banter he quickly lost sight of them again. Another witness claims to have seen them together in Juneau Park. Over the next two months Eddie made frequent reference to the 'movie producer', and one might conjecture that Dahmer had proposed taking some pictures and that Eddie had fondly exaggerated the significance of this. Unusually, Dahmer did not on that occasion pursue the idea. Eddie told the barman, 'he's cute'.

He introduced his brother Henry to Dahmer in a local (not gay) bar. 'I didn't believe he was capable of putting together a portfolio,' said Henry. 'He was not flamboyant enough to be a producer. Too quiet and introverted. No style.'

Eddie Smith's search for the good life led him into two dangerous cul-de-sacs. He was inclined to be promiscuous, smoked a great deal of marijuana and inhaled 'poppers', a liquid nitrite much used for heightened sexual excitement or for abandoned dancing at the night-clubs. He was, secondly, far too trusting a character. His personality was so infectiously light and effervescent that he made friends easily and improved the atmosphere wherever he went; he added spice and enjoyment to the company, and

145

was a well-built and attractive man despite a protruding collar-bone. It is impossible to know whether his dreams might one day have been realised in some degree, but he certainly deserved better than he got.

The Sheik's future collided with Jeff Dahmer in the early hours of Sunday, 24 June, at the Phoenix Bar. Dahmer need not have offered him money to come home – he was willing enough without it. The rest is now familiar, and the reader will be spared relentless repetition of these increasingly tragic events. Once more, Dahmer took a number of photographs of the corpse, ritualising drama and turning life and death into a graspable object – in fact draining them of any meaning beyond the necrophilic fantasy. The result did not please him, and he destroyed the photographs by cutting them into small pieces. Dahmer hoped to find a better way of preserving the skeleton and skull. The former he placed in his new freezer for a few months; it would not dry out properly, stubbornly retaining moisture, and was ultimately acidified. For the latter he devised a new solution. He turned the oven up to 120 degrees and put Eddie's skull in it for an hour, thinking thus to dry it more efficiently. After a while he heard loud popping noises. The skull was in the process of exploding, flakes of bone grotesquely flying out to hit the sides of the oven. The plan was abandoned and the skull later acidified.

Dahmer told police officers in 1991 that he felt 'rotten' about the destruction of Eddie Smith because he had kept nothing of him and his death had been a true waste. Implicit in this remark is the assumption that, had he been able to save a skull or a penis, death would *not* have been wasteful. There is no better indicator than this of Dahmer's total moral degeneration and his irretrievable distance from reality. His alienation has deteriorated to such an extent that he is literally in a world of his own, unmarked by feeling or sanity. It is hard to believe that a man's isolation could go much deeper.

In the ensuing months, Eddie's brother Henry stood

outside the 219 Club and the Phoenix Tavern, showing pictures of his brother to anyone who cared to look, asking if they had seen him or had any idea what might have happened to him. At the trial in February, 1992, his sister Theresa one day came and sat next to me and showed me those same pictures. She carried them in her wallet, as we might carry holiday snapshots of husband, wife or children, and share them with inquisitive strangers. Eddie was past any help that I could offer, but Theresa wanted me to see them nevertheless, Eddie smiling, laughing, lounging, being alive. I don't think I ever knew a moment so poignant or distressing in the whole trial, nor one which more vividly conveyed the stark tragedy of it all. A few feet away from us in the courtroom sat Jeff Dahmer. Theresa detested what he had done, but before the end of the trial she was coming to the view that he was insane, and this helped her not to hate.

In 1992 I went with Theresa and Henry to the Oxford Apartments, where they were astonished to find that this entrance, habitually used by Dahmer, backed on to a house where their brother Johnny had once lived. 'The souls of twelve men inhabit that place,' said Theresa, 'including my brother Eddie's.'

During the two weeks which followed this murder, Dahmer had a meeting with his probation officer, a group therapy session at De Paul, and a meeting with his counsellor there. He spent Saturday at the Unicorn Club in Chicago, and the following Friday, which was his next available time off work, he met Luis Pinet. The encounter with this young man is curious indeed, and potentially very instructive. Dahmer had seen him often before at the 219 Club, where he worked clearing glasses and sweeping floors, and had reasonably assumed that he was of legal age; in fact, he was fifteen and the job was part-time. They had never spoken before. On 6 July, Dahmer saw him at the Phoenix late at night, no doubt after the 219 had closed, and approached him with an offer of $200 if he would come back home, pose for some nude pictures

147

and have some sex. Why so much? 'I thought it would take that much to peak his interest,' he says. They went to the apartment in a taxi, had their photo session and some 'light sex', and fell asleep in bed together. It was the first time since Tuomi that a partner had willingly stayed the night with Jeff Dahmer, albeit probably as a result of excessive drinking. The next morning they agreed to repeat the experience, and Luis said he would meet Jeff at twelve o'clock.

Dahmer had decided that he would kill the boy and keep him, but he had run out of sleeping pills and could not at that moment afford a further prescription. He would have to render him unconscious some other way. He first went to the army surplus store and bought a rubber mallet, then at noon went for his rendezvous. 'He didn't show up, so I thought he was just kidding, he's not going to meet me.' This was Pinet's second escape. That night, Dahmer was back at the bars where by chance he bumped into him again outside the Phoenix. Pinet explained the misunderstanding; he had assumed the arrangement was to meet at twelve midnight, not twelve noon, and he did not intend to back out of it at all. So they went to Dahmer's apartment for a second night. While Pinet was posing for photographs, lying face down on the bed, Dahmer struck him a blow with the mallet on the back of the neck.

'Obviously he got upset about that,' says Dahmer, laconically. Not upset enough, it seems, for after an argument and explanation to the effect that Dahmer was afraid he was going to take the $200 and leave without giving fair exchange, which Pinet accepted, he went out without the money and slammed the door behind him. That was his third escape. Ten minutes later, he was knocking at the door again. Dahmer asked him in. He said he needed a little money to catch a bus home, and would Dahmer let him have a couple of dollars. Dahmer says he was feeling panic creeping on at this stage, either because he would lose the boy again, or because the boy might report the incident; perhaps a little of both. He therefore grabbed him from behind and they fought on the floor for some minutes, with Dahmer's hands around his neck. 'I guess I intended on strangling him, but he was too strong.' He was also fully conscious, an advantage not given to any of the victims who had died. 'Let's talk,' said Dahmer, upon which they ceased wrestling and sat on the edge of the bed, calming down and discussing the attack. Astonishingly, while they were thus poring over the night's events, Dahmer persuaded Pinet to have his hands tied behind his back. He quietly wriggled free of the ligature and made to depart again, at which point Dahmer showed him the knife which he used for cutting flesh, without, of course, revealing its function. They continued talking until seven in the morning, when Pinet promised that he would not tell anyone what had happened. They then walked to the bus-stop together and Dahmer paid for his taxi home. On his fourth escape from he knew not what, he was at last free.

'I just didn't have the ability to do him any harm,' says Dahmer. 'Why, I don't know.'[5] The obvious answer was that he was sober and the victim was awake, but a more subtle explanation suggests itself. The length of time that the two were acquainted is significant. After the first night they spent together, Pinet was quite willing to return to him for more, and happily made an assignation which he kept. There was, then, no need for Dahmer to kill him in order to retain him, and any normal person would have seen this as the possibility of a continuing relationship, freely engaged in by both partners without coercion. But Dahmer was incapable of such 'normal' reasoning because the partner was not at that stage a person to him at all, but a putative object, a 'thing' to stimulate his fantasy. During the course of their night-long discussion, the object gradually took on being, the fantasy dissolved, and Dahmer found himself face to face with a human being. He told the police that as he began to sober up he got to know Luis on a more personal level, which is true as far as it goes. What it means is that Dahmer was rescued (and the boy saved) by the gradual intrusion of reality to conquer and dispel the unreality of dream. However one may interpret the alteration, it is beyond doubt that the Jeff Dahmer who bade goodbye to the boy at the bus-stop was no longer the Jeff Dahmer who had wanted, hours before, to kill him.

By another terrible irony, Luis Pinet did inform the police, and a False Imprisonment complaint was filed. He told them three different stories, however, each apparently more crazy than the others, and the police simply did not believe him. He could easily have led them to Dahmer's apartment, as he had found it by himself the night before, and they would certainly have found incriminating evidence had they searched it. One loses count of how many times Jeff Dahmer might have been stopped if events had taken a slightly different turn.

Months later, Luis Pinet saw Dahmer at the Grand Avenue Mall and initiated a conversation with him. They exchanged pleasantries with no display of resentment or grudge. His next encounter was in the courtroom, when he gave evidence against him at the trial.

Dahmer had an appointment with Donna Chester the day after his all-night talk with Pinet. He spoke openly of suicide and frankly conceded that he was homosexual, although he did not know why. He told her that his sexual tensions were relieved by regular masturbation. On the page, it looks like a timid admission indeed, hardly worthy of remark, but it was a signal step for this locked man to share any inch of his problems with prying professionals. The theme of suicide would crop up with increasing frequency in the coming months, parallel with his frenetic embrace of murder. Miss Chester will note his decline into slovenliness and his acute depression, and she will conclude that he is a chronic complainer with a negative attitude. A salient characteristic she will discern is the constant inability to manage finances. Jeff never has enough money, is always in debt, always over-spending.

She thinks he is a compulsive buyer and hints at the possible psychological implications of such a condition: yawning emptiness must be filled by ever-diminishing treats.

The truth was, he owed $2,000 in various doctors' and hospital bills, including $1,000 to De Paul Hospital for therapy ordered by the court. His weekly pay-check amounted to $275, out of which he paid $115 for rent and utilities. The rest went on food, drink and pornography.

Perhaps a probation officer should not be expected to explore the psyche of his or her charges; their function is to be vigilant for delinquency, not probing for explanation. Donna Chester did not therefore address herself to the question why the very idea of a relationship with another human being, of either sex, was entirely inconceivable to Jeff Dahmer. Perhaps he would not allow her to. She was face to face with a man whose intangible threads connecting him with his fellows had all been severed, a man alone and alien, who watched other people form bonds and did not know how it was done; whose counterfeit version of bonding was to drug a person senseless and hold him; whose only intimate relationship was with a corpse, because he knew no other way.

All the Dahmers assembled at the house in West Allis for Thanksgiving in November, 1990 – Shari and Lionel from Ohio, David from Cincinnati, Jeff from Milwaukee. He told Donna Chester that he was not looking forward to it because he felt ashamed of his life-style and knew he had nothing to contribute towards the levity of a family gathering. All he did, he said, was to go to work for twelve hours, come home, and go to work again. He sometimes visited the bathhouse in Chicago, packed tight with other men seeking touch without connection, and wandered the streets. Or there were the bars. There was desolation in each five-second pause when he said, 'I did my drinking alone, and bar-hopping alone . . . no one . . . no one.'[6]

Generally, he was home from work by 8 a.m., would make a little breakfast and turn on the television. That's when an abusive and childish chat-show by Geraldo appears, and Jeff loathed the host's strategy of trying to make his guests feel bad about themselves. 'He just wants them to feel as guilty and as lousy as possible. The guy is such a prick.'[7] He would then try to sleep a little, and go out for lunch to the Grand Avenue Mall more often than not. There are a number of self-service restaurants in this two-block-long covered shopping arcade – French, Chinese, American – to suit every taste. He was particularly fond of McDonald's and a chicken-and-chips establishment on the first floor called Apricot Annie's. He would turn up there in the early afternoon and always go to his favourite stool at the bar; if the stool was occupied, he would walk around until it became vacant rather than take another one. He liked the coffee best at the French Café.

He would go home by bus, or occasionally by cab. One taxi-driver recalled that Dahmer had invited him in for a beer, but he declined because he could not drink on the job.

At last, Jeff Dahmer found an innocent interest he could indulge. He bought a 30-gallon aquarium from The Fish Factory at West Oklahoma Avenue, some tropical fish and some books on the subject. He used the black table, destined to be his altar, as a pedestal for the fish tank, and spent time and care on setting it all up properly. 'It was nice, with African cichlids and tiger barbs in it and live plants, it was a beautifully kept fish tank, very clean . . . I used to like to just sit there and watch them swim around, basically. I used to enjoy the planning of the set-up, the filtration, read about how to keep the nitrate and ammonia down to safe levels and just the whole spectrum of fish-keeping interested me.' He would wander around the fish-store, fascinated by the shapes and colours of rare specimens, and in recollection it was only when talking about fish (or press misrepresentation of his case) that his voice became animated. 'I once saw some puffer fish in the store,' he relates. 'It's a round fish, and the only ones I ever saw with both eyes in front, like a person's eyes, and they would come right up to the front of the glass and their eyes would be crystal blue, like a person's, real cute.'

He developed a great enthusiasm for trigger fish as well. After his arrest, he would look back with nostalgia on this last attempt to do something ordinary, normal, harmless. 'It's a fun hobby,' he said. 'I really enjoyed that fish tank. It's something I really miss.'[8] Dahmer did not say so, but there is an inescapable serenity in an aquarium which contrasts dramatically with the tumult still raging in his own weird world. That tumult erupted once more at the beginning of September in front of the bookstore on North 27th Street, where he met Ernest Miller from Chicago.

It is as well to point out here, perhaps, that by no means all the people Dahmer approached accepted his enticement of money for sex. Police amassed over a dozen instances of individuals who were propositioned by him and declined, a few of them more than once.* They each have reason to thank Providence for their strength of character. But Ernest Miller said yes.

Dahmer was about to enter the bookstore at about 3 a.m., after the bars had closed, when he spotted Miller standing outside – black, twenty-three years old and well built, wearing a yellow sweatshirt with striped sleeves, and white tennis shoes. He offered $50, and they walked the two blocks to the apartment. Dahmer lay on top of him, hearing the sounds and ticks and beats pulsating beneath him. He listened, entranced, placed his ear and lips to the stomach, then went down to find the phallus. 'That'll cost you extra,' said Miller. Dahmer got up and went to the kitchen to make his potion, gave it to Miller who fell asleep about half an hour later.

* Vincent McHenry, Robert J. Pettis in the Grand Avenue Mall, both in October; Perry Woolsay in November; Allen Matthews in January at the 219 Club; Leonardo Rodriguez in the Grand Avenue Mall in February; Douglas Jackson in April, McHenry again in April; Reginald Ball in May, Matthews again in May.

Dahmer was immensely proud of his acquisition. For the rest of the night he fingered him, fondled him, gazed upon him. He walked around the room, drinking beer, occasionally glancing at him, then went into the kitchen and returned at leisure to find him still lying there, a perfect body, all his. He touched the sleeping form, withdrew for another beer, came back and touched it again. He masturbated himself in such a way as to have his hand touching Miller's body at the same time, as if it were participating in the act. There was just one thing wrong. He had only been able to give him two sleeping pills as he had run out, and the body might very well stir soon and want to wake up. It was too late to strangle him without a fight. How could he devise a way to keep him there?

His solution was effective, but catastrophic, and for him quite novel. He drank some more alcohol to smother fear and residual inhibition, then with the knife he used for dissection he neatly severed Miller's jugular vein. He avers that he knew this would be painless and quick, that Miller would not suffer, and with the medical knowledge acquired in army days he would certainly know exactly where to inflict a mortal wound. 'It took him maybe about a minute before he died.' Blood gushed out on to the bed and walls and carpet.

Worse was to follow. Having hauled the body on to his black table (the aquarium was not yet in place at this point), he took about twenty photographs of it in various positions and once more caressed it adoringly. Next he put it in the bathtub and began the process of dismemberment. Once he had severed the head he kissed it and talked to it, apologising for having had to do this, 'but I couldn't think of any other way'. He took more pictures of the decapitated body at various stages of dissection, and of the head itself, which he placed in the fridge. In the coming days he would take it out from time to time and masturbate before it. For the final photograph he pushed the eyelids up to obtain a more life-like image (the fact that the eyes were closed must mean, one hopes, that Miller did not regain consciousness before he died).

Meanwhile, Dahmer had completed dismemberment in the bathtub. The method is best described in his own words: 'I separated the joints, the arm joints, the leg joints, and had to do two boilings. I think I used four boxes of Soilex for each one, put in the upper portion of the body and boiled that for about two hours and then the lower portion for another two hours. The Soilex removes all the flesh, turns it into a jelly-like substance and it just rinses off. Then I laid the clean bones in a light bleach solution, left them there for a day and spread them out on either newspaper or cloth and let them dry for about a week in the bedroom.'[9] He stored parts of the legs, arms, heart, kidney and liver in various bags in the freezer for later use.

Dahmer had formed the intention of using the complete skeleton to adorn one end of his shrine, and went so far as to try reassembling it, once he had disposed of all remaining flesh, with glue. This proved to be too laborious a task, so he placed the skeleton in the bottom drawer of his cabinet in the bedroom until another day. Once he had removed flesh from the head, he spray-painted it and coated it with enamel. 'I had three of them by that time that I wanted to keep, so when they were dried I glued the teeth in to make sure they were fastened.' These three skulls were on display, and looked fake enough to remain on display even when subsequent victims were present. Their final resting-place was in the top drawer of the cabinet.

Meanwhile, they were surprised at the Joe Hall Dance Studio in Chicago when Ernest Miller did not show up for his first session on Tuesday; he had been granted free admission.

For the first time we now come upon a disturbing innovation, when Dahmer ate some of the flesh he had saved. We shall leave until later a discussion of the significance of this behaviour, which increased as the months went by, since it is inadequate to ascribe it to sheer curiosity and it does bear an interpretation which fits a coherent scheme of his pathology. Nor does it help to specify exactly which portions were eaten, although such details were to be given in open court. The reader will perhaps allow me, from this point onwards, to be generally less precise concerning the fate which befell the remains of each individual. Most of what has been said so far was revealed in court, even to the baking of Eddie Smith's skull, but some of the more lurid details were not then known, and the families of those who died have borne more than enough without having to learn of *post-mortem* indignities. I shall therefore describe Dahmer's actions without, for the most part, indicating which victim was the object of them.

David Thomas, twenty-two years old, died in the early hours of 24 September, 1990. Curtis Straughter, nearly eighteeen, died on 17 February, 1991. He was waiting at a bus-stop near Marquette University when Dahmer spotted him, jumped off the bus and approached him. Errol Lindsey was nineteen years old when he died on 7 April, and Tony Hughes, who was killed on 24 May, was thirty-one. All were black, and two were heterosexual but co-operative. Tony Hughes was especially to be pitied as he was deaf and dumb, and thereby deprived of the ability even to protest to his assailant. Hughes, who was homosexual, met Dahmer at the 219 Club and asked three of his friends, two girls and a man, to give them a ride back to where Dahmer lived. He and Dahmer sat in the back seat writing notes to each other. Tony wanted to bring the whole company in for drinks at the apartment, but Dahmer indicated that he was inviting Tony by himself. Tony then relayed this information to his friends in sign language, and they understood the situation well enough. He did not seem at all afraid of Dahmer.

Tony Hughes was never seen again, but his presence was strongly felt in the courtroom less than a year later when his mute friends turned up to demonstrate solidarity in grief. Most impressive of all was his mother, an elegant, trim, quiet and dignified lady in mourning. She was there every day, unsmiling and unconquerable, yielding neither to bitterness nor rage, in silent celebration of the closeness she and Tony had enjoyed in life. I never spoke to Mrs Hughes, but I felt the strength of her commitment.

These unfortunate men came across Jeff Dahmer's path at the point where he was beyond repair. He told Dr Judith Becker that his 'moral compass had been shot' and that he lived only for the weekends. He had begun watching the movie *Exorcist II*, which cost him $90, on a regular basis, as soon as he came home from work, both before going to the bars and with his victims on returning from the bars. He was, he said, thoroughly corrupt and evil by this time. Perhaps the tiniest chink of light still danced upon his soul from time to time; there was an occasion when he took home a man and had light sexual contact with him, kissing and masturbating, and the man left next day in the normal way. Why? He says that when he sobered up he realised he did not like him as much as he had thought. On the other hand, one might be permitted to hope there was more to it than that; there is no evidence either way.

As his disorder deepened, so did Dahmer's peculiar experimentation escalate. He bought a pair of handcuffs to heighten the fantasy of power and control, and Curtis Straughter actually fell asleep with them on. He also bought a black leather strap as a tool for strangulation, thinking it would be quicker than the manual method; one of the four was murdered this way with a bag over his head. Another was killed because he was going to wake up soon and would be angry. With all of them, however, Dahmer fell into a cuddle immediately after death, holding them close and placing their arms around him to simulate the intimacy of embrace.

With one of them, he decided he wanted to keep the entire skin. This he effected with a small, sharp paring knife, making first an incision at the back of the neck, slicing up to the crown, and then pulling the skin on either side of the incision. It was like skinning a chicken one was about to cook, he said. The outer layer peeled away from the muscle tissue if handled with care and the whole operation took about two hours. Dahmer told the police exactly how he did it; the bland account in the confession, narrated with formal third-person detachment, is at least precise. The skin 'would completely pull right off the skull of the individual. He related that the only time he needed to do any real cutting would be around the facial features, that being the eyes, nose, lips and mouth. He related that the entire skull portion of the skin came off in one complete piece and while it was off it actually looked somewhat like a mask you can buy at a party store.'[10]

Dahmer placed the skin of the entire body in a solution of cold water and salt, hoping to preserve it intact for his shrine. But after three weeks it was obvious that it would not work, as the skin was disintegrating. Reluctantly, he broke it into pieces by hand and flushed it all down the lavatory.

Meanwhile, he lay the flayed body on a plastic sheet on the bedroom floor and photographed it. He does not appear to have been repulsed; on the contrary, to him it was an object of beauty.

In the first chapter of this book we learnt how police officers, alerted by Tracy Edwards, found photographs of bodies in various stages of dismemberment in the drawer of Jeffrey Dahmer's chest and suddenly recognised that they were genuine and original. It is time now to see how those photographs were taken and what was their purpose.

There is a head-and-shoulders picture, with the subject's arms folded behind his head, which could resemble any ordinary snapshot were it not for the obvious fact of his death, and it was taken for much the same motive as an ordinary portrait. 'I just wanted to get a good picture of his face so I could remember how he looked,' said Dahmer. Most of the others, however, do not admit of so mundane a purpose.

Those taken before dismemberment were positioned on the black table in order to show off either the chest or the belly. While they are all stretched out, some have the chest thrust forward, and Dahmer has been to some trouble to arrange the pose in this manner. One has the head at the bottom of the picture, the chest spread out at the centre and ends at the top of the picture with the pubic hair. The legs hang down from the table out of range of the camera, as if they were useless appendages to the thing of beauty. He was thinking, 'How nice he looked, how I wish I could have kept him another way'. After these kinds of poses, he would ejaculate on to the chest as a kind of morbid signature before dragging the corpse to the bathroom.

Those taken in the bathtub have likewise been carefully positioned. One has the victim draped over the edge of the bath, his head and arms hanging outside, the arms stretched above his head, and the lower part of the torso sitting cross-legged in the tub. This, too, accentuates the chest area, Dahmer's primary source of fetishistic excitement. On another picture, the mouth of the victim is open; Dahmer says he opened the mouth himself so that he could place his penis into it.

It is when one comes to the second area of sexual interest – the belly that he had listened to while the victim was alive – that dismemberment begins. There is a photograph of a man who has been opened up, with a cut from the neck right down to the groin, revealing all the internal organs. When asked why he should do this, Dahmer said, 'I wanted to see what someone looked like inside.'[11] That turned out to be a disingenuous reply, for he subsequently revealed that he would plunge his hands into the intestines and feel them, occasionally still warm to the touch. If there was room, he would get an erection and lower himself on to the open body to have intercourse with the viscera, placing his penis literally *within* the body and ejaculating among its organs. When it was too cramped in the bathroom to do this, he might pull the intestines out and rub them on his penis, using them as a masturbatory aid.

159

Every time he wanted to take a picture, he had to stop and wash his hands.

These photographs were kept in order to be used as a stimulant at a later date. Others, however, seem to serve no purpose other than talismanic. There is a picture taken in the kitchen sink of a man's head, resting on ice, with a pair of hands, palms upward and fingers spread, at either side of the neck. A bottle of washing-up liquid stands incongruously on the side of the sink. Dahmer says he used the sink because the blood would drain away more easily (indicating that this was a pose manufactured shortly after decapitation), but he is unable to explain why he should arrange them in this grotesque manner. Similarly, another side view of the head, displayed with hands alongside and severed genitals below, including pubic region, has been taken with the pieces on a towel. They seem to be totems or icons of a kind, weird salutations to a sinister god dredged from Dahmer's own imagination.

A photograph of a headless torso in the bathtub has the skin pulled back to reveal the rib-cage, and the fingers of the hands are sticking up. 'I don't know how that happened,' said Dahmer. 'I didn't position them like that or anything. After the wrists were cut, the tendons must have pushed both top fingers out.' In the light of this, it is decidedly superfluous of him to admit, 'My desires were bestial, obviously.'[12] Another day, he said, 'I think my emotions were pretty well seared at that time, as far as any decent emotions,' and he clearly felt discomfort in recollection. 'I always feel a little uneasy talking about this,' he said. 'No matter how many times I go through it, it's just as sickening every time I do.'[13] It is interesting that he should use such a word, denoting awareness of the effect such scenes may have upon normally constituted people. The fact remains that he did not feel sick while he was doing it, was not repulsed by activity that would cause many people to faint.

The best commentary on these dreadful pictures was

given inadvertently in the courtroom by Judith Becker. Asked whether she had viewed a selection large enough for her to form an opinion, she paused before answering, then said simply and quietly, 'I do not care to see any more.'

'True, it didn't satisfy whatever craving I had,' said Dahmer, 'or I would have stopped doing it. Things just went from bad to worse.' In a photograph of a semi-dismembered corpse one can see another body lying in the tub behind; they had begun to pile up.

Once the picture-taking had been exhausted, Dahmer set about final disposal. Having first removed the internal organs, 'I noticed that all the blood tends to collect in the chest area, so I drained that off. You just lift the torso part up and it drains out, down the bathtub drain. Then you slice up the liver into smaller pieces, it's quite large. You start cutting off the flesh, in the leg area or the arm area and just work your way down. Then when I was saving the heads I'd cut the neck bone, sever the head.' This would eventually be placed in a saucepan of water. The eyeballs just boiled away, he said; the flesh took longer to dislodge. He used a dessert spoon to scoop out the brain material so as to be left with a perfect unblemished skull.

The inevitable consequence of these activities was a very strong smell which, from time to time, pervaded the apartment building and brought dozens of complaints upon the head of the building's manager, Sopa Princewill, who used No. 102 as his office. It was difficult at first to locate the source of the smell, and there was a suspicion that somebody in the building might have died and lain undiscovered. The police interviewed every tenant, and getting no answer from No. 205 they kicked the door down. To no avail; the tenant was not dead but in jail. In Dahmer's bathtub, meanwhile, lay half a torso. On another occasion the police called to find the tenant of No. 308 had been strangled, and again interviewed everyone in the block. It was the people who lived opposite

Jeff Dahmer who were finally convinced that the odours emanated from No. 213, and Mr Princewill confronted Dahmer with the complaint. He said that his freezer had malfunctioned and some meat had been spoiled. Mr Princewill inspected the freezer, saw some ordinary supermarket bags on top, but did not investigate below where the unorthodox contents lay hidden. The freezer was full, he remembers. Dahmer's explanation was accepted, especially as he was contrite about the embarrassment he had caused.

The smell did not entirely evaporate, however. Some prospective tenants were being shown Apartment 313, directly above Dahmer's (there were three storeys to the block), when an apologetic Mr Princewill had to give up and abandon the inspection because the smells coming from below were too nauseating. Once more, he confronted Dahmer, and was told that the fish tank had gone wrong and some of the fish had died. Dahmer, apparently trying to be helpful, directed Princewill towards a grey barrel in the hall closet. When Princewill opened it, the odour was so overpowering that it brought tears to his eyes and threw him back. He was very angry. '*This must go,*' he told Dahmer emphatically. The next day he noticed that the offensive barrel had been dumped in the large trash dispenser, and felt satisfied. The third time Princewill spoke to Dahmer about smells occurred the day after Tony Hughes died, and two days before the attack upon his next victim. Hughes' body was lying on the bedroom floor at the time.

The smell of decomposition can be alleviated by immediate *post-mortem* disposal, but Dahmer was by this time so careless and slipshod that he would often leave a body two or three days before beginning dismemberment. When a body is first opened after such a delay, the bowels surge out, pushed by gases, and the smell is indescribably awful. One is bound to wonder how Dahmer was able to live within that permanently polluted air, how he slept with the smell in his nostrils, ate with the odour of putrefaction hovering around him. Unless he was so deranged as actually to *like* it – sheer indifference is impossible to conceive. And still he went on taking pictures of it all; there are some of the body whose bowels had fallen out, as described above, which implies that the photographer was working in conditions of unspeakable foulness.

Why? Because the taking of photographs is an inherent part of the compulsion itself. It was strong enough to banish the smells, render them impotent and unable to interfere. We recall that police officers found seventy-four polaroid pictures in Dahmer's drawer, which does not take into account the scores he had taken and subsequently destroyed. This was not a hobby, it was an imperative – pressing, impatient, ineluctable. Dahmer was by no means the first to photograph his victims. Bittaker and Norris in California in 1979 took pictures of the girls they raped and killed to capture their terror on celluloid. The Moors murderers of the 1960s, Brady and Hindley, did much the same. Leonard Lake, arrested in 1985, had an underground film studio and made his own pornographic videos of victims. The point is, the camera *completes the objectification* of the victim, destroys the last vestige of his individuality, robs him of his independent being. Just as murder creates a compliant corpse, so the photography of that corpse demonstrates total ownership and control – it is a step further in the same direction. The person, once threateningly alive, now exists only in so far as the photographer allows him to exist through images of *his* creating. It is the translation of life into death, of sentience into petrification, of will into object, the dissolution of all into one triumphant *thing* – the photograph.

Erich Fromm has analysed what he calls the necrophilous character, which may show itself in seemingly innocuous acts. Men who feel more tender towards their cars than their wives are demonstrating the dangers of inanimation (literally, *soullessness*). They wash it lovingly, even when they could afford to pay someone else to do it, they may give it a nickname, they caress it and gaze at it.[14] The car has become, in such cases, almost a love-object, which does not, unlike a love-subject, occasionally refuse one's attentions. The murderer is doing precisely the same in turning his love-object into a still image, turning love (aliveness, mutuality) into pornography (passivity, self-gratification). With his camera, he conceptualises and conquers that which was once a free being, and in this way uses the camera as a kind of weapon or instrument of control. The camera is a thing which records things, framing them, solidifying them.

It is important to recognise that the camera does not enhance, it reduces (in so far as the person photographed is now no more than an image), and it insultingly proclaims ownership, too. It has become a substitute for involvement, and, in that regard, Dahmer's photography of *his* corpses, *his* dismemberment, *his* trophies, is a loud signal of the condition which afflicts him – necrophilia.

Chapter Seven

The Frenzy

Necrophilia is not against the law, in so far as there is no statute which proscribes it. Legislators have presumably thought it so rare or inconceivable that it was not worth forbidding, rather like Queen Victoria, who, refusing to believe that lesbianism was possible, struck all reference to it from the bill Parliament had put before her for royal signature in 1885; in consequence, male homosexuals were made criminals *per se* while female homosexuals, protected by ignorance, could behave as they chose. Likewise, our understanding of necrophilia is so limited that Jeffrey Dahmer could only be tried for murder, which he did not deny, while the real clue to his conduct was given muddled attention because it did not constitute an offence.

The Greek words *nekros* (corpse) and *philia* (love, liking, friendship) combine to make a condition loosely translated as 'love of the dead'. It covers a variety of forms and has been the subject of many attempts at definition. One instance of it is a refusal to accept the fact of death, as Romeo displayed so dramatically when he leapt into Juliet's tomb and held her body to his breast. In this case, 'love of the dead' is a desperate extension of mourning and is not unknown to history. According to Herodotus, Periander continued to have intercourse with his wife after her death, and another story has King Herod sleeping with the corpse of his for seven years. Similarly, in parts of central Europe until the seventeenth century it was permissible for a man to consummate his marriage by sexual intercourse even if his bride had died before her wedding-day. This is clearly not the branch of necrophilia with which we have to deal here.

The more perverse necrophile does not so much deny death as embrace it. Far from grieving over a lost love, he celebrates a new-found one, for he cannot love, or at least go through the physical manifestations of love, unless his partner is dead. This is to put the case at its most extreme, for the *desire* to behave in a necrophilic manner is far more widespread than most people care to admit. There are brothels in Paris wherein the whore will obligingly make herself up to look corpse-like and lie in a coffin waiting to be ravaged; such places do not want for customers. Less overt is the man who asks his wife to 'play dead' and keep quiet while he performs the act of love without her assistance; I know some happily married women who are pleased to gratify their spouses in this way and simply be 'taken'. I have already had cause to point out that one of the first sexual fantasies that occurs to the pubescent boy is that of a girl who will simply lie there and let him explore her body; mutuality in sex comes at the next stage, once his confidence has been established. In this sense, non-active necrophilia is a kind of arrested development, a child-like fear of the dangers of sharing, and as such is not in itself harmful. We have been able to follow Dahmer through these early stages, from the fantasy of the jogger through the stealing of a mannequin to the drugging of partners, each a step in the escalation towards full-blown homicidal necrophilia. True, it had already exploded once when he was eighteen and been kept at bay for nine years, but for the purposes of description these *pseudo*-replacements en route towards disaster retain their validity.

Dennis Nilsen made himself up to look like a corpse long before he killed anybody. He wrote that he must be in love with his own dead body, and the thought frightened him. Other men masturbate in graveyards or habitually watch funerals. Some seek employment in a morgue to be near the stillness of death. In ancient Egypt so many embalmers were caught abusing female corpses entrusted to them that the job was passed to women. We would be astonished how many people today are able to satisfy their unusual needs without arousing suspicion or committing any crime. A medical student, with quite legitimate access to skeletons, is on record as having frequently taken a skeleton to bed with him, cuddled it and kissed it.[1] The fact that there are so few necrophiles who progress into homicide, accounts for the paucity of clinical evidence which might clarify the condition. Rosman and Resnick's study found only fourteen instances of necrophilic homicide from which they could usefully extract data. In comparison, there were twenty-one cases of people who had used an already dead body for sexual pleasure (a category to which they gave the unfortunate name 'regular' necrophilia).

There is yet another category, *necrophagy*, which we shall have to examine separately in its place. Necrophagy is the consumption of dead human flesh, an even rarer manifestation of the disease and one which erupts at the final stages of its evolution.

Part of the difficulty in understanding this kind of aberration is the assumption that it is unique or without precedent. It was an assumption widely held in Milwaukee, even within the courtroom, during Dahmer's trial, and shared by Dahmer himself. He had not read about the subject, nor was he interested in it as an area of study or a blueprint for emulation. He once asked Dr Becker whether there was anyone in the world like him, or was he the only one. There are, alas, only too many examples of people who have committed acts of which Dahmer's are merely an echo. It might help to place matters in perspective if we consider some of them.

Andrew Bichel, born about 1770 in Bavaria, killed young girls and handled their intestines before cutting them in half. He admitted to feeling 'excitement' as he

167

opened the bodies up. Sergeant Bertrand, a twenty-seven-year-old soldier in the 74th Regiment, dug up the corpses of young women in 1848 in Paris and tore out their entrails. Sometimes he hacked off their limbs or achieved congress with them. Interestingly, he appears to have been a chronic masturbator in adolescence, indulging up to seven times a day, a characteristic we have already noted as precursory to serious deviance in adult life. Jack the Ripper is the most notorious case of the Victorian period, whose activities again indicate a fascination with viscera – his mutilation of the prostitutes he attacked was ferocious; Peter Sutcliffe was thus appropriately dubbed the 'Yorkshire Ripper' in 1978, because his purpose was not merely murder but degradation of the victim's internal organs. Easier to grasp, perhaps, is the case of John Christie in London in March, 1953. His address, 10 Rillington Place, remains almost as famous today as Buckingham Palace. The bodies of three women were found in a secret cupboard behind wallpaper, another under the floorboards, two more in the garden. An ineffective and quiet man, Christie would lure women to his home and get them drunk, then kill them *in order to* possess them sexually; he could do it no other way. Other points of comparison with Dahmer are that Christie would frequently masturbate on to a corpse, and that his compulsion grew in intensity with the years, to the point where his last three murders were committed by a man gone berserk and quite incapable of worrying about the possibility of detection.

Peter Kürten terrified Düsseldorf in the 1920s with his loathsome needs, and killed men, women and children alike for the purpose of sexual gratification. If no victim presented himself and the urge was great, he would turn to animals instead, and once killed a swan and drank its blood. One of his victims was hastily buried by him, and later dug up and violated both vaginally and anally. When he was arrested, his neighbours and workmates were convinced a mistake had been made, for the Peter they knew was quiet and well behaved at all times. The most uncomfortable comparison is that of Ed Gein, arrested in Plainfield, Wisconsin, in 1957, and presumed largely forgotten by local inhabitants until Dahmer's arrest. They did not appreciate the reminder, for they considered that Gein, another polite and self-effacing man, had brought shame upon the State. In the woodshed of his house was the naked, headless body of a woman hanging upside down from a meat-hook and opened up down the front. The head and intestines were discovered in a box, the heart on a plate in the dining-room. The skins from ten human heads were preserved, and another skin taken from the upper torso of a woman was rolled up on the floor. There was even a belt fashioned from nipples and a chair upholstered in human skin. Incidentally, Ed Gein was found to be insane, but was never released from custody for the rest of his life, a fact worth bearing in mind when Jeff Dahmer's ultimate destination was decided.

On the other hand, Edmund Kemper, who shot his grandparents dead when he was fifteen, was released from a maximum security hospital four years later and launched upon a particularly hideous murder spree. He, too, would retain the heads of victims for masturbatory purposes, but probably his most vivid and awful act was, having killed and decapitated his mother, to tear out her larynx and throw it into the garbage so that she would not scream and yell at him any more! In 1935, Albert Fish was tried for murder, but it was his necrophilia which drew attention to him. His victims were children, and the body of one little girl was used to make stew. He was found sane and executed in 1936.

There is more, and worse. Dr J. Paul de River has made a study of some of the more outlandish cases, including one of a morgue attendant whose necrophilia was so pronounced that he performed hideous acts upon the corpses in his care.[2] And the most unpleasant case known to me is that of Richard Chase, the so-called 'Vampire of Sacramento', whose madness was so intense that he placed the

169

viscera of pigs and rabbits in a blender and mixed them to eat. His treatment of his victims challenges description. The point I am making is that Jeff Dahmer's behaviour, awful though it be, is not without precedent, nor is it the most nauseating manifestation of necrophilia on record. But it is one whose development it is possible to trace, with some effort and not a little conjecture, and whose roots might thereby be uncovered. Dahmer does not stand alone; he is part of a long gallery of human beings whose emotions have been distressingly diverted towards a love of the dead.

It is for this reason that Dahmer's insistence that he did not enjoy killing should be given due credence. Murder was not the point of the act, but its avenue. Many necrophiles kill for the subsequent pleasure of dismemberment, what von Hentig called *lebendige Zusammenhänge* (to tear apart 'living structures').[3] Dennis Nilsen maintained that in his case dismemberment was merely functional (in an all-too-graphic remark he referred to it as 'the dirty platter after the feast'), and Dahmer initially claimed that he, too, derived no pleasure from the activity. It is likely, however, that this was his last defence, the final twitching of a moribund morality, as he subsequently admitted that he would pause during dissection to gaze upon his work. I still think it is true that his primary aim was to achieve a desired object, not to destroy it; the destruction was his way of *keeping* something of the body whose company and solace he had sought.

Fromm attempted a catalogue of characteristics which together might define a necrophilous personality, a list much criticised by professionals because of its reliance upon speculation and imaginative insight. It is still pertinent for us to consider this list and see how it might be applied to Jeff Dahmer. The habit of breaking matchsticks in half must not be taken too seriously, or it might condemn half the population to morbidity. There are other points which carry more conviction. For instance, the conversation of a necrophile is bland, without intonation or colour. 'He remains stiff, cold, aloof; his presentation of the subject is pedantic and lifeless. On the other hand the opposite character type, the life-loving person, may talk of an experience that in itself is not particularly interesting, but there is life in the way he presents it; he is stimulating; that is why one listens with interest and pleasure. The necrophilous person is a wet blanket and a joy killer in a group; he is boring rather than animating; he deadens everything and makes people feel tired, in contrast to the biophilous person who makes people feel more alive.'[4] It is beyond question that Dahmer's conversation lacks liveliness.

It is also true that Dahmer lacks the capacity for free, joyous laughter. He essays a smile, or a smirk, but there is an absence of mobility or expression in his face, as if the smile is appended to something which it does not fit. His substitute for laughter is a kind of single guttural grunt, again tentative and 'killed' at its inception. His complexion is pallid and sallow. All these are characteristics advanced by Fromm as typically necrophilous.

When he comes to childhood signals which may presage a necrophilous future, we recognise some discordant and contradictory echoes. The biophilous child is interested in toys which represent life and enhance his enjoyment of it – such as dolls and pets – whereas the necrophilous infant only responds to mechanical things, dead structures. At a very early stage Jeff Dahmer had his share of life-enhancing activities, with his little pets and cuddly toys to take to bed, but they gave way after a certain age to the fascination with the way objects function. His favourite toy was a set of Styrofoam building blocks, and we have already seen how his interest in animals degenerated into an obsession with how they *worked*, what was their structure and form. The skeleton, heart, liver, lungs, were all objects to him which could be put together, like a jigsaw puzzle, to make an animal. All children rightly learn from the mechanical approach to life and ultimately combine it with the spiritual and emotional to gain a composite understanding. The adult Dahmer never really emerged from his childhood thing-making fog.

If one or both parents are obsessed with ill-health and the struggle against it, this, too, according to Fromm, may help create a negative influence. The mother is most important in this respect. She must notice her child's growing responses to the rich world around him, encourage them, draw them out, make adventure from them and thus instil a forward-looking optimism. The mother who notices instead everything that is wrong with the child, sees each sneeze as a setback, every illness as a failure, is likely to create an atmosphere of negativity. 'She does not harm the child in any obvious way,' writes Fromm, 'yet she may slowly strangle his joy of life, his faith in growth, and eventually she will infect him with her own necrophilous orientation.'[5] Jeff became alarmingly self-sufficient, almost autistic in his lack of connection, imprisoned in total isolating narcissism. There is a possibility, to put it no higher, that Joyce Dahmer's absorption in her own health and mental well-being, and especially the absence of hope which accompanied it, may have contributed to his gradual sinking into that silent brooding sludge which is the nest of necrophilia. There is, however, no evidence whatsoever to support this idea.

Finally, there is a dangerous point when adolescence begins and the first sexual stirrings are experienced. At the trial, Dr Dietz was to make reference to the (literal) coincidence of Dahmer's first exposure to the internal organs of a mammal (when he brought the pig's head home from school) and his first masturbation, implying that this collision forced the one interest to fertilise the other. This is quite possibly true. A boy may become fetishistically fixed on a particular towel if that was the object with which he was drying himself when he experienced his first ejaculation, and for a while refuse to use any other. Dahmer's awakening sexuality happened to occur at the same time as his unhealthy thoughts about viscera and the two became fused. Add to this the memory that his own viscera had been handled by somebody else when he was four, and still more that there was a depressive dark mood around the house when he entered puberty, and one has a very dangerous cocktail of influences. Necrophilia may to some extent derive from 'a libidinal association between first orgasms and a depressed, morbid state due to family disruption', write Smith and Braun.[6] In other words, it matters hugely what *state of mind* the boy is in, whether joyful or harassed, adventurous or aridly curious, when the first orgasm is experienced; the associations may remain for life.

None of this is to say that every mother who takes too many pills will nurture a necrophile, nor that every child who is interested in skeletons will want to make a living person into one. It is the confluence of all these matters, their collision and combined strength which exerts a phenomenal hold on the personality. Any one influence would, by itself, be risibly inadequate to produce so catastrophic an outcome as happened in Jeff Dahmer's case. The fact remains that there is very little evidence, in his childhood, through adolescence, in personality and interests, of a biophilous character, one eager to find fun and beauty in life, to move forward and upward on the spiral of adventure. His were the downward-turning, inward-looking, suffocating spirals of Infinity Land.

The world's literature does not exactly abound in examples of necrophilic behaviour, despite some particularly florid and implausible passages in de Sade and Baudelaire. A little-known story by C. M. Eddy, however, matches the development of Dahmer's necrophilia to an uncanny degree. The narrator describes his infancy thus:

> My early childhood was one long, prosaic and monotonous apathy. Strictly ascetic, wan, pallid, undersized, and subjected to protracted spells of morbid moroseness, I was ostracised by the normal, healthy youngsters of my own age . . .
>
> Had I lived in some larger town, with greater

173

opportunities for congenial companionship, perhaps I could have overcome this early tendency to be a recluse . . . My life lacked motivation. I seemed in the grip of something that dulled my senses, stunted my development, retarded my activities, and left me unaccountably dissatisfied.

The first corpse he sees is that of his grandfather, a moment he describes as 'that portentous hour', and his life is changed forever. 'A baleful malignant influence that seemed to emanate from the corpse itself held me with magnetic fascination. My whole being seemed charged with some ecstatic electrifying force, and I felt my form straighten without conscious volition.' The narrator goes on to become a killer, with increasing frenzy as one murder follows ever harder upon another; he is ineluctably bound by a compulsion to seek constant renewal of that terrible thrill which comes solely with the proximity of a corpse. 'I knew, too, that through some strange satanic curse my life depended upon the dead for its motive force; that there was a singularity in my make-up which responded only to the awesome presence of some lifeless clod.'[7]

Fiction, yes, and overblown fiction at that, but possibly more instructive than most factual accounts of what are nowadays called 'serial killers'. Jeff Dahmer might himself have written the words quoted above, or at least would recognise their veracity. The descent into necrophilia can only be achieved at the expense of true emotional realisation of what one is actually doing, and this stifling of residual emotion has to be carefully nurtured. Dahmer prepared himself by getting drunk. He needed alcohol to give him courage to go seeking at the bars, alcohol to smooth the rite of drugging, more alcohol to smother his inhibitions against murder and drive up his urge to keep someone, yet more to cope with dismemberment. But alcohol could not do it alone. There was in addition the much longer preparation of secrecy, as he fought to protect what he knew was a degenerate personality from the interference of morality. For a time, until 1987, he had struggled in the opposite direction, to turn his life around, as he put it, and break free of the death-love which infected him. But that was gone, shattered; all his efforts now were bent towards feeding the bitter appetite of his dark inhabiter.

'The destruction of the dams of shame, disgust and morality, which must take place in the erection of necrophilia,' wrote A. A. Brill, 'requires more psychic labour than in the construction of any other perversions.'[8] Dahmer's dams of shame had been breached after the murder of Steven Tuomi and were subsequently sunk beneath a flood of diseased imaginings. With the death of his fourteenth victim, this flood was about to give way to manic frenzy and cumulatively derisory experiments. He thought he might find a way to keep somebody without having to kill him. One of those he would like to have kept was a boy called Konerak.

On Friday, 24 May, the day Tony Hughes died, Konerak was involved in a fight at Pulaski School with another boy. It was little more than a schoolboy scuffle of no great moment, but such scramblings for status tend to assume the role of major events in playground life, and there was talk the fight would resume that evening at Mitchell Park Domes. It never did. Konerak, colloquially known as 'Khum' or 'Kolack', was a friendly, high-spirited youngster who did not make enemies. The next evening, Saturday, 25 May, he went to a party at Crystal Palace with Laotian friends. On Sunday morning he took a shower at 10 a.m., then went downtown. That was the last time his brother saw him. The brother was called Somsack; for Konerak Sinthasomphone was about to be the second member of this immigrant family to fall into the hands of Jeffrey Dahmer, Somsack being the boy whom he had sexually assaulted in 1988.

That Sunday Dahmer had left the body of Tony Hughes

on his bedroom floor and gone to the Grand Avenue Mall for lunch at the Spiesgarten. He afterwards idled around window shopping until about five o'clock, with no apparent intention of looking for a companion; it was, after all, not the time of day when he would usually prowl, and he had not fortified himself with alcohol. He left by the main entrance on Wisconsin Avenue, about to cross the road to catch his bus home, when Konerak walked in, wearing bib jean shorts and black tennis shoes. On an impulse, Dahmer stopped him and asked if he would like to earn $50 by posing for some pictures. Konerak was initially reluctant ('He hemmed and hawed a little bit', said Dahmer), but eventually consented to go home with the man. One is bound to wonder whether he remembered what had happened in similar circumstances to his brother three years earlier; if he did, the recollection did not deter him. They took the bus together.

At the apartment Dahmer took two photographs of Konerak posing in his underwear, one standing up and the other lying down. Then he prepared the drugged drink and Konerak passed out for several hours, during which time he was caressed and fellated, and Dahmer fell asleep for a while as he cuddled him. It was in the course of this long Sunday evening that he proceeded with his latest and most pitiless experiment, one which he had in fact already attempted unsuccessfully on two previous victims and would employ on yet more before he was caught. Having discovered that a corpse was only satisfying for a short period, and that he would much prefer to have somebody who was alive but stayed with him, having also determined that nobody would stay under the conditions he would impose, he came upon the idea that he could perhaps destroy a person's will by surgery, and keep him in a zombie-like state deprived of independent thought. 'I didn't want to keep killing people and have nothing left except the skull,' he said.[9]

To this end, while Konerak was deeply unconscious, he took his drill and bored a narrow hole through his

176

cranium, at the top, three-quarters back on the crown and slanting forward. His intention was to reach the frontal lobes, but his understanding of their location was necessarily only approximate. With a marinating syringe which he had bought at Lecter's Kitchen Supply, he then injected muriatic acid into the brain, inserting up to two inches of the needle. Relating this aspect of his crimes, Dahmer was uncharacteristically embarrassed. 'This is going to sound bad,' he said, 'but . . . should I say it? . . . I took the drill while he was asleep . . .' It is a shard of a moment when his 'dams of shame' have not been totally breached, and the moral conscience flickers briefly. We shall have more to say about this attempt to create a 'zombie' when the matter is raised in court.

Very late at night, about 1.30 on Monday morning in fact, Dahmer left Konerak naked and asleep in the sitting-room while he went out to a local bar for a beer. He was gone about half an hour, nearly had a second glass, but thought it better to get back and see how his captive was progressing.

Meanwhile, Konerak had woken up and found his way out of the apartment. Johnny Laster was driving down the street with his girlfriend next to him when they were astonished to see a naked young man lurch across the road in front of them, then walk into a tree. He looked as if he was drunk. An unidentified black man helped him to his feet and moved on. First two, then three black girls came to Konerak's rescue. They were Tina Spivey, Nicole Childress and Sandra Smith. Konerak could not talk and was obviously disoriented. He kept holding his head in his hands, sitting down on the kerb, getting up again and staggering. The girls thought he had been taking drugs. They also said they saw blood on his testicles and pubic hair, as well as coming from his anus, but none of these observations was ever corroborated. They certainly did not see any blood on his head. Konerak had a generous head of hair, hanging almost to his shoulders, which obscured any damage they might have seen on the skull.

177

One might imagine that drilling through the cranium would produce a great deal of blood outflow, but a narrow hole might have no such effect and be completely dry. This means that nobody present realised what had happened to Konerak, and he was in no state to be able to tell them.

Jeff Dahmer turned the corner and saw Konerak faltering and being questioned by the girls. 'My first thought was to get him back to the apartment,' he said, 'because he was naked.' He also admits to being 'scared' at that point. Telling the girls that he would look after him, he took him by the elbow. Konerak resisted, swinging his arms about and dragging his feet, at one point clinging on to a tree. The girls were by now even more seriously alarmed. How could they be sure this man even knew the boy? In the mêlée which ensued, Dahmer pulling Konerak down the alley behind the apartment building, the girls trying to stop him, he referred to Konerak by three different (fictitious) names, which convinced them that he was lying. One of the girls said Konerak cried out, 'No, no', when Dahmer got hold of him and marched him off in a full nelson headlock. Miss Childress said the boy was 'stumbling, trying desperately to get away'. She would argue no longer; she ran across the road and called the police.

Officers Joseph Gabrish and John Balcerzak in Squad Car 36 received the call 'man down' at 2.06 a.m. They were on the scene within four minutes, and by this time found a crowd of over fifteen people watching the struggle. As soon as the police car arrived, Dahmer's attitude and demeanour relaxed. No longer using force, he was seen by the officers to be walking with the naked man, while others around were screaming at him. They asked Dahmer what was wrong with his friend, and sat Konerak on the hood of the squad car, covering him with a yellow blanket. He said nothing, and there was no evidence of any injury to him or any blood visible. Dahmer proceeded to explain that the man was a friend of his, and that he frequently behaved in this erratic manner, running around naked, when he had had too much to drink. That evening, he said, he had been on Jack Daniels whiskey. His name was John Hmung. No, he did not have any cards to support this identification, because John received his mail at another address. The strong implication was that he frequently stayed with Dahmer (who gave his own correct name and address and showed his Ambrosia card) and that they were homosexual lovers.

Tina, Nicole and Sandra were convinced that he was 'just a kid', whereas Dahmer told the officers he was twenty years old. In the report subsequently made to the District Attorney's office on the conduct of the officers it is revealed that there were a variety of estimates as to his age, ranging from thirteen to twenty. In fact he was fourteen, slim, and 5 feet 3 inches tall. 'The Asian people, they look young. It's hard to tell their age,' says Dahmer. Gabrish and Balcerzak were satisfied they were dealing with a young man over sixteen. They were also satisfied that Dahmer, with his quiet, consistent manner, was doing his best to be co-operative, while the loudly protesting girls were, in their view, interfering with their enquiries. For their part, the girls were intensely frustrated that the police should seem to pay more attention and lend greater respect to this dubious white man while they, the black girls who were doing their civic duty, were being ignored. Nicole tapped one of the officers on the shoulder, at which he 'exploded' and yelled at her to 'shut the hell up' and not interrupt, not to tell him how to do his job.

The officer shone a flashlight into Konerak's eyes, but would not, as Miss Spivey suggested, examine his anus. Spivey also said that Konerak was playing with his penis, but no other witness has supported this observation. At length the officer said, 'Madam, this is a domestic thing' and bade her let the matter rest. They invited Dahmer to take his boyfriend back indoors, and when Dahmer appeared tentative in grabbing hold of the boy, they suggested that he would have to be firmer. Dimly realising what was about to happen, Konerak started struggling

179

with the police officers as well. 'So one took his one arm on one side and the other took his other arm on the other side and they escorted him back up, about half a block to the apartment,' said Dahmer. In this manner was Konerak Sinthasomphone delivered to his executioner.

In the apartment, Dahmer showed the police the two polaroid pictures he had already taken of Konerak, which paradoxically supported his contention that they were intimate. This, together with the fact that Konerak's clothes were neatly folded on the sofa, and that he sat quietly, apparently contented, for the five minutes or so that they were there, convinced them that they had not come upon anything improper. In the bedroom a few feet away, behind an unlocked door, lay the body of Tony Hughes, already bloated up. An officer noted that there was a smell of excrement in the apartment, but did not think to investigate further. 'He was on the floor and I had the light off in there,' recalls Dahmer, 'and one of the officers sort of peeked his head around in the bedroom but didn't really take a good look or anything.' They then left, with the cheering remark, 'Well, you just take care of him.'

In the light of the fact that the officers in question were suspended when the Dahmer case broke, it is worth remembering that the call 'man down' is a routine one which might occur any number of times in one night. Records show that on 27 May Gabrish and Balcerzak responded to calls at 1.26 a.m., 1.40 a.m., 1.50 a.m., 1.59 a.m., 2 a.m. and 2.30 a.m., as well as to Konerak's distress at 2.06 a.m. It was a normally busy work-load.

Within an hour of their departure, Konerak was dead. Dahmer injected his brain with a second syringeful of acid, hoping thereby to keep him, but against this new assault he stood no chance. He decapitated him, opened him, photographed him. The body was taken apart and disposed of along with that of Tony Hughes, their discarded torsos acidified together when the killer had retained the parts of them he wanted to keep.

Konerak was reported missing the next day. His school

locker was searched for clues. His brother Somsack was interviewed, but he made no connection between this sudden disappearance and his own experience in 1988; there was no obvious reason why he should. The filed missing person dossier declared that no foul play was suspected. On 30 May, Konerak's portrait was published in the *Milwaukee Sentinel* and was immediately recognised by Miss Childress. She called the F.B.I. and was advised to notify the Milwaukee Police. This she did, telling them not only that this was the boy whom she had tried to save three days before, but that she had since seen the man he was with, in the Grand Avenue Mall, and would identify him again without difficulty. It is, to say the least, a thousand pities that these various strands were not spotted by somebody and tied together. They would have had the suspect's name and address as well as circumstantial witnesses had the log-book of Squad 36 been pulled and the identity of 'John Hmung' (now correctly identified by Miss Nicole Childress as Konerak Sinthasomphone) been investigated. 'Man down' and 'missing person' are separate matters which do not normally cross, and so Childress' alarm went unheeded.

As for Dahmer, who also saw the photograph in the *Sentinel*, he still had no idea that he had murdered the brother of the boy whose complaint had sent him to the Work Release Center. 'If I'd have known who I was dealing with,' he said, 'I sure as hell wouldn't have bothered asking him back, that's for sure.' Even so, what was his motive for killing him? Or did he not intend to kill him? He was not looking for anyone that day. Konerak walked into his path by the purest chance; he was not homosexual or consenting to anything more than posing for money. The poses were, however, taken with his hands behind his neck and his chest thrust forward, the very position in which Dahmer always placed his corpses when he was picturing them. It is more than likely that this pose triggered the fetishist in him and excited him to convert Konerak from a model to a personal possession. When the boy posed in that position, he was doomed. Dahmer says that he did not plan on killing him when he was out at the bar having a late beer, but concedes that it was very probable that the mood would come. Would he have let him go if he had not escaped on to the street? 'No, I hadn't let the others go, I don't see why I would let him go. I doubt that very much.'

A further motive presents itself, one more calculating, callous and cold. Now that the boy had been seen with him, by police and neighbours alike, he had become potential evidence and had to be rubbed out for that reason alone. 'I just didn't want him saying anything,' he admits obliquely. 'I couldn't afford mistakes like that, so I was scared even then.' It is at least possible that Konerak died, not to keep Jeff Dahmer company, but to keep his mouth shut.

On 28 May, Dahmer took a day off work to devote himself to the disposal of two bodies, and the following day reported to his probation officer, Donna Chester, that he had 'no major problems'. The first signs of imminent collapse were beginning to show. On the one hand, he was taking too much time off from the chocolate factory and had to be warned that he would soon run out of 'points' and risk dismissal. On the other, Mr Princewill warned him that the smells emanating from his apartment were intolerable and he risked eviction. Donna Chester was growing concerned about him; she sent him to Dr Crowley who, on 11 June, took one look at him and prescribed some powerful anti-depressant pills. It was all too late. Jeff Dahmer could lose job, home, health, and still not be able to shake off the obsession which now governed his every waking hour. He was about to be consumed by it.

There was still the loving, sweet presence of his grandmother on the distant periphery of his life, who might just redeem him from the brink of bleak insanity. She was involved in a car accident as she was driving home, which wrecked the car and left her with slight scratches. Suddenly, Jeff Dahmer was wrenched from his nightmare to be reminded of ordinary, healthy concerns. He went to see her to 'help out' and expressed a hope that she might stay with her cat and not attempt to drive again. 'It'll be a lot safer for her,' he said. It was a rare moment when he was able to externalise, to think of somebody other than the self which drove him and monopolised his energies. Weeks later, Detective Murphy would bear the task of calling upon this old lady to break the news that her grandson had butchered three men in her basement.

The unequal battle reached its apogee in July. On 30 June, Dahmer met twenty-year-old Matt Turner at the bus station in Chicago, brought him back to Milwaukee and strangled him. He was not reported missing. Five days later, also in Chicago, he met Jeremiah Weinberger, a twenty-three-year-old half Puerto Rican, half-Jewish man with an adust complexion, who died probably on 7 July after a long ordeal. Police had an accurate description of Dahmer as being the last person seen with Weinberger, and an artist's impression of his face. It was on 12 July that he bought the 57-gallon blue barrel in which to dump the accumulating remains of mutilated bodies. On 15 July he met twenty-four-year-old Oliver Lacy in the street, took him home and strangled him. Lacy was a handsome black body-builder whose head and skeleton Dahmer fancied to keep to adorn his shrine. He was reported missing by the fiancée he had dated for many years, Rose Colon. The same day, Ambrosia Chocolate suspended Dahmer pending a review of his record on attendance.

It made no difference. Dirty and unshaven, he told Donna Chester that he was seriously thinking of suicide. (He had thought of injecting himself with formaldehyde, but was afraid it might take too long to have effect.) He was running out of money and would have to leave the apartment. He did not know where he would go or how he would live. She contacted the Salvation Army on his behalf and placed him on their list for emergency accommodation. She also gave him addresses of food banks where he could secure a free meal. He was degenerating into a tramp.

That same day, Thursday, 18 July, he went from Donna Chester's office to see Dr Crowley again. Crowley noted that he was 'tense, anxious, and very depressed', and privately thought him to be in a very bad way indeed. He had no hesitation in offering more anti-depressants, but the prescription was never presented to a chemist. Instead, Dahmer's behaviour on his way home was, in the circumstances, incredible. He approached a black man named Ricky Thomas and invited him back to his apartment for a drink. Thomas declined. Dahmer was no longer able to think sequentially or to act with logic. He was a hostage to his compulsion. At his lowest point, the only solace he could imagine was another body.

On Friday, 19 July, he had word that he was fired. 'As I told you yesterday,' wrote Allen Zipperer, 'the company has completed its investigation and has decided to convert your suspension to a termination for excessive absenteeism. Jeff, it is truly unfortunate that you did not take corrective action to improve your attendance record. This is something that you alone control. If you have any personal belongings on company property please arrange for its removal no later than July 25, 1991.' Upon receipt of this news, Dahmer went out and spied twenty-five-year-old Joseph Bradehoft at a bus-stop near Marquette University. A married man with a two-year-old daughter, Bradehoft was known to have bisexual inclinations. He was estranged from his wife, who had filed for separation and placed a restraining order on him not to visit. He went home with Jeffrey Dahmer, was strangled and dismembered.

The scene at Apartment 213 in that week from 12 to 19 July was more lurid than Giotto's vision of hell on the wall of the Scrovegni chapel in Padua, which depicts devils munching on the intestines of the fallen. When Oliver Lacy was being massaged in one room, the headless body of Jeremiah Weinberger was floating in a bath of cold water and bleach next door. Dahmer was obliged to take a shower with two corpses in the tub. He took one photograph of Matt Turner in a standing position after death, because rigor mortis had set in and he was able to position the body properly. Other pictures show a headless Oliver Lacy hanging by a strap from the bar of the shower-curtain, and the same mutilated corpse, also with the rib-cage exposed, lying on top of the decapitated body of Weinberger. Both heads were separately preserved in the fridge and freezer, along with two others. A bag containing internal organs was stuck to the bottom of the freezer. Hearts were in the fridge, and a whole bicep, large enough to cover a plate, had been fried and eaten. The drum in the bedroom contained the remains of three people. Bradehoft was murdered on the 19th. Dahmer left his body on the bed and covered it with a blanket for two days. He does not say where he slept during this time, but we may assume it was beside the corpse. On 21 July, he uncovered the body to find the head was covered in maggots. So he cut it off, cleaned it, and placed it in the freezer. We are fast approaching the denouement.

These are not the actions of a man in possession of himself, but rather of one 'possessed' by demonic force; they are the wild, perplexing, irreducible acts of raging dementia. He says he was too tired to keep up with the tasks of dissection he had imposed upon himself, but his exhaustion did not interrupt plans for his shrine. He completely 'defleshed' (his word) the body of Oliver Lacy in order to have the second of the two skeletons he needed to guard each end of the altar (the first was Ernest Miller). He even investigated the cost of a freeze-drying machine, in the vain hope that he might be able to 'keep' people whole by preserving them in perpetuity. But a machine large enough for the purpose would have cost $30,000. Embalming he would not consider, because the embalmed body does eventually decay. The two griffins had been damaged in a fight, when one of the victims kicked the table and knocked them over, but he did not discard them;

they were essential to an aim far dearer to him than maintaining a job or leasing an apartment. Thus far had his grasp of reality evaporated.

Incidentally, the admission that the griffins were damaged in a struggle casts a grim light on the way in which victims of this final frenzy died. No longer is it always a matter of deep sleep and unconscious oblivion. The murderer has become sloppy, careless, lacking in concentration, and this one man had to be subdued by brute strength. At what stage was he resisting? 'As strangulation was going on.' He wasn't sleeping, then? 'Not quite asleep, no, not quite.'[10] So he fought for his life, albeit with reduced power. It would not help to identify him, but it is obvious that this was no cosy search for company, but a contest won by overwhelming forces. Jeffrey Dahmer's mind had turned to compost.

When asked whether he felt remorse for what he had done, Dahmer said, 'Yes, I do have remorse, but I'm not even sure myself whether it's as profound as it should be. I've always wondered myself why I don't feel more remorse.'* There were three that he picked out for especial contrition, though in the first two cases it is more a question of pity for himself than for the victim. He regretted Steven Hicks because of the shock: 'I wish I hadn't done it'; Steven Tuomi because 'I had no intention of doing it in the first place'; and Jeremiah Weinberger because 'he was exceptionally affectionate. He was nice to be with.'[11] That is a devastating comment, at once pathetic and replete with implication. I hope it may permit a closer examination of exactly what happened to Jeremiah.

Aaron Weinberger adopted the Puerto Rican/Jewish little boy and brought him up under his own name. He knew that Jeremiah was homosexual and wont to stay

---

* Dennis Nilsen: 'Words like sorry hold little comfort for the bereaved. I mistrust my own inner sincerity to bear even to utter them.'

away from home for a night or two, but he always telephoned to let him know where he was. He lived with his father in order to save money for college, and had ambitions to seek a career in art design. He was good-looking and very self-conscious about his physical appearance. At weekends he would go to Chicago gay taverns such as Carol's, Roscoe's, Sidetracks, to meet friends and socialise, but during the week he regularly stayed at home. On the evening of 5 July, he stopped by a restaurant at 10.30 p.m. to see a friend who worked there, Ted Jones, and told him he intended to go dancing at the Vortex, and would meet Ted after work at Carol's Bar on 1355 North Wells Street. Ted got to Carol's Bar by about 2.30 in the morning.

There he saw Jeremiah in animated conversation with a blond man, animated at least on his part – the blond was rather quiet. Jeremiah came over to him and said, 'This guy wants me to leave here and go to Milwaukee for the weekend. What do you think?' Ted replied, 'He looks okay, go for it. You don't have anything else to do this weekend.' Jeremiah returned to the blond man and sat beside him at the bar. Shortly afterwards they went to a dark backroom where they kissed and embraced. 'He was very affectionate in the bar,' recalled Dahmer. 'He was giving me blow jobs right in the bar and everything.' There is surprise in his voice, the surprise of a man to whom this degree of unforced attention was novel. It might be that here was somebody so keen on Dahmer's company that he would stay with him of his own accord! They walked back to the bar area, where Dahmer sat on a stool with Jeremiah on his lap. Jeremiah called Ted Jones over and spoke with him for half an hour, while Dahmer moved to an adjacent stool and brooded, saying nothing. In that moment, perhaps, the spell was broken. Jeremiah could not, after all, be his and his alone, because he had connections, he was tied by friendships to other people like this man, he *belonged* to people. That was an intolerable thought.

Last call for drinks was at 3.45 a.m. Ted Jones said, 'I'll call you tomorrow to see if you want to go to a picnic this weekend. If there's no answer, I'll assume you went for the weekend.' Dahmer and Weinberger took the Greyhound bus to Milwaukee, a ride of an hour and a half during which Weinberger made love to his new friend all the way. 'He was all over me on the bus ride home.' The damage was done, the trust dissipated, back in Carol's Bar. Besides which, it was questionable whether at this stage Jeff Dahmer could see anything for what it was. Jeremiah was genuinely attracted to him, and had made advances to nobody else. That was not enough for Dahmer, however.

When they got home, they embraced and had oral sex, after which Dahmer prepared his treacherous mixture of drink and sleeping pills. 'I wanted to see if I could find a way of keeping him with me without actually killing him.' The irony is, he would probably have stayed, as he had told Ted Jones that he would be away for the whole weekend and his enthusiasm was evident. While this kind and decent man slept, Dahmer drilled through his skull and, for the first time, the acid injections having resulted in fatalities, he squirted boiling water into his brain.

'He woke up at the end of the day, the next morning, and he was sort of groggy and everything. He talked, it was like he was dazed and I thought I would be able to keep him that way.' Jeff helped him take a shower. Jeremiah said nothing about his head. There was no blood or liquid effusion of any kind. He was up for about six hours, just sleepy and indecisive. He made no effort to leave the apartment. Of course, he did not know what had happened to him, and could not understand why he felt so comatose. 'He was walking around, going to the bathroom, but I had to go to work the second night, at the end of the second day, and he was still walking around so I gave him another dose of pills and another shot of boiling water in the same hole.' He left Jeremiah lying on the bed.

188

The next morning he returned to find him dead. He had fallen off the bed and was lying on the floor, his eyes wide open. Dahmer was surprised the eyes should be open like that, as all the others had died with their eyes closed. One must only hope that Jeremiah did not wake up and endeavour to save himself from this madness into which he had fallen.

Dahmer took seven pictures of him, the first as he lay there on the floor, staring in disbelief, the others after decapitation. The headless torso lay in cold water and bleach in the bathtub for a week.

In the meantime, Aaron Weinberger reported his son missing, and Ted Jones, Allen Patrykus and Chuck Plimmer coincided in their description of the man he had accompanied to Milwaukee. Based on this, police artist John Holmes drew a likeness of the suspect which was to be circulated among Chicago's gay community in the hope somebody might know him. Events over the next twenty-four hours were to render that drawing superfluous.

Dahmer's career was reaching its climax. He was dominated by his aberrant desires, held captive by them to the point where they banished every other thought. 'Nothing else gave me pleasure towards the end, nothing, not the normal things, especially near the end when things just started piling up, person after person, during the last six months. I could not get pleasure from going out to eat, I just felt very empty, frustrated, and driven to continue doing it. None of these are excuses for what I did, but those are the feelings I had in those last months, really intensive. For some reason, I kept doing it. I knew my job was in jeopardy around February. All I would have had to do was just stop for several months at a time and space it out, but it didn't happen that way. I was just driven to do it more frequently and more frequently until it was just too much – complete overload. I couldn't control it any more.'[12]

If there was one moment at which the fatal decision was made, it was at 9 a.m. on 15 July. Dahmer had a partially drugged Oliver Lacy in the apartment and a beheaded Jeremiah Weinberger in the bathtub. He had tried putting Lacy to sleep with chloroform, but it didn't work, which surprised him because 'it worked okay on fruit flies in biology class at school'. He knew he would have to go to work in about an hour, but he liked Lacy and wanted to keep him, just one more, just this one. How was he to choose what to do? If he went to work Lacy would have recovered by the morning and would almost certainly not want to stay – he was not gay anyway. Dahmer called Ambrosia Chocolate and asked for a 'personal day', that is an extra day's leave. It was granted, but the next evening, with Lacy dead, he was told that he had exceeded his permitted number of 'personal days' and was henceforth suspended. Oliver Lacy was 'the one who started the dominoes falling'.[13]

'If I'd been thinking rationally I would have stopped. I wasn't thinking rationally because it just increased and increased. It was almost like I wanted it to get to a point where it was out of my control and there was no return. I mean, I was very careful for years and years, you know. Very careful, very careful about making sure nothing incriminating remained, but these last few months, they just went nuts.'[14]

He thought back to Chicago. Maybe he shouldn't have gone there. Maybe that's when it started going wrong. He would probably not have lost his job if he had pulled on the brakes then. 'It just seemed like it went into a frenzy this last month. Everything really came crashing down. The whole thing started falling down around my head.' In the final week, he had to think. He was going to have to vacate the apartment, and that must mean abandoning his shrine, the two skeletons, the eleven skulls and heads, all that beauty he was creating. 'That was the last week I was going to be in that apartment building. I was going to have to move out and find somewhere to put all my possessions. Should I get a chest and put what I wanted to keep in that, and get rid of the rest? Or should I put an end to this, try to stop this and find a better direction for my life? That's what was going through my mind that last week.'[15]

One of his workmates, Richard Burton, was driving with a friend when he saw him standing on a street corner and gave him a ride. Dahmer said he wanted to get out of Wisconsin and go to Florida. Burton wished him luck, and he got out. To his friend, Burton said he thought Jeff had 'lost it all' – no job, no friends. A little later he spotted him again talking to a black man at a bus-stop.

On 21 July, after dismembering the body of Joseph Bradehoft, he was wandering around the Grand Avenue Mall where, in two separate incidents, he propositioned Hispanic men with the invitation to earn money by posing for pictures and watching videos. They were Joseph Rosa and Ricardo Ortiz. Both refused.

The events of 22 July depict a mind at once unfocused, listless, and delirious, unhinged. Dahmer got up late, in the midst of his human debris, and went out for a beer. Sopa Princewill accosts him in the corridor with a 40-ounce bottle, and warns him that he may not last until his lease runs out at the end of the month – he may be evicted sooner because his place smelt so awful. He listens, but does not react in any noticeable manner. He goes downtown and is walking along 3rd Street near Wells Street at 2 p.m. when he sees a black man sitting on a sidewalk bench. This is twenty-year-old Ormell Holmes. He asks Holmes if he wants to earn $50. What do I have to do for that? asks Holmes. Pose for pictures and drink some rum. Holmes indicates that he is not interested in that kind of thing, and Dahmer moves on. He approaches another man in the same street, with the same result.

He now goes to his favourite haunt, the Grand Avenue Mall, and has some fast food. He is seen there at 3.30 talking to a man on one of the benches. A little later, he asks a sixteen-year-old black boy called Anderson to come home with him and watch movies, and his offer is again declined. At 4.30 Dennis Campbell, who works at Milwaukee's famous German restaurant, Karl Ratzch's, is in the Mall with his girlfriend Julie Weyer, and goes to the men's room on the first floor. Having urinated, he is drying his hands on a wall dryer when the door opens and a scruffy white man with several days' growth of beard walks in and stands behind him, then moves beside him. There is no long preparatory choreography. The white man says straight out, 'Do you want to make fifty dollars real quick?' 'Doing what?' says Campbell. 'Come to my apartment and watch videos.' 'I don't think so,' says Campbell, and the man, whom he thought 'weird, creepy and very unusual', says, 'O.K.' He told Julie about it afterwards and she laughed.

He has a quick pizza and some beers and half an hour later is by one of the side entrances when he sees three men together, one of whom has spoken to him twice before in the preceding weeks, just to ask for a cigarette. This is Tracy Edwards, who has been in Milwaukee only since early June, having previously lived with his mother in Mississippi. He has many old friends here though, as he once lived in Milwaukee for four years. The two people with him are Jeff Stevens and Carl Gilliam. Dahmer falls into conversation with them, tells them he is 'real bored', and offers them $100 each if they will come to his house and keep him company. (He is at this stage virtually penniless.) One of them asks if there is sex involved, and Dahmer says he just wants to handcuff somebody. They agree to walk with him to a liquor store on 7th Street, a few blocks up Wisconsin Avenue, and the four men are outside the store before 6 p.m. Dahmer walks in, leaving the other three on the sidewalk. Tracy's twin brother, Terrance Edwards, who is with his girlfriend at a bar across the road, comes to greet them, and they tell him of this odd guy who will pay them just to have a good time. Terrance strongly advises against it. Dahmer comes out, there is some more talk, whereupon Stevens and Gilliam wander off to find their own ladies. Dahmer and Tracy get in a cab outside the Greyhound Bus Station. It is too late for Terrance to stop his brother, but he manages to catch up with Carl. Dahmer has told them that he lives at the Ambassador Hotel.

Terrance and Carl walk to the Ambassador with the intention of intercepting Tracy and stopping him from doing anything foolhardy. On arrival, they wait for one and a half hours before giving up. They now have no idea where Tracy could be, and are seriously worried.

Tracy is in 213 of the Oxford Apartments on 25th Street, with an eerily threatening man who seems only half aware of where he is and what he is doing. He had to disengage alarm systems to get into the apartment, which emitted a foul odour amid a weird ambiance, despite being fairly neat and clean. On the floor were four large cartons of muriatic acid, which Dahmer said he used for cleaning bricks. Tracy is already sorry he has got himself into this mess, but if he keeps his wits about him he may be able to get out of it. He must keep the man talking. Dahmer says he remembers they talked about gay bars in Chicago, and he recalls showing him the knife, but after that everything went 'fuzzy'. Edwards says Dahmer clapped a handcuff on him while his back was turned as he looked at the fish tank. 'What's happening?' he said. Dahmer said he was only joking, and he would get the keys to the handcuffs which were in the bedroom. They walked into the bedroom, where the video of *Exorcist II* was playing, as if planned, and Tracy noticed a big blue drum in the corner and posters of naked men on the walls. 'I won't hurt you if you let me handcuff you and take some pictures,' said Dahmer. 'You have to be nude.'

Tracy realised he was dealing with a volatile character, one moment conciliatory, one moment menacing, sometimes cold and determined, sometimes vacant and pathetic. Edwards made sure that he kept his two hands far apart all the time, so that it would not be easy to handcuff him totally, and kept Dahmer talking about it. Why did he want to use handcuffs? 'I'll be in control,' Dahmer said. Then the knife was brandished.

Tracy said he would let him take the pictures if only he

would put the knife away. He would go into the bathroom and undress. To show he intended compliance, he took his shirt off, not knowing that this – the exposed chest – was the trigger which sealed the fate of Steven Hicks thirteen years before, which made him tear into Steven Tuomi's ribs in 1987, and which had led to the death of fifteen more men since. Fortunately for him, Dahmer had fallen so far off the edge of sanity that his sense of the present was fragmentary and defective. He told Tracy that he was very beautiful. He appeared suddenly relaxed and 'laid back'. He sat on the edge of the bed watching *Exorcist II* as if in a trance, rocking and chanting the while. The alterations in his personality and behaviour were sudden and extreme. When he lay his head on Tracy's chest and listened to his heart, Tracy finally knew he was in the company of a mad man.

There was some manoeuvring, during which Tracy contrived to push the knife under the bed and make his way into the living-room while Dahmer was at the fridge looking for a beer. He told Dahmer to trust him, and that he would do what he wanted as soon as he took the handcuff off. Dahmer said he would find the key, and went to the bedroom, whereupon Tracy made a dash for the front door. Dahmer caught up in time to grab his arm and plead with him to come back in. Tracy Edwards fled.

The rest is now history, as police officers Rauth and Mueller were flagged down by Tracy Edwards who subsequently led them to Dahmer's apartment and its terrible secrets. For the first time since Luis Pinet, Dahmer had a man in his den with no sleeping pills with which to paralyse him. What could he have thought he was doing? The pattern was broken, shattered. He did not seem to care any more. He made only a half-hearted attempt to retain Tracy Edwards, and even when the police came to the door, he did not refuse them entry. He did not prevent the police officer from going into the bedroom, knowing what he would find there. It was only when he was arrested that Jeff Dahmer awoke from his reverie and was rudely hauled back into the real world.

'Something stronger than my conscious will made it happen,' Dahmer says. 'I think some higher power got good and fed-up with my activity and decided to put an end to it. I don't really think there are any coincidences. The way it ended and whether the close calls were warnings to me or what, I don't know. If they were, I sure didn't heed them.'[16]

'If I hadn't been caught or lost my job, I'd still be doing it, I'm quite sure of that. I went on doing it and doing it and doing it, in spite of the anxiety and the lack of lasting satisfaction.'

On 22 July he was not drunk (by his own standards), he did not black out, but his conduct was so loose and haphazard that capture was, at last, practically inevitable. 'How arrogant and stupid of me to think that I could do something like this and just go about my life normally as if nothing had ever happened. They say you reap what you sow, well, it's true, you do, eventually . . . I've always wondered, from the time that I committed that first horrid mistake, sin, with Hicks, whether this was sort of predestined and there was no way I could have changed it.

'I wonder just how much predestination controls a person's life and just how much control they have over themselves.'[17]

Chapter Eight

The Question of Control

The query posed by Jeffrey Dahmer at the end of the previous chapter goes to the very heart of the debate about criminal responsibility and the exercise of free will. Put starkly, there is no free will in nature, and the concept of freedom of choice, the basis for every moral edifice and all notions of conscience, is man-made and man-imposed. Morality is the civilising influence which mankind has erected to shield himself from the appalling vacuum of chaotic nature, where blunt caprice prevails. The question is whether Dahmer's acts are the product of tyrannical nature, and therefore unmanageable by him, or the issue of choices freely made by a man who has rejected the moral constraints of his fellows. If the former, then his behaviour is not subject to his control; if the latter, then control is its very essence. Whichever the case, *control* is the key-word which will dominate proceedings at the trial, and it is a word which is also a major preoccupation of Dahmer's thought and conversation.

Control systems, whether we call them morality or behaviour modification, have evolved with the development of mankind into an organised social being, and we can see their origin in the 'displacement activity' of other creatures as they find a way out of the anarchy of individualism into a method of group responsibility. The work of ethologists, Tinbergen and Lorenz in particular, has been crucial in this regard. They observed that geese, for example, go through a ritual of neck swaying and hissing rather than enter into a destructive combat, and that male sticklebacks, when in dispute, stab furiously at the sand to direct their frustrations onto it rather than at each other. These are embryonic and successful attempts at a control system or 'morality', designed to ensure the greater good of the community at the expense of freedom of the individual. Seen from this point of view, Dahmer's control systems were severely impaired, unless we assume he deliberately turned away from them to revert to the brute selfishness of untamed elemental nature.

The control system of moral choice obviously belongs to the conscious part of the self; the uncontrolled Dionysian expression of pre-moral urges equally obviously belongs to the subconscious self. Freud called the subconscious *das Unbewusste*, which literally means 'the unapprehended'. It follows that what cannot be apprehended by the consciousness cannot be controlled by it. The idea of negation is also foreign to the unconscious – it has no truck with the word 'no'. Conscious morality says 'thou shalt not', forbidding all manner of acts which are not conducive to social ease and interaction. The unconscious says 'thou shalt', in order to obey a deeper imperative. I am not suggesting that Dahmer was in some way 'unconscious' at the time of the murders, but that the motive force which led him to them rose from the deep untouchable recesses of *das Unbewusste*.

All of which is a restatement in different terms of the opening proposition as to whether free will can be said to operate, in any *profound* sense, in a case such as this. We are experimenting with language in the hope of grasping the essential dilemma at the core, and merely finding different ways of saying the same thing. Does one control, or is one controlled? Are we active agents, or passive twigs? Can we ever understand the tangled motives which entwine the roots of what we do, or are they buried beyond sight, condemning us to behave robotically in their service? These are philosophical questions beyond the

197

walls of psychiatry (which deals with the results of aberration, not the theory of volition), and way beyond the scope of a court of law. Lawyers habitually make a distinction between the irresistible impulse and the impulse not resisted, but the whole question of control is far subtler than that, having to do with the feeling of fundamental compulsion, not momentary impulse.

When there is conflict between deep-seated compulsion and residual moral resistance (between being controlled and controlling), the murderer often resorts to alcohol as an ally, releasing the former and annihilating the latter. This applies to Jeff Dahmer as it did to Dennis Nilsen and to dozens of others. Sometimes the murderer is engaged in a Herculean struggle to resist the compulsion, as with Theodore Bundy, who gave the impression of being master of himself and of all he surveyed; privately, he recognised the dark urgings which consumed him and he tried to keep off the streets when he felt them rising, so that no woman would stray into his ken. The compulsion grew, and 'Bundy felt himself slipping under its control again and again'.[1] In the end, he found himself committing the most heinous acts in obedience to a self which raged unreined inside him. Ian Brady provocatively called this the 'higher' self – the fact of its tyranny remains. He has said that it cannot be resisted, that one is compelled to do its bidding because the 'higher self' is incomparably stronger than the mind.

Now listen to Jeffrey Dahmer. 'I was completely swept along with my own compulsion,' he said. 'I don't know how else to put it. It didn't satisfy me completely so maybe I was thinking another one [murder] will. Maybe this one will, and the numbers started growing and growing and just got out of control, as you can see. I got to the point where I lost my job because of it.'[2] The paradox is that Dahmer sought to control his world and the individuals who blundered into it, but was all the time controlled *by* it. The propensity to murder lurks, incessantly, insatiably, in his bowels. Then, when its hunger gasps and reaches out, 'it breaks loose from its moorings, takes charge of the individual who formerly had some hold over it, and goes on to murder itself, like a powerless rider of a runaway horse'.[3] To talk of free will in such circumstances is an absurdity. One might as well try to fall upwards.

It has been possible in Dahmer's case to observe the birth of this monster within, its gradual poisoning of the psyche, the incipient attempt to contain it, and the desperate internal struggle with it after the murder of Steven Hicks in 1978. It is worth insisting on this, for a gap of nine years between the first killing and the second is extremely unusual. In all other similar cases, once the obstacle of the first one has been conquered, the need to repeat is overwhelming, and subsequent murders come rapidly in its wake. The very fact that Jeff Dahmer held his murderousness in check for nine years testifies to the intensity of his fight to control and not be controlled. After the death of Steven Tuomi in 1987, which he did not expect and does not remember, his struggle was lost. He says himself that his morality was shot, that he gave up trying to resist, that he surrendered to the monster. It was easier to go on than go back. Like Macbeth, he was 'in blood Stepp'd in so far, that, should I wade no more, Returning were as tedious as go o'er'.[4]

This notion of control is so slippery that its subtleties threaten to confuse. Though the murderer is, in this sense, a victim of his master, he does unconsciously collude with him, for murderousness is in some cases a personal safety-valve which may prevent something 'worse' from occurring, such as utter disintegration of the psyche. 'What the world sees is the figures whom he destroys but not the invisible figure whom he protects . . . His ethical goal is individual, personal and remains unseen by those around him and by himself also.'[5] In his inner torment, the murderer must sacrifice others to save himself, and in that respect the idea of control shifts from the passive to the active. Being himself controlled by a nameless, mysterious power that he did not understand was, to Jeff Dahmer, frightening. His response was to exercise control over his victims, in other words to grab the initiative. Time and again we have heard him say that what he most wanted, in his 'empty' life, was to be in control of *something*, and only when he was alone with his prey did he experience that feeling of being 'on top'. This is another paradox, for his way of countering the intolerable helplessness of being controlled is to impose that same helplessness upon his victims. It is a straight transference, a kind of retaliation.

Speaking of the British psychopath Patrick Mackay, Dr James Stewart said, 'Patrick might be excited by the knowledge that someone was at his mercy, and . . . in such a situation he would probably be incapable of restraining himself.'[6] In this context, it is also important to note that strangulation as a method of killing offers a more tantalising opportunity for control than any other, the victim being wholly at the mercy of the amount of pressure the murderer chooses to exert. It may take five minutes to squeeze the life out of someone, but that time can be prolonged by the diminution of pressure and its gradual reimposition. In such a circumstance, the murderer is in total control of life and death – he can grant life to his victim as well as despatch him into the afterworld. Dennis Nilsen did precisely this with Carl Stottor, whom he nearly killed and then reprieved, leaving Stottor confused as to whether he was his executioner or saviour. Dahmer seems to have exercised similar power with Luis Pinet. While he has been consistent in admitting that control was his aim, he has never said that he enjoyed the act of killing, and the image with which he has left us is that of a lover choking his unconscious mate before wrapping him in his arms. He did let slip, however, that one victim was not fully unconscious and had to be subdued, which might indicate a pleasure in the act of slow strangulation which he is still unwilling to concede. Only Dahmer will ever know the entire truth behind this.

Nor is it inappropriate to be reminded how deeply embedded in our history is the acceptance of this notion that the loved one should be controlled and subdued. Krafft-Ebing pointed out that in prehistory a couple's first copulation came about as the direct reward for pursuit and overcoming (as it still does with other animals), and to this day cartoons crudely depict the caveman as clubbing his mate and dragging her to his lair. We retain an echo of this ancient rite in the modern Christian marriage, when the bridegroom-predator picks up his 'conquest' and carries her off to his domain.

It is also to Krafft-Ebing that we owe another insight – that there is a corollary between defloration of a virgin and the sex-murderer's cutting of the flesh, both actions of piercing, stabbing and entering. One might also suggest that in the most orthodox love-making there is a desire on the part of the man not merely to enjoy sensual pleasure but to thrust as far *into* his mate as he can possibly reach; the act is mimicked by a habit of some homosexual men called 'fist-fucking', in which the arm is pushed deep into the partner's rectum. The point of these reflections is to emphasise that the grim aberrations of a man like Dahmer are not all that different in kind from a spectrum of behaviour from so-called normal to extremely eccentric. Dahmer's acts, however abhorrent, place him within the scope of human experience, and his wrestling with control only exaggerates similar preoccupations faced by many of us who are not regarded as dangerous.

That Dahmer should become dangerous while the majority of people (including those who have bizarre fantasies) remain harmless needs some explanation. Clearly, his emotions and his psyche did not proceed to maturity in the expected way; their development was arrested by some event or other of cataclysmic importance. This event would be likely to have taken place at the time when he was very young, when mother and infant were still one unit, allied against the world, and the infant's dependence was total. As Melanie Klein has shown, the infant goes through a phase when his psychic peace is extremely fragile and any loss suffered is acutely felt and likely to reverberate long into the future. Is it possible to discern any such crucial loss suffered by the young Jeff Dahmer?

I believe his double hernia operation at the age of four changed the course of his life. It is well documented that children under six suffer significantly more from the trauma of surgery than their elder siblings, because their understanding of what is happening to them and its possible effect upon their bodies is severely limited. The infant is striving towards independence, towards the ability to exist in his own right without constant maternal nourishment, and he is enjoying his first tentative steps towards control of his own destiny; there are things he can do, of his own volition, which will achieve a desired effect. What then happens in hospital, a place to which he has never been before and which he does not choose to go to now? Suddenly, his embryonic autonomy is shattered by a rude invasion; his little powers of decision are roughly withdrawn and he becomes an *object* in the hands of strangers. *His ability to maintain control* is undermined, disregarded, even perhaps cancelled. He experiences 'loss of control, autonomy, and competence'.[7] And he does not know why.

Not knowing why, he will wonder and invent. His capacity to handle his emotional reactions to trauma and threat *when alone* is still very insecure, and his understanding of this, his body, how it works and what one may do with it, is tiny. 'His knowledge of his own physiology and anatomy is meagre and is confused with weird speculations about the inside of his body.'[8] Jeff Dahmer's own imaginings about the insides of people's bodies began with his hernia operation and the intrusion into his. The atmosphere in hospital cannot help but be terrifying, because it is so unfamiliar. Add to this the anxieties of parents and the proddings of strange men, the feeling that something dreadful, unknown and unspoken, is about to happen, and the imperative that in the face of all this he must be passive and compliant, and the child is overwhelmed. 'He has fantasies of what did happen to him which are far in excess of the actual facts,' writes a learned paediatrician, and he is further convinced that 'the injury will continue to increase and make him entirely different from anyone else in the world'. Both these observations seem to apply with peculiar accuracy to the case of Jeff Dahmer. And there is a third, slightly chilling in its prophetic implications: 'He may abreact the fear by playing that he is performing the operation on another child.'[9]

The memory of the fear and fantasies which preceded the operation may then be repressed, with the result that unconscious recollections begin to infect the growing child's perceptions of the world and of people, and every new experience assumes the threat of a repetition of the old. This is a heavily buried reaction, of course; one would not suggest that Dahmer thought everyone he met was a surgeon in disguise, but, never wanting to see or be touched by that surgeon again, he would presume that everyone was implicitly dangerous – his responses would be deeply coloured by the experience. 'Emotional shock may not express itself openly for some time . . . Just as physical shock may result in death, so emotional shock may result in a lifetime of unhappiness.'

It is often very difficult to see the connections between an adult's unusual behaviour and the surgery he endured as a child, but in Dahmer's case the avenue from cause to effect is strikingly clear. The history of a four-year-old who was given a meatotomy (to widen the urethral opening) without anaesthetic shows some parallels.[10] His play thereafter was to do with cutting people up, and cutting off his own face, hands, and penis, all clearly derived from the fear of castration which the operation had engendered. Jeff Dahmer's operation involved opening his abdomen with fairly deep incisions, feeling his insides, exploring within him, at a time when his ability to count upon his mother, with her own insecurities and nervousness, was already in jeopardy. He asked her afterwards whether his penis had been removed (so he told Dr Becker), and the post-operative pain would feel exactly as if it had. The fear of castration is not only, or even mainly, sexual, and here we must come to the most telling inference. When Dahmer was cut open by the surgeon, in his own mind he lost control of his own body once and for all, and his crimes in adulthood were a belated attempt to reassert himself and regain control. They expressed a desperate wish to reclaim that power which, unconsciously, he thought the surgeon's knife had removed.

Hence the importance of *control* in his vocabulary, and its significance as the leitmotif of his trial. Control was something lost in infancy and never recovered. With his victims, he at last placed himself in a position where he could control not only what happened to them, but *what happened to their bodies*. At last, he was the surgeon and they the passive child on the table. He could handle their intestines as his had been handled, cut them in the same place as he had been cut, restore to himself that autonomy of which he had been robbed, by stealing theirs. The tactile intimacy of the operation had at the same time mingled the feeling of sexual privilege with that of corporal invasion, which is why he chose to regain control and restore his stolen potency not with enemies, not through hatred, but with a loved object. The combination was disastrous.

Now do we begin to see the subconscious significance of Dahmer's black table, which was to form the centrepiece of his temple or shrine. In a sense it was his altar, and we shall later investigate the possible meanings of this as a ritual symbol. But for the moment it must have another dimension. Why did he buy a table, and not something lower or smaller or more ornate, as one might expect an altar to be? And what did he use the table for? It was on the table that he draped the naked corpses of his victims, on the table that he photographed their chests, abdomens and genitals, on the table that he sometimes made the first incision before dismemberment in the bathtub. What else, then, is Dahmer's black table but the memory of that hospital operating table upon which he had been summarily emasculated in the most intimate manner?

It need hardly be said that one does not wish to argue from the particular to the general and fall into the absurdity of suggesting that every child who has a double hernia operation is bound to grow into a necrophile. Conversely, that the development is not universally true does not invalidate its truth in a particular instance; this, I think, is one such.

That, at least, is the case for predetermination. It will be objected that a theoretic view of mental history like this entirely absolves Dahmer from any responsibility for his conduct and is thereby unacceptable. We all have Original Sin, it is said, and are cluttered with flaws. We may choose whether or not to indulge those flaws or deny them, to acquiesce or resist. Dahmer's own story indicates that he did resist for a while, thus supporting the thesis that he, like the rest of us, was daily presented with choices which he was able to evaluate and act upon. By this reckoning, he was not driven by an irresistible unconscious urge to control, but made decisions either to avoid desires which he knew to be depraved, or to give in to them. Every one of us has to make such choices, admittedly of a less devastating nature than his, and take the consequences for them. His freedom to choose right or wrong was inviolate, despite the peculiar nature of his problem. He had the will, he had the power, he had the potential to do good. He killed because he *decided* to kill. So it would be fiercely and repeatedly argued in court by District Attorney E. Michael McCann.

There is one thing seriously wrong with this point of view. While it is possible to make decisions which are in every obvious sense voluntary and logical, they may be made in order to achieve an end which is in itself involuntary ('driven') and illogical. Put another way, one may make sane sequential moves towards an insane and inconsequential purpose. The point was scarcely addressed at all in court. Had Jeffrey Dahmer killed to assuage hatred of blacks or homosexuals, he would have succeeded, in so far as his hatred would have been assuaged. Had he

205

killed to revenge himself upon some person who had insulted him, he would have succeeded, in so far as he would have been avenged. Had he killed for financial gain, he would have succeeded, in so far as the robbery would have improved his finances. These would all have been decisions freely made to achieve a discernibly possible end. But if he killed to make a friend, if he killed to own a body, if he killed to compensate for infantile surgery, if he killed to create a zombie, if he killed to invest a private shrine with power, he would have failed in each regard, for none of these aims is attainable by such means. Hence his decision to kill is the result of magical or delusional thinking, and though the decision itself might be free, the thinking is imprisoned in madness.

Lawyers will have nothing to do with such dialectics, which they consider suspect. They are reluctant to accept that free will can be diverted by anything less than a severe and easily recognisable illness. Doctors, on the other hand, are equally reluctant to admit that freedom of choice can escape from the restraints of biochemical make-up or psychological influence. Doctors say we are how we are made; lawyers say we are what we do. It is an existential debate, incapable of resolution, which is why lawyers and psychiatrists, speaking different languages, always collide in a court of law. They range on either side of the argument with which we began, prompted by a reflection of Dahmer's, namely the degree of control exercised by him or over him. It is germane to the even more passionate argument, as to whether Dahmer was sane (in control) or insane (controlled) at the time of the murders, and it is no wonder that the legal interpretation of insanity has gone through so many hoops in its desire to pin the criminal to his acts and deprive him of excuses.

Contrary to the view sustained by popular prejudice, a working insanity defence helps ensure that the majority of defendants are held accountable under the law. In clarifying the rare grounds for exemption from the principle

206

of criminal responsibility, the principle is itself thereby strengthened. The concept of absence of free will is the origin of the insanity defence. It is a mark of civilised life that a mad person (like an infant or an idiot) should not be held responsible for his conduct. Lord Hale established the principle in 1736 – 'where there is a total defect of the understanding, there is no free act of the will' – and Alan Dershowitz, professor at Harvard Law School and fearless defender of the apparently indefensible, has put it succinctly thus: 'It is a deeply entrenched human feeling that those who are grossly disturbed – whether they are called "madmen", "lunatics", "insane" or "mentally ill" – should not be punished like ordinary criminals.'[11]

One has only to ponder the alternative, that a lunatic should be hanged by the neck until dead or locked up in a concrete cell for his lifetime, to see how repellent it is to common humanity. So, when the defence of insanity is called, the jury will be asked not to consider what the defendant did, but what kind of man he is.

Historically, they have always found this difficult on emotional grounds, and have sometimes reached strange conclusions. At the trial of sixty-five-year-old Albert Fish in 1935, the jury heard overwhelming evidence of mental derangement, including his habit of eating his own excrement and driving needles into his scrotum which he left there to rust. He killed a little girl, made her arm into a stew and ate it. The defence attorney pleaded insanity, but the jury would countenance no such thing and found him guilty without mitigation. He was executed in 1936. Richard Chase, the Sacramento man who mixed viscera in a blender and ate the stomachs of dogs and pigs before he started to attack people, was (alarmingly) declared sane by two court-appointed psychiatrists; the jury were relieved to be able to find such a monster guilty of first-degree murder rather than have to admit that he was one of the maddest people the courts had ever come across.

There are occasions when one is bound to feel sympathy

for jurors who are asked to deliberate upon unspeakable acts. A twenty-six-year-old Londoner called John Bowden killed Donald Ryan in 1982 by striking him on the head with a machete, then dropping him still conscious into a bath of scalding water, where he fainted; he carried Ryan into a bedroom and proceeded to cut off his arms and legs with an electric carving-knife while he was alive. And so it went on. The photographic evidence was so unpalatable that the trial had to be adjourned when four jurors fell ill. In such circumstances, it is little wonder that they are loath to resort to the psychiatric 'excuse'.

There is an additional danger against which jurors must arm themselves – that a defendant may successfully plead insanity by pretence. It almost happened in the case of the so-called 'Hillside Strangler', Kenneth Bianchi, who convinced psychiatrists for months on end that he was mad, only to be revealed as a fraud at the last minute. In passing sentence, Judge George commented, 'Mr Bianchi had faked memory loss; he had faked hypnosis; and he had faked multiple personalities. This action by Mr Bianchi caused confusion and delay in the proceedings. In this, Mr Bianchi was unwittingly aided and abetted by most of the psychiatrists who naively swallowed Mr Bianchi's story hook, line and sinker, almost confounding the criminal justice system.'[12]

In the last analysis, society must rely upon the common sense of the jury, who are the ultimate arbiters of what the community will allow. In this, they may override instructions and advice from the judge in their zeal to represent the ordinary unsophisticated conscience. There is, however, yet another danger in this, for the easiest and most convincing argument to common sense is that of *res ipsa loquitur* ('the thing speaks for itself'), which holds that a man who commits disgusting acts must be insane, otherwise he would not commit them. This is a circular argument, and fallacious, for the conclusion is implicit in the premise. On such roller-coaster logic, any conviction for murder would be rendered almost impossible. As Jack

Levin neatly put it, one must not 'confuse what is sick with what is sickening'.[13]

The jury also has the right to return a mixed verdict, a possibility which is of particular interest in relation to the Dahmer case. In Hamilton, Ohio, James Ruppert was charged with eleven homicides. He was found guilty of aggravated murder in regard to the deaths of his mother and brother, but not guilty by reason of insanity in regard to the other nine slayings of his sister-in-law, nieces and nephews. They were all killed by shooting. The reasoning behind this suggests that Ruppert *became* mad after the first two murders. The reader has learnt enough of Jeff Dahmer's offences and their dizzy escalation in June and July of 1991 to appreciate the virtues of such a mixed verdict. The expectation was that, as the evolution of his mental condition was tracked by the evidence, he might be found guilty on the first ten or twelve counts, and insane on the remainder. Ruppert's crimes were all committed on the same day (Easter Sunday, 1975), whereas Dahmer's extended over a period of years, offering a much more convincing case for gradual or creeping insanity.

Jurors at the Dahmer trial would need to be given a working understanding of some definitions, if only to know which to discard, but they were in the event offered very little in the way of guidance. Nobody mentioned the word 'psychopath', though an appreciation of its meaning and import was crucial to their deliberations upon what might constitute an 'abnormal condition of the mind'. The first definition of the term was given by Sir David Henderson, Professor of Psychiatry at the University of Edinburgh, in his *Psychopathic States* (1957), and debated by the Royal Commission on Capital Punishment, whose report led to the Homicide Act of 1957 in England. In *Killing for Company* I avoided using the word because it seemed to me to apply to any criminal whose motives were inaccessible, and to describe a deed, not a condition. No one could recognise a psychopath before he committed a psychopathic act, which implied the ridiculous corollary that he was not psychopathic until his condition sought expression. The Royal Commission took account of the psychopath's visible 'normality' by specifically excluding such a condition from its understanding of mental disease. An abnormality manifested only by repeated criminal or otherwise antisocial conduct would not constitute a mental disease. Psychopathy is, the report stated, 'a statistical abnormality; that is to say, the psychopath differs from a normal person only quantitatively or in degree, not qualitatively; and the diagnosis of psychopathic personality does not carry with it any explanation of the causes of the abnormality'. In other words, to explain a psychopath only by his acts is to fall into the *res ipsa loquitur* fallacy.

Nobody put forward the proposition that Dahmer was a psychopath presumably because, even had it been accepted, it would not have changed the issues at stake under Wisconsin law (to which we shall come later). But the Royal Commission exclusion *was* invoked erroneously in support of a different contention, without the mistake or the original purpose being explained to the jury (the judge clearly did not understand such distinctions anyway).

Nor was it suggested that Dahmer was antisocial or, to use the ungainly word which has replaced psychopath, a 'sociopath'. Such a person is on the periphery of the society of which he should form a part, he obeys a personal code out of tune with that of the rest of the community, he has a low sense of guilt and a low frustration tolerance, and he exists only to gratify himself no matter what the cost to others. In other words, he has had his conscience ripped out. Such a definition might seem appropriate to Dahmer, who himself told the police that his offences were the result of a warped desire for self-gratification, and the District Attorney came close to applying it. Defence, however, would steer clear of this term, since, again, sociopathy was understood by professionals to be a personality disorder and not a mental illness; mental illness would allow an insanity defence, personality disorder would not.

What, then, would constitute a proper insanity defence? Since biblical times society has been reluctant to regard a person as blameworthy if he could not tell right from wrong. The principle was finally given legislative muscle by the so-called McNaughten Rule of 1843, the most important milestone in the history of legal definitions of insanity. Daniel McNaughten had been acquitted of the murder of the Prime Minister's secretary by reason of insanity (he suffered from the delusion that everyone from the Pope downwards was out to get him). The public was outraged,* and a fierce debate in Parliament ensued, as the result of which judges were asked by the House of Lords to define insanity once and for all. Lord Chief Justice Tindal obliged with the McNaughten Rule, according to which a criminal is not to be held responsible if, by reason of a disease of the mind, he either does not know the nature and quality of his acts, or does not know that they are wrong. Every ruling since then has been a variation on this theme, the twin-pronged aspect of the defi-

---

* Ye people of England! exult and be glad,
  For ye're now at the will of the merciless mad.
  Why say ye but that three authorities reign –
  Crown, Commons, and Lords? – You omit the insane!
  They're a privileg'd class, whom no statute controls,
  And their murderous charter exists in their souls!
  Do they wish to spill blood – they have only to play
  A few pranks – get asylum'd a month and a day –
  Then heigh! – to escape from the mad-doctor's keys,
  And to pistol or stab whomsoever they please.

  Now, the dog has a human-like wit – in creation
  He resembles most nearly our own generation.
  Then if madness for murder escape with impunity,
  Why deny a poor dog the same noble immunity?
  So, if dog or man bite you, beware being nettled,
  For crime is no crime – when the mind is unsettled.
  (T. Campbell, 'On a Late Acquittal', *The Times*, 8 March, 1843)

211

nition enduring, though its wording and emphasis have shifted. The McNaughten Rule remained on the Statute Book in England until 1957, and is still the only yardstick of insanity in sixteen of the American States.

Jeffrey Dahmer would probably not have met the requirements for insanity under this definition, for he knew the nature and quality of what he was doing, and knew that it was wrong. But perhaps 'knowing' is an insufficient description of the cognitive process, and an emotional understanding should form part of it. In 1954, a new standard was adopted by some States, following an opinion by Judge David Bazelon in the District of Columbia. Known as the 'Durham Rule' (after a mentally-disturbed criminal called Monty Durham), it held that a man could know right from wrong but either be deficient in emotional appreciation that what he did was wrong or be unable to control his behaviour because his unlawful act was 'the product of mental disease or mental defect'. On both counts, it is likely that Dahmer would qualify as an insane person; his emotions were certainly awry, and his crimes were just as surely the 'product' of mental defect, if such mental defect could be established (in the event, it was).

The American Law Institute further adapted these perceptions in 1962 to establish a test for insanity which is now applied by the majority of States, including Wisconsin. According to this A.L.I. test (Section 4.01 of the Model Penal Code):

A person is not responsible for criminal conduct if at the time of such conduct as a result of mental disease or defect he lacks substantial capacity either to appreciate the wrongfulness of his conduct or to conform his conduct to the requirements of law.

This was the test which Dahmer would have to meet if he intended to plead insanity. His counsel would be required to prove first, that he suffered from mental disease or defect, and second, that the disease or defect reduced his emotional understanding and/or made it impossible for him to control his behaviour.

The first half of the test is much derided by lawyers, especially since the Hinckley verdict which found the defendant insane when he attempted to assassinate President Reagan. The trouble is, more and more disorders of personality are being put forward as mental diseases in line with the growing sophistication of psychiatric insights. The renowned British jurist Lord Devlin is on record as disapproving of this – 'the concept of illness expands continually at the expense of the concept of moral responsibility', he wrote.[14]

A mental disease is defined as 'an abnormal condition of the mind which substantially affects mental or emotional processes'. Despite the fact that instructions to the jury continue to maintain that 'you are not bound by medical labels, definitions, or conclusions as to what is or is not a mental disease', it is not practically sensible to expect a jury to deliberate without guidance, and the Dahmer trial was therefore replete with labels, definitions and conclusions through which they had to sift. For this purpose, lawyers use the *Diagnostic and Statistical Manual of Mental Disorders*, known in shorthand as *D.S.M.-III* and colloquially as a 'cookbook'. The mental disease which was adduced as applicable in Dahmer's case was identified by a word which nobody in the courtroom had ever encountered before.

The second half of the test, as to whether Dahmer was able to control himself, would present the jury with an equally tangled task, for 'experience confirms that there is still no accurate scientific basis for measuring one's capacity for self-control or for calibrating the impairment of such capacity'.[15] On matters like this, juries are bound to fall back on *moral* opinions rather than *medical* ones (not *why* he failed to control himself but *should* he have done), and in that area they are ultimately on their own. The psychiatric experts would do battle with one another over whether

213

Dahmer was or was not in control of himself, but they were not much better equipped to reach conclusions on such gossamer distinctions than individual members of the public. The American Psychiatric Association admits the dilemma with a nice reflection: 'The line between an irresistible impulse and an impulse not resisted is probably no sharper than that between twilight and dusk.'[16]

Basically, then, prosecution and defence would broadly agree that there was something deeply wrong with Jeffrey Dahmer, that his disorder of personality was severe; the prosecution would claim that it did not, however, amount to a mental disease, and did not rob him of free will, whereas defence would insist that there was a disease, and that it transformed him into an automaton. Otherwise stated, Mr McCann would seek to prove that Dahmer chose not to resist the impulse (compulsion), and Mr Boyle that he could not.

In their respective endeavours, they would call five psychiatrists, and the court two more. Psychiatrists who testify as to criminal responsibility, known as forensic psychiatrists, are a rare breed, forming only 3 per cent of the total number practising in the United States. They tread a tortuous path between legal and medical jargons, and the adversarial system in a court of law sometimes causes them to meander into foreign territory where they risk humiliation and obloquy. The wisest of them will not accept a brief from prosecution or defence which might oblige him to tailor his opinion to suit his employer, but those who make a living out of giving testimony might find they are poorer if they do not. (Of the eight experts who examined Jeffrey Dahmer, only one, Dr Kenneth Smail, declined to give evidence because he could not support the defence case for which his advice had been sought.) It is a pity this should be so, because forensic psychiatrists agree in their diagnoses 80 per cent of the time; it is only courtroom manners and (occasionally) commercial considerations which make them appear to be constantly at one another's throats.

Their involvement would be necessary in the second of the two projected trials which Wisconsin law demanded. The purpose of the first trial would be to determine whether or not the defendant did that of which he was accused; this would be solely an examination of fact, the *actus reus* (state of affairs caused by conduct of the defendant). If a verdict of not guilty was returned, that would be the end of the matter and the defendant would walk free. In the event of a guilty verdict, he would then face his second trial to determine *mens rea* (state of mind of the defendant at the time of the offences). In this trial, the traditional roles of prosecution and defence would be reversed, in that the burden would fall upon the defence to prove Jeffrey Dahmer was insane, while there would be no corresponding burden upon the prosecution to establish his sanity.

Dahmer pleaded guilty to the facts and waived his right to a first trial. He would not deny that he had done what he had done. Indeed, he did not want to contest anything at all, and would have preferred sentence to be passed without the necessity to delve into his state of mind. Once his long confession to the police was complete, he sank into a fatalistic torpor. His first request to Detective Murphy was to be supplied with a Bible, which was granted, and he was convinced that Old Testament notions of retribution were justified in his case. He knew he deserved the death penalty (which does not obtain in Wisconsin), because 'it executed justice quickly'. What of the morality of adding one more (judicially sanctioned) murder to the seventeen he had already perpetrated? 'If it wasn't moral it wouldn't be in the Bible as far as I'm concerned,' he said, 'but that's for the theologians and the philosophers to debate.'

He was, however, persuaded that he had the right to have his sanity tested in court, even if he did not have the desire, and that the due process of law and fairness would best be served by his agreeing to stand trial on the issue. Still, he was reluctant to participate. 'I'm not going to get up on the bench and say anything, that's for sure, no way. As far as I'm concerned, there is no defence. I see no hope. It's just completely hopeless from my standpoint. I'm not going to sit up in front of all those people and try to answer questions.' Dahmer's sense of humiliation and shame was intense at this stage, and his fear of exposure deep. If he could have had his way, they would have held the trial without him.

His one duty, as he saw it, was to identify the people who had died under his trust, and the greatest anxiety was detectable in his voice during the two weeks which elapsed before the final victim was named. He had another concern, too. He wanted to write to his grandmother, by now in a nursing home, to tell her how much he loved her and how much he regretted the sorrow he had caused. He could not, because he was not permitted a pen lest he use it as a weapon with which to harm himself.

There was a real degree of unburdening in the long sessions he had with all the psychiatrists, although Dahmer is not the most articulate of confessors. His habitual reticence fought with his desire to get it 'all out on the table'. 'It's a relief not to have any secrets any more,' he said. There remained the nervousness which anticipated his first meeting with his father since the arrest, when he would have to face the heavy silent rebuke of a God-fearing, disappointed and shaken man. The interview went off without incident, however, and Lionel Dahmer was much admired for the steadfast support he gave his son in the midst of shrieking expressions of public horror.

Once the identifications were complete, Dahmer felt that life had well and truly come to an end, that his past was irretrievably lost, blown away, and himself with it. 'It's just like a big chunk of me has been ripped out and I'm not quite whole,' he said. 'I don't think I'm over-dramatising it, and I'm certainly deserving of it, but the way I feel now, it's like you're talking to someone who is terminally ill and facing death. Death would be preferable to what I'm facing. I just feel like imploding upon myself, you know? I just want to go somewhere and disappear.'

The long days in a prison cell offered ample time for reflection, which he tried hard to avoid. 'When you've done the type of things I've done,' he said, 'it's easier not to reflect on yourself. When I start thinking about how it's affecting the families of the people, and my family and everything, it doesn't do me any good. It just gets me very upset.' But the mind cannot stop itself working, and thoughts cannot be turned away at will. Dahmer, battered by enforced introspection, quickly fell into dejection. A panic attack would be heralded by shallow breathing, sweating, tightening up, and then would spiral downwards to the pit of despair, parodying (or fulfilling, perhaps) his imaginary descents into Infinity Land as a child. He admitted that the nothingness of infinity would be sooth-ing, 'nice', and it sounded like the plea of a child for a warm blanket. What occurred instead was a 'deep, clawing depression' and a nothingness which was not soothing but menacing. It was 'the sense of total, final hopelessness. That's quite a sensation. I imagine it's a bit what hell is like.'

Indeed, it is. Jean-Paul Sartre in *Huis-Clos* depicted hell as the permanent and inexorable contemplation of oneself as fixed, defined, finished, known, utterly bereft of the freedom to change or evolve. Dahmer could only look forward to becoming the inactive object he had forced others to be, without their (questionable) advan-tage of actually being dead. 'A life of nothingness,' was how he put it; 'years and years of bland desperation.'

He thought of suicide, often. 'If I could just stop that little throbbing muscle in my chest,' he said one day. 'Give me a cyanide pill,' on another. 'Better be with the dead,' said Macbeth, 'Whom we, to gain our peace, have sent to peace, Than on the torture of the mind to lie In restless ecstasy.'[17] He knew he would not have the courage to take his own life, but it would be quite proper 'if I was killed in prison. That would almost be a blessing right now.' It was not that he did not know how to commit suicide if he

217

wanted to. 'All you have to do is make a good slit, right where that large artery goes through your leg there, where it joins the hip, and you bleed to death within a couple of minutes, before they could get anyone to you.' There were other prisoners stabbing themselves in the arm and stomach with pencils, which was why Dahmer was not allowed any writing materials on remand. Pencils would be useless, he said, 'all that would do is create pain and I have enough of that already'. He did not think that suicide was necessarily wrong, especially when set beside his crimes. 'I can't do much more wrong than I've already done, can I?'

Aware that Dahmer's (improbable) suicide would be a procedural embarrassment, guards kept watch on him twenty-four hours a day. There were three looking at him as he urinated (and laughing as well), and the light in his cell was kept permanently switched on. Flashlights were regularly trained on his face when he tried to sleep. One day he sharpened his toothbrush in protest against what he thought unreasonable treatment, and he had in consequence to sleep on the concrete floor in his underwear. He was subjected to frequent taunts and death threats, but as the weeks went by, and guards gradually recognised him as a tainted human instead of a museum specimen, small signs of geniality occasionally emerged. A guard who had to desert his post for fifteen minutes in the middle of the night said to him, 'Now don't do anything stupid, Jeff.' It was a tiny moment of connection.

Prison routine encouraged depression. Breakfast of one small square of oatmeal and a piece of bread was served at five in the morning. One cup of coffee was permitted per day, and three showers per week. Between meals there was 'nothing to do but watch the ants crawl around on the floor'. The cell was small, allowing three steps from wall to wall, and the bed bugs were plentiful. 'You feel them overnight jumping on your eyelids and nose.' Above all, there was the boredom. One inmate started screaming and yelling during the night. 'They had to chain him up and he just really went nuts for a couple of hours. I can see why now. It does get to you – the boredom.' Being notorious was an added difficulty for somebody as private as Dahmer. He had to get used to hearing his name whispered and people staring when they passed him. 'It would be nice just to sit down anonymously with someone and not be known and strike up a conversation about the weather or something; not to have to talk about this.'

Before the trial he started to have fitful dreams. They never concerned the incidents with which he was charged, nor the men whom he had butchered, which surprised him. They were pleasant homosexual dreams accompanied by feelings of warmth and calm, with no violence or stress. Even these he distrusted, however, and declared his intention to free himself from them. First, the Bible forbade homosexual behaviour, and he hoped he would in time be able to banish homosexual thought. Second, it was the homosexuality in him which led to his becoming a murderer. Had he not encouraged it, none of this might have happened. Nor would he encourage it now that it was too late to make any difference. It was possible, at least, that in the depths of his being his orientation was not homosexual at all, but that it had been diverted onto that path by his extreme social awkwardness as a child. Dahmer's rejection of his homosexual dreams may have reflected a subconscious wish to rediscover his earliest self.

There was another dream which involved the police digging up some bones and attempting to incriminate him in suspected foul play when he was completely innocent and ignorant of the bones' presence. This may not even have been a dream relating to his criminal activities, though surely inspired by them; it was a common anxiety dream of impotence in the face of unblinking power, and it was hardly surprising that Dahmer should have his night invaded by such dreams as the date of his trial and ignominy approached. Perfectly guiltless people have this kind of nightmare. One night he dreamt of an old man in a dark cape who came floating up from the pond at the house in Bath, Ohio, accusing him of stealing plywood which he was sawing. He put the saw down and left. Was this the grim reaper? Or Jeff Dahmer's conscience? Or merely a troubled and turbulent mind?

'I should have got a college degree and gone into real estate and got myself an aquarium, that's what I should have done.'

The hours of talking to policemen and psychiatrists had at least exorcised, to some extent, the evil which had seemed to propel him for so long. He had never before talked at such length about himself and the interviews provided some of that connectedness he had always lacked. 'I still have the guilt, I'll probably never get rid of that, but yes, I'm free of the compulsion and the driving need to do it.' What remained was the depression, all the greater for being born of belated self-knowledge. 'I don't think I'm capable of creating anything,' he said. 'I think the only thing I'm capable of is destroying . . . I'm sick and tired of being destructive. What worth is life if you can't be helpful to someone?'[18]

Chapter Nine

The Trial

The Safety Building on West State Street in Milwaukee is a scruffy, discouraging edifice of bleak corridors built as a featureless square surrounding the county jail at its hub. In every hallway sit several forlorn figures, sleepy and distracted and nearly always black, waiting for something to happen or someone to notice them. One looks in vain for a coffee bar, a splash of colour, or a winning smile. It is a grim place for grim business.

On the fifth floor, unexpectedly found behind a simple door down the hallway, is the courtroom of Judge Laurence Gram. It would be familiar to anyone who has seen cinema or T.V. representations of American trials – the Judge's Bench against the back wall, a witness-box to his left and bailiff to his right, flags proudly decked behind him. Facing him in the well of the court are two unpretentious tables, as plain as one might find in a dentist's waiting-room, where the prosecution and defence teams sit in comfortable swivel-chairs. Among the defence personnel is, of course, the defendant himself.

It is one of the glories of the American system as opposed to the English that the defendant is visibly and not just theoretically treated as an innocent man until the jury should decide otherwise. Instead of being isolated high in a dock flanked by two policemen, the very architecture of the room proclaiming his apartness, here he is seated with decorum and propriety next to other free men charged with presenting his case to the court. Though Jeffrey Dahmer's crimes would be loudly condemned by both sides, Jeffrey Dahmer himself would throughout the proceedings be treated with courtesy, his right to be consulted held in solid respect.

To the right of the courtroom are the jury benches, and behind the counsel tables, again facing the judge, are public seats. At this point, however, Judge Gram's court differed sharply from other courts, for between the public and the rest of the room was erected an eight-foot-high steel and lexan wall, effectively cutting the room in half. Specially built for Dahmer's trial, the see-through wall was meant to protect the defendant from potential anger in the community, but its consequence was to exclude the public from participation in what should be a democratic process. They would be reduced to the status of *voyeurs*, gawping guiltily across a divide, unable to hear what was going on and watching a mute ritual as if on a faulty television set.

That was, perhaps, the hidden purpose of this ugly construction, for reality is, in America, only acceptable when seen at one remove, filmed and made to resemble the Hollywood style as closely as possible. In tacit confirmation, there was a robot camera, and still and video cameras placed beyond the forbidding wall inside the court, so that the T.V. eye had freer access to due process of law than mere people. It was a not very subtle admission that the ethics and values of television counted for more than the principle of accountability to the local community, and, further, that the trial would be splendid entertainment.

Secluded behind the partition were twenty-three seats for newspaper reporters, to be shared on a rotating basis between about 150 individuals representing scores of 'media' organisations; thirty-two seats open to the public on first-come first-served basis; and the greater number of forty seats reserved for family relations of the young men who died.

Born in West Allis, Laurence Gram was sixty years old when the Dahmer trial came his way, and he had been a judge for nearly twenty years. A silver-haired, avuncular, jolly man, he looked as if he would be more at ease reading fairy-tales to his grandchildren than presiding over a searching analysis of soul. There would be occasions during the following three weeks when Judge Gram's endearing geniality seemed sadly incongruous. The Dahmer case deserved rigorous attention to philosophic and legal niceties and promised to raise questions which would reverberate down the years. Judge Gram's courtroom was not an adequate theatre for bold ambitions of this sort; it was essentially parochial.

The District Attorney, Michael McCann, had held this important post for nearly a quarter of a century, since his early thirties. Both he and his opponent in this case, Gerald Boyle, were Catholic, but they had rather different views about sin. McCann, a graduate of the University of Detroit and Georgetown University Law School, with a Master's in Law from Harvard, was a deeply moral man whose passionate advocacy reflected his outrage and did not have to be contrived. He personally took one or two 'high-profile' cases a year, but otherwise kept to his desk and would be clearly uncomfortable dealing with sexual deviance. Murder he understood perfectly well, human frailty distressed him.

Gerald Boyle, for the defence, was an entirely different animal. Against McCann's austerity he personified ebullience and cheerfulness, with a warm, friendly manner and a habit of making the jury feel that he was one of them, learning with them rather than teaching them. His faith was more Christian than Catholic, and imbued with a profound sense of natural justice. Graduated from Loyola University in Chicago and Marquette University Law School, Boyle's weapons were common sense and kindness, but he had little patience with the fine distinctions of argument and had a distaste for preparation. Whereas

McCann relied upon meticulous groundwork, Boyle looked for swelling inspiration.

McCann's assistants were Carol White and Greg O'Meara, while Boyle was supported by Wendy Patrickus and Ellen Ryan. Both men, however, were to take the lion's share of their briefs' questioning and cross-examination, leaving minor witnesses to their respective teams.

Although judge, counsel and jury did not see them for the most part, a prominent role on the periphery was played by the small army of mothers, brothers and sisters who turned up to occupy 'victim family' seats. I have already referred to the unforced dignity of Mrs Hughes and the touching confidence of Theresa Smith, but there were many others, daily pinned against the wall in the hallway with microphones thrust under their noses and cameras zooming into their misery. They did not seem to mind.

Jostling for attention were the professional protesters whose sole purpose in life is to hold a placard aloft and chant its message. One of these was well known in Milwaukee for demonstrating against everything under the sun as a more or less full-time occupation. For the opening day of the trial, his slogan was 'Milwaukee Government Supports Dahmer's Gay Life Style', above quotes from Galatians and Leviticus and the bald assertion that government officials had publicly issued proclamations in favour of lesbianism, homosexuality and sodomy. The exhibition was frivolous and childish, as was the press attention it attracted.

In their defence, it must be said that the press, being over-represented as well as undernourished, were obliged to resort to interviewing one another in the long empty days of jury selection, and would have filmed a cockroach had it been anywhere near West 25th Street. Their frenetic activity was barely contained in a room three floors below the court, a jumbled mess of cameras, cables, computers, microphones, telephones, people, sandwiches and noise. The room buzzed with the energy of ambition, and that sense of urgency which is a journalist's lifeblood. It was odd that so much of the world's press should congregate for this trial, as there was unlikely to be drama or surprise in a series of dry psychiatric reports. Perhaps there would be an outburst from the defendant, or even an appearance in the witness-box. There might be an unexpected witness, since the State was rumoured to have fifty-one potential witnesses lined up before proceedings began. If all else failed, the two counsel would descend to the Media Room at the end of each day's evidence to tell the reporters how well they had presented their cases.

The trial was scheduled to begin at 8.30 a.m. on Monday, 27 January, 1992. It did not start on time. There was first a delay caused by the bomb-sniffing police dog, Blitz, assigned to check the courtroom for explosives, then difficulties in transporting prospective jurors across town. For two hours the public and press benches faced an empty room; some incipient friendships formed.

When the defendant finally walked in, necks craned to peer at him. Pressmen asked each other what they thought of him, and victims' families looked on with a sullen hatred mingled with curiosity. The charges were well known by now. What about the man himself? The shock registered by Dahmer's ordinariness was palpable. He wore an open-neck shirt and brown jacket, walked straight to his chair, looked either straight ahead or down at the table, and showed no signs of self-importance or diabolic character. He might almost have been a spectator at the play rather than its principal actor. In the five months since his arrest, prison diet and inactivity had combined to put on weight, so that his jacket looked as if it might tear at any moment. What nobody realised was that he had been taken to the courtroom strapped and handcuffed to a wheelchair and released only at the last minute, nor that he had purposefully left his glasses outside so that he could not see what was going on or who might be looking at him.

Prospective jurors were marched in and sat around the edge of the court while the judge addressed them. The publicity which had preceded the trial and promised to attend it would make it necessary that the jury be sequestered for a period likely to exceed two weeks. Anyone who anticipated that this might prove an intolerable burden was invited to say so. Out of seventy men and women called, twenty-five gave reasons why they could not serve, from one who claimed that he wouldn't have the stomach for it, to a woman plaintively declaring that, 'I've got to feed the birds. There's no one else to do it, and they'll starve.' Judge Gram excused them.

Mr Boyle and Mr McCann then questioned those who remained, first generally and then individually in judge's chambers, in a process known as *voir dire*. The purpose was apparently to learn in advance what each juror felt and thought about the charges, so that either counsel could disbar him if he threatened to have thoughts which they might find prejudicial or inconvenient. Mr Boyle was anxious to discover their attitude towards psychiatry, the defendant's right to remain silent, homosexuality, and 'the phantom fear that Mr Dahmer will ever be free in society'. Mr McCann's concern was that they should not be seduced into thinking that the enormity of the offences must itself be indicative of mental illness, and that they would follow the judge's instructions even if they did not agree with the law as it stood in relation to such offences.

Both speeches were eloquent and persuasive, Boyle's particularly in his imprecation to jurors to deliver a fair and impartial verdict without fear or favour. But the outcome of this procedure meant that, instead of having a random collection of men and women bound by civic duty to serve, McCann and Boyle contrived to have sworn in an unrepresentative team vetted by them both. The system even allowed them to strike off potential jurors without offering any reason. After three days, they had pared the numbers down to the requisite twelve (among whom there was one black man) plus two alternates. But what they had, in place of a jury, was a joint committee.

* * *

226

On Thursday, 30 January, the trial finally began, with Gerald Boyle's stark opening statement promising a journey into Hell. Counsel is not permitted, in the opening statement, to argue his case or attempt to convince the jury. His function is to tell the story, to give them a basic narrative of events which will be corroborated and elaborated later by the evidence to be set before them. Boyle warned that he would hold nothing back, that he would equip the jury with all they needed to reach a decision. Dahmer himself, he said, would not give evidence, but he would speak through his confession, which would be read in every detail by police officers. 'You will have to listen.'

Having established that this was not a case about homosexuality, nor about race ('Mr Dahmer's obsession was to body form, not colour'), Boyle proceeded to rehearse, in broad terms, the history of his client from puberty onwards, with reference to the jogger, to the pig's head and to the gruesome defilement of Steven Hicks. At this point, the pained hush in the room caused Boyle to interrupt his story with an apology. 'This is a sad commentary,' he said. 'I take no delight in telling you this. I grieve for the family. I tell you these things because I must, because you have to know.'

Mr Boyle traced the haunted four years which followed the murder of Hicks, and identified the incident in West Allis library as the 'critical moment in Jeffrey Dahmer's life', when his 'control fell apart'. He did not shirk the unpleasant images of Dahmer using severed heads as sexual stimulants, and introduced the worrying theme of cannibalism. 'He took them from life through dying, into death, through death, and back into life again – they became alive again in him.' In fact, the cannibalistic aspect of his conduct was a fairly late development, and not applicable to all the victims. Mr Boyle drew attention to the cannibalism, but neither he nor any of the witnesses expatiated upon this primitive conduct, which, as we shall see, holds one of the clues to his derangement.

Boyle appeared to be defensive as he reached the end

227

of his peroration. He asked not to be blamed for taking the case on, that it was his duty so to do, and that his defending Mr Dahmer should not be interpreted as in any sense exculpatory. On the other hand, he was determined the case should be properly aired. 'I make no excuses for my representation of this young man,' he said, and finished on a note which aptly summarised the defence's position: 'This was not an evil man, this was a sick man.' There were few in court, at this point, who would disagree.

It then fell to Mr McCann to address the jury with his opening statement, from which emerged, as one would expect, a quite different portrait of Jeffrey Dahmer. The defendant was characterised by a total 'want of candour', he 'always undertook to deceive'. Quoting from Dahmer's conversation with the prosecution's expert Dr Dietz, he established that, after 23 November, 1987, and the unexplained death of Steven Tuomi, he gave in to his desires and did what he pleased. 'I, too, have struggled with sexual impulses,' confessed Mr McCann, inviting us to see the defendant as nothing more than a degenerate hedonist. McCann also insisted upon those words which he would wish the jury constantly to bear in mind – 'control', 'decision', 'preparation', 'deceit', 'cunning' – words designed to draw the portrait of an evil man rather than a sick man.

Thus were two conflicting accounts of Jeffrey Dahmer presented to the jury in the same day, and as yet nobody could be sure which was the more accurate. Judge Gram then read out the criminal complaint, State of Wisconsin versus Jeffrey L. Dahmer, a litany of fifteen homicides which piled up to form an apparently insuperable mountain. Mr Boyle's task, not to deny the murders but to explain them, was daunting indeed. Mr McCann, on whom no burden of proof rested, need only repeat them. Dahmer himself sat quietly and vacantly, rocking slightly, occasionally scratching his forehead, not looking left or right. He was, to say the least, enigmatic.

The first witness to be called for the defence was Detective Kennedy, who started to read the 178-page confession which Dahmer began on the morning of 23 July, 1991. It proved to be a terrifying document, but the reading of it would assist the defence case in two respects – first, to underline the sheer awfulness of Dahmer's conduct and suggest, by implication, that this could in no measure be the confession of an ordinary criminal; and second, to emphasise his willingness to co-operate, his compliance and total absence of obstruction. In the course of this reading, a third Jeffrey Dahmer emerged before the court, not the evil man, nor the sick man, but the lonely man. 'He had no company himself,' said Detective Kennedy, 'and these individuals would keep him company.'

Detective Murphy replaced his colleague in the witness-box as he had in the interview room, and told the court in remorseless detail everything that Dahmer had said in a series of meetings stretching to sixty hours. The fact that Dahmer did not need to be persuaded to talk, but usually asked for a meeting with the detective, was brought home to an increasingly bemused jury just before court recessed for the day.

On 31 January, Murphy continued with his evidence by admitting that he had, in showing photographs of missing persons to the defendant, purposefully included some of those individuals who were alive and well, to see if he was inventing incidents and identifying people at random. He came to the conclusion that Dahmer was utterly truthful and could be trusted to remain so.

That does present a difficulty, because one of the statements he made in confession was to the effect that he had not injured Konerak Sinthasomphone in any way before the arrival of the police, whereas we now know that he had by that time already drilled a hole through the boy's skull. In line with this discrepancy is his claim to the police that all the drilling had been done *post mortem* as a way of emptying the corpse's skull of brain matter, which he would scoop out with a spoon and pour down the sink.

This does not accord with his later admission that the drilling was done while victims were alive in order to prevent their mustering the will to leave him, nor with the smallness of the holes themselves. The question would assume greater importance in a few days, when a court-appointed psychiatrist would assert that he believed the confession rather than its subsequent elaboration, i.e. he thought that Dahmer drilled holes after death.

When Detective Murphy finished his evidence we were left with the impression of a defendant aware that he had done wrong, astonished that it had happened, anxious to make amends, and pervaded by an intense sense of loss each time he placed the remains of a young man in the garbage and watched him be carried away to extinction.

At 2.15 in the afternoon the first lay witness was called. Tracy Edwards was already well known to a number of people in the room, for he had appeared on two nation-wide T.V. chat shows and had become somewhat of a celebrity by virtue of his being the-one-who-escaped and brought Jeff Dahmer to justice. He did not say on television (nor, for that matter, would he in court) that he had flagged down the police on 23 July only in order to have handcuffs removed and not to report Dahmer (who would have gone undetected a little longer had the police officers possessed the right handcuff key). It was not in Mr Edwards' interest to attract attention to himself. When he appeared on the chat show he was recognised by police in Mississippi as the man they wished to question with regard to the assault and battery of a thirteen-year-old girl, and was promptly arrested. (When Dahmer learnt this he made the rueful comment, 'Well, God got two birds with one stone that night, didn't He?')

Edwards was smartly dressed and dapper in court, like a sharp sporting promoter. His account of what happened on the evening of 22 July did not differ substantially from Dahmer's. He insisted that the invitation was to pose for nude pictures only, and that there was no mention of intended homosexual activity. 'He didn't come across that way,' he said. 'He was just like a normal everyday person, friendly.' It was as he came to the moment when Dahmer suddenly changed character that Edwards' guileless, compelling description had spectators leaning forward; the whole room realised we were listening to a man with the unique experience of watching madness come and go before his eyes. 'This guy's so nice,' he said, 'and all of a sudden he's pulling knives on me. What's going on? He's not the same person. His face structure and body structure are different. He's a totally different guy.'

Edwards had quickly intuited that he would need to keep his wits about him. 'I tried to let him know I was his friend. He said he didn't want people to leave him or abandon him.' Watching the *Exorcist* film Dahmer began rocking back and forth and muttering. 'I couldn't understand what he was saying. The preacher in the film impressed him and he wanted to mimic him. He kept changing moods, was a different person from one moment to the next. He was transfixed by the movie.' For one and a half minutes Dahmer lay with his head on Edwards' chest, listening to his heart-beat, then when Edwards went to the bathroom and returned, 'he reverted to the person I first met. He felt sorry for himself, had lost his job, and thought nobody cared about him. I wanted him to feel that I wasn't going to leave, that I was his friend.'

Another abrupt change occurred when Dahmer said that he was going to have to kill him, and Edwards unbuttoned his shirt again to make the man feel more at ease. Mr Boyle asked whether these mood-changes appeared to be induced by alcohol. 'No,' said Edwards, 'it was an inner mood, a person change. He began going out of himself.' The description of what Frederic Wertham called 'catathymic crisis'[1] and the churchmen refer to as possession could hardly be more vivid.

There had come a moment when Dahmer lost interest in the handcuffs which were dangling from Edwards' wrist and withdrew into reverie. 'It was like I wasn't even there any more.' Edwards took his chance, struck Dahmer, and escaped. What impression did the actions and conduct of the defendant make upon your mind? asked Boyle. 'That he was a crazy guy.'

In cross-examining Tracy Edwards, prosecuting counsel was anxious to discredit him and thereby dilute the powerful vision of derangement which his testimony had conjured. Much was made of his television appearances in an attempt to suggest that he had worked up his story for financial gain and was prone to exaggeration. The ploy was successful in one particular. Edwards had said that there were seven locks on Dahmer's door. Mr McCann, prepared as ever, held up a photograph of the door which clearly showed there were only two. Edwards left the witness-box a nervous and chastened man, and proceeded to give a press conference in the Media Room flanked by his heavily protective lawyer, a thick arm round his shoulder.

Mr Boyle wanted next to call Robert Ressler, an expert with the Behavioural Science Unit of the Federal Bureau of Investigation, who had specialised in the study of 'serial killers' and written widely on the subject. Ressler's experience was frequently called upon by overworked police forces struggling with conflicting clues in their hunt for a repetitive murderer. Combining evidence from the condition of bodies, the method of attack, the place, time, and frequency of murder, and a mass of other disparate detail, Ressler was able to construct a profile of the sort of man the police should be looking for, his age, appearance, character and even profession. Boyle would invite the expert to describe the kind of man who had committed such acts as Dahmer confessed to, and, perhaps, surreptitiously plant the idea that such a man was not quite what he appeared to be.

Mr McCann rightly objected to such evidence being heard, on the grounds that it would be theoretic and irrelevant to the case in hand, and he questioned Ressler's competence as an expert witness. The Judge ruled in favour of Mr McCann because Ressler's knowledge was not needed at the trial. You should not argue backwards

232

from the defendant, who is identified, to the profile which
might identify him; that at least was the import of his
decision. The jury were out while these matters were being
discussed, so they never knew what they were missing,
but the press heard it all and brought Mr Ressler down
to the Media Room for the obligatory press conference
despite his disbarment. No one pointed out that he was
essentially a statistician, a painstaking assembler of facts
rather than a shrewd observer of people.

Court recessed for the weekend and reconvened on
Monday, 3 February, at 8.30 a.m., with the resumption
of Detective Murphy's testimony (he had been excused
on Friday afternoon to appear in another court). For the
first time we heard Dahmer's own explanation for his
crimes in a pungent phrase which the State's counsel
would use as chorus to his oratory throughout the coming
weeks; they were the result of 'my own warped selfish
desire for self-gratification', he told Murphy. We likewise
heard his voice when he remembered the sickening experience of his schoolfriend's running down dogs: 'I never saw
such a look of terror on an animal's face as that beagle
puppy.' We heard panic ('frantic attempt to undo what
I'd got myself into'), loneliness ('they always wanted to
leave'), and regret ('I wish I could turn back the years'),
but there was a stark absence of full-blooded remorse.
The confession was that of a man drained of the emotional
juices, a man adrift.

With a series of quick, short questions to the detective,
Gerald Boyle elicited the information that none of the
dead had been tortured, and that none were known to
have been victims of murder until Dahmer confessed.
Cross-examination was conducted by Carol White, a cool,
dignified, rather aloof young lady with a deceptively gentle
voice. She established that Detective Murphy had no
reason to doubt anything that Mr Dahmer told him, then
strayed into areas on which his opinion should not properly be sought. 'Was Mr Dahmer ever out of touch with
reality?' 'No, he wasn't.' 'Did you feel he could make

people believe anything he wanted?' 'Yes.' Mr Boyle, surprisingly, raised no objection; relaxed and mischievous, he gave the impression that he had something up his sleeve which he would produce in his own good time. Meanwhile, he was not going to be ruffled by Carol White. Let her ask what she might. Only when she invited the detective to say whether he thought Dahmer was 'out of control' did Boyle object (sustained).

The State then made a blatant lunge for jury support by producing portraits of each victim in the indictment and passing them to each juror in turn. It would not have been permitted in an English court, but Mr Boyle did not seem to mind (probably he knew well enough that the judge would not sustain him). The strategy had no legal point to it, for the victims' identities were not in question, nor was it disputed that they died at the hands of the defendant. The only possible excuse was to remind jurors that real people were destroyed by this horror, and that they should not allow their concentration upon ideas to smother their human sympathy. With this in mind, the display of portraits was nicely timed to precede Mr Boyle's first expert witness, who would necessarily be talking about ideas.

Dr Fred Berlin came to the witness stand with impressive credentials. Director of the Sexual Disorders Clinic at Johns Hopkins University, he had seen over 2,000 individuals with deviant sexual desires and treated several hundred of them. He had worked at the famous Maudsley Hospital in London and was on the sub-committee which defined sexual disorders for the diagnostic manual *D.S.M.-III-R*. There could be no doubt that he was a specialist in the very field which would most likely illuminate Jeff Dahmer's condition. For all that, however, Dr Berlin was little short of a disastrous witness. He looked unkempt, with a disorderly thatch of hair unparted and uncombed, a tie not properly knotted, a hand-knitted blue V-neck jumper under an ill-fitting jacket. One felt sure he would have been happier in a jogging suit. None of this would have mattered (and is, anyway, deeply unfair and irrelevant), could it have been put down to the professorial eccentricities of brilliance. But Dr Berlin also appeared frivolous, chuckled too often, was too pleased with himself, was pugilistic in manner, gabbled to the degree that his words could not always be caught, constantly scratched his eyebrow and nose, and perspired too readily. To the jury he might seem not only to lack *gravitas*, but stability as well.

When Mr McCann questioned him on his record, he quickly established that Berlin was not board-certified in Forensic Psychiatry, and more damagingly yet, that he had never before in his life testified in a murder case on the question of criminal responsibility. Remorselessly, McCann attacked his competence, experience and qualifications, as well as the reputation of his much-lauded clinic at Johns Hopkins. Boyle objected once or twice, to be over-ruled by the judge and retire to his chair, lounging and quietly contemptuous. 'I'll just jump in when I think I should,' he said. For his part, Dr Berlin was well aware that he was being insulted and was understandably rattled. Unfortunately, his displeasure came across as petulance.

With Fred Berlin discredited before he even started, his evidence would have to be strong indeed to win back a wary jury. For the next few hours, Mr Boyle put to him questions which (rumour had it) Berlin had himself devised and given to the attorney in a certain order, the better to marshal his arguments in ascending sequence.

He began by explaining the function of the two 'prongs' of the insanity defence, cognitive and volitional. The cognitive clause asked whether the defendant knew right from wrong, the volitional clause asked if he could manage his behaviour in accordance with such knowledge. It was Dr Berlin's view that, 'when left to his own resources, he cannot conform because he suffers from a mental disease'. And the name of that disease? 'Paraphilia.'

It was not a word likely to trip off everybody's tongue. It was not a word much used even in medical circles until quite recently, having fallen into desuetude since its invention by I. S. Kraus at the beginning of the century. But it was a vast envelope of a word, into which could be packed all manner of peculiarities and aberrations of emotional desire, anything which seemed to be sexually eccentric, and it was therefore adopted by American category-shifters to be included in the famous *D.S.M.* 'cookbook' in 1980. Initially, as defined by Wilhelm Stekel in the 1920s, paraphilia was a perversion, the acting-out of sexual desires which were deviant from the norm. If parapathy meant neurosis ('a mental state during which the distinction between reality and fantasy is temporarily lost. The patient hovers between reality and dream'[2]), then paraphilia was the 'picture' of this mental state, its expression in thought or deed.

One characteristic of a paraphilia is its solitariness. It is essentially a cryptic form of masturbation and is indulged in fantasy to the exclusion of everything else. The imagination becomes hypnotised by one aspect of sexual desire, and cannot rid itself of the fixation in order to develop more free expressions. Freud said that it was the fate of all of us to have our mothers as objects of our first sexual fixation. We generally survive infantile imprisonment undamaged, but have to pass through many perilous stages before we can emerge into the sun of mutual love. Some of us get blocked along the way. The pederast, who can only be excited by children, is stuck in his own pubescence, so paralysed by the memory of innocent affections that he is unable to move forward. His impairment counts as a paraphilia, specifically named 'paedophilia', or the love of children. Another paraphilia is the desire to expose oneself in public ('exhibitionism'), another the desire to rub one's body against a stranger in a crowded place ('frotteurism'), and there are dozens of others which fixate upon an object ('fetishism').

The fetishist is essentially a specialist. He will be excited by a certain colour of hair, or style of dress, or perhaps merely a shoe. Adler called fetishism 'fear of the sexual partner', and it is certainly true that the fetishist contrives to render the sexual partner superfluous by achieving sexual gratification without him/her. There is a sense in which pornography is fetishistic, substituting the image for the real thing, and Jeffrey Dahmer's fascination with chests, stomachs and intestines was an extreme example of fetishistic deputising which merits a definition of its own – 'partialism', or the desire for a part rather than the whole. The lust murderer has recently been given a special category under the awkward name 'erotophonophilia', coined by a leading sexologist in the field;[3] the word was not mentioned at this trial.

Even in this brief résumé, it will be clear to the reader who has come this far that Dahmer could be assigned to several of these classifications, but the dominant one in his case, necrophilia, is regarded as so rare and clinically difficult that in *D.S.M.-III-R* it is unhelpfully tucked away in a sub-category, devoid of elaboration or definition, as a paraphilia 'not otherwise specified'.

Other characteristics of a paraphilia are its compulsive need to repeat and its irresistibility. 'Every form of gratification requires repetition as well as enhancement', wrote Stekel, and immature gratifications are more prone to repeat because they need to rediscover the euphoria of the first time, like an infantile regression. Stekel had no hesitation in defining paraphilia as a disease. He called it a 'spiritual parasite which incapacitates its host for any other form of mental endeavour'.[4] We have only to recall Dahmer's words, when he spoke of the compulsion which would not leave him alone and occupied his every waking thought, to recognise the aptness of this dramatic description.

We must revert to Dr Berlin's evidence. He assured Mr Boyle that one does not excuse misbehaviour by calling it an illness, but in this case Dahmer's affliction amounted to 'a cancer of the mind', 'a broken mind', and it was facile to suggest that he could simply stop thinking about it and it would go away. 'We cannot always *choose* what

237

to have on our minds,' he said. Necrophilia does not arise from a voluntary decision; it was not a matter of waiving various options. Boyle asked what could have caused it in the first place, and Dr Berlin was unable to give a satisfactory answer. 'We have found no cause either biological or environmental,' he said.

This reply gave the unfortunate impression that Dr Berlin was happiest constructing a theory and then finding specimens to fit it; he had the effects before him, and found them sufficient proof of the condition. Mr Boyle tried hard to rescue his witness from the muddle he had got himself into ('I guess I'm rambling a bit,' Berlin said), and guided him to the conclusion which he needed to focus the jury's attention, namely that willpower alone cannot control behaviour, and that 'if necrophilia is not an impairment of the mind, I don't know what is'. But Mr McCann had spotted the sophistry and was ready to expose it.

In cross-examination, McCann sought first to ridicule the witness, to diminish his stature and thereby provoke his simmering irascibility. He told the jury what it knew already, that the witness was 'extremely verbose', and determined (by implication, to help them) that he would curtail this verbosity and limit Dr Berlin to short answers. His questions would try to make it clear that Berlin was not a man of experience.

'How long did you talk [with Mr Dahmer] about family history?'

'Fifteen minutes.'

'From zero to age eighteen?'

'I'm not writing a biography of him.'

'What did you then talk about after family history?'

'Personal history.'

'How long did that take?'

'Half an hour. My examination covered five hours in all, maybe six. I'm not trying to be evasive.'

'The record indicates four hours and forty-five minutes. If you spent forty-five minutes talking about family history and personal history, that leaves four hours, so you spent fifteen minutes on each homicide.'

This was demonstrably unfair, for the doctor was not a police officer bound by the rigours of investigation, and it was foolish to suppose that he could only examine a patient on strictly factual matters. This, however, was the inadequate level at which much of the trial was to be pitched, and the 'cross' of Dr Berlin easily confirmed his incompetence to the jury. McCann went on to ask the witness about the defendant's fantasy life.

'Did he fantasise about murder?'

'Yes.'

'How?'

'Gosh, I don't remember exactly. Early on, he had fantasies which included killing. Themes were what I was interested in, not details.'

'Did you ask him how killing occurred in his fantasies?' The District Attorney was pinning Dr Berlin down to admit that he did not in fact explore the meaning or even the content of the defendant's fantasies, but accepted on simple trust everything Dahmer told him. It was an accusation which could well be applied to most of the psychiatrists on the case, on either side, but for Dr Berlin it was particularly galling, as he had spent less time than anyone with Dahmer and was being portrayed, successfully, as slovenly and unthorough.

'It is ridiculous to think that you can do it in four and a half hours,' said Mr McCann disdainfully. Visibly stung, Dr Berlin answered, 'I don't tell you how to do your job.' We risked descending to a playground squabble. Berlin then admitted that he was 'getting mad', and manfully justified himself by pointing out that it was the quality of work which counted, not the amount of time spent on it. 'My integrity is being questioned,' he moaned. 'No, doctor,' came back Mr McCann, 'your inexperience.'

Knowing he had the embattled expert against the ropes, the District Attorney pushed home his advantage with relentless vigour. He said the witness had not 'bothered' to ask certain questions of the defendant, and therefore did not know enough to reach any worthwhile view of his state of mind. 'Did he say he preferred live persons?' 'At times he said that.' 'What words did he use?' Berlin could not answer this and attempted to evade. Several times Mr McCann invited the witness to consult his notes, and waited in triumphant silence for up to five minutes while Dr Berlin rustled his papers aimlessly. It soon became apparent that his notes amounted to a few pages on a jotting pad. McCann suggested that the doctor did not think he required more than this, because his conclusions were based upon his own ideas and not upon the evidence. His manifest discomfort was relieved only when the court recessed for the day.

There was more of the same when McCann resumed his cross-examination the next morning. Dr Berlin's tactic was now self-assertive, offering long discursive answers to questions designed to elicit simple facts. This was no more effective, for it confused the jury and made it seem as if the doctor was defensively displaying his knowledge. McCann cleverly allowed him to go on with it, before finishing by getting Berlin to admit that Dahmer was a liar.

Gerald Boyle concentrated his brief 'redirect' examination of the witness on establishing the important point that one did not have to be 'dumb or stupid' in order to be mentally ill. In other words, Dahmer could be a manipulative liar and still be sick. Dr Berlin was then mercifully excused.

Setting aside the shambles of his presentation and delivery, Dr Berlin had successfully conveyed the idea that the defendant had been prey to a compulsion the rest of us would find difficult to comprehend. There had been some altercation over the question as to whether necrophilia was a true compulsion or not. *D.S.M.-III-R* blandly excluded all paraphilic disorders from its definition of compulsion, on the grounds that their indulgence promoted pleasure, whereas a true compulsion was pointless.* A lot of this is semantic jigsaw-building, but there is a fine distinction which needs to be drawn between doing something for the relief of agonising (imaginary) symptoms (such as perpetual hand-washing) and doing something to repeat an experience which has become indispensable to one's happiness (such as getting drunk). Both are compulsions. A compulsion does not have to be involuntary to be real. *D.S.M.-III-R* disagrees with this, and the District Attorney was concerned to underline its authority; otherwise, as he later told a news conference, anyone might claim a compulsion to excuse any kind of behaviour.

It should also be self-evident that compulsion must be *against* moral judgement or it is meaningless. If there is no moral realisation of the wrongfulness of one's acts, then one does not need to be compelled to do them. One would act in a cretinous moral void. It is only *because* Dahmer appreciated the wrongfulness of his acts that the notion of compulsion enters into the argument. You are compelled against your better judgement, not in support of it. These matters would rise again in discussion with a prosecution witness the following week.

Something else which this first expert witness disclosed gave cause for nagging disquiet. It was clear that he had taken Jeffrey Dahmer's account of himself at face value, that he had not challenged him or looked behind his words. Of the seven psychiatrists who would give evidence, six of them would likewise accept the defend-

---

* 'Some activities, such as eating (e.g. eating disorders), sexual behaviour (e.g. paraphilias), gambling (e.g. pathological gambling), or drinking, when engaged in excessively, may be referred to as "compulsive". However, the activities are not true compulsions because the person derives pleasure from the particular activity, and may wish to resist it only because of its secondary deleterious consequences.' *Diagnostic and Statistical Manual of Mental Disorders*, American Psychiatric Association, p. 246.

ant's own estimation of himself, and only one would introduce a note of scepticism. I talked with Dr George Palermo after the day's proceedings. 'I like Jeff Dahmer,' he said, 'but he is quite cunning. He uses his charm and the helplessness of his situation as weapons. He is establishing a view of himself which he imposes on his questioners. You have to be wary.' Even if that were so, however, the very duplicity of Dahmer was a part of him which needed to be explored, not merely dismissed as a 'weapon'. Dr Palermo's scepticism was, I thought, excessive.

Neither was 'charm' a quality which would immediately spring to mind when listing Dahmer's attributes. He was too passive for that, too diffident; charm requires attack. On the other hand, his vulnerability was undeniable, and was felt, in this second week, throughout the courtroom. Spectators had ceased to regard him as a curiosity, and had gradually come to look upon him as human. Comments were made if he seemed tired or dishevelled. Even the victims' families, who detested him, noticed when he hadn't washed his hair or changed his suit. Shorn of the distorted dramas of his past, he looked distinctly fragile, even a trifle scared.

He had some vestige of humour. One day he did not bother to shave and was being wheeled down the corridor when a woman passed, recognised him, widened her eyes, threw her hands up to her face, and screamed. Unperturbed, Dahmer told the guard, 'I guess I should have shaved.'

He rarely talked to his defending counsel, but sat compliantly between Wendy Patrickus and Ellen Ryan day after day, answering monosyllabically when either addressed him. These two young ladies in fact knew him very well by now. They had seen him on a regular basis for over six months and had shared the gradual revelation of his iniquity. They had talked to him longer and more often than anyone else. Miss Ryan, who had been abroad for a year before she was engaged to help with this case, first saw the photographs of butchered and dismembered bodies when she was in Dahmer's company, and had to struggle hard to contain her revulsion. It was a terrible shock. She succeeded in banishing all reaction from her face, however, and recovered slowly, by herself.

It took a long time for she and Miss Patrickus to gain Dahmer's confidence, or rather his relaxed acceptance of them. At the beginning, he had behaved as someone totally unfamiliar with human contact. He did not know how to find it or deal with it, especially with two young women. He was docile, polite and accommodating, but in no way socially forthcoming. They felt that he was capable of friendship, and had never been offered it before. So they persevered, quite apart from the demands of the job, in getting him to relax without bullying. After six months they conceded that he was 'a nice guy', a long way from the manipulative dissembler portrayed by Dr Palermo. He would pay gratuitous, slightly embarrassed compliments, such as (to Miss Patrickus) 'You look nice today', or (to Miss Ryan) 'That's a snappy necklace you're wearing.' He was like a novice learning the social graces. Ellen and Wendy said it was 'lovely to see him open out and relate'. For his part, Jeff Dahmer told them, 'You know, you are the closest friends I have had in my entire life.'

They helped prepare him for the visit to court of his father and stepmother. He was deeply anxious about their intended presence in court, and derived little comfort from the obvious moral support which their presence implied. Jeff knew they were aware of the broad outlines of his crimes and the strange obsessions they portrayed, but he was embarrassed that they should have to listen to the squalid details.

In the event, they listened with admirable impassivity. Arriving through a private door, Lionel and Shari Dahmer sat in the back row on the public side, expressionless and intent. Unmolested by the press (who did not know where they were staying and never attempted to approach them in court), they neither wept nor evaded. A few feet away from the relations of the dead, they watched and listened in silent acknowledgement of their duty not to shirk the damage that had been wrought, and in loyalty not to abandon their son to this exposure of his life. Dr Dahmer appeared a shy, dignified man, whose pain was private but whose modest nobility showed. Mrs Dahmer looked like a big-hearted woman, warm and social, whose presence would be a comfort to anyone. Here, however, she was reticent and solemn, now and again slipping her hand into her husband's as he faced an incredible ordeal.

The second expert witness for the defence was Dr Judith Becker, professor of Psychiatry and Psychology at the University of Arizona, whose speciality was the evaluation and treatment of paraphiliacs, and whose profession involved the training of physicians to recognise a paraphilic disorder. Assistant District Attorney Carol White interrupted the rehearsal of Dr Becker's impressive *curriculum vitae* to point out that, despite this, she had never before testified in a criminal case.

After twitchy, arm-waving, energetic evidence from Fred Berlin, Judith Becker's presence in the witness-box was like a cool, calming breeze. Pretty and elegant, with an utterly disarming smile, she combined grace with true professional acumen, was compassionate as well as thorough, decent as well as detailed. It was she who first explored Dahmer's childhood, and offered to a fascinated court the stories of tadpoles drowned in motor-oil, of Frisky and the countryside. She presented an entirely new side of Jeff Dahmer, the man who cried tears of terror after the death of Steven Hicks, who was shy about sex and did not know how to meet people, and who fiercely protected his parents ('It's not Dad or Mom's fault, it's my fault.').

There were, however, two fresh elements in her evidence which positively demanded proper examination and were passed over. Dr Becker reported Jeff's hernia operation, which we had not heard of before, and, on gentle questioning by Boyle, suspected that it might be signifi-

cant. She went no further than that. She also told us about
the game of annihilation called 'Infinity Land' without
pursuing its possible import. We were left with it in limbo,
a curiosity not to be tampered with. It is only now that
these two aspects of Dahmer's history have been considered, and one wonders if their significance might have
had some weight with the jury in determining the state of
Dahmer's mind.

Dr Becker repeatedly referred to the defendant as 'Jeffrey', a lapse for which in cross-examination she was chided
by Carol White, who attempted to turn her transparent
niceness and compassion against her by insinuating a lack
of professional detachment. This took no account of the
fact that Detective Murphy's report of the confession is
littered with references to 'Jeff', and nobody dared suggest he was getting too close to the murderer.

Then there was the brief moment, referred to in an
earlier chapter, when Judith Becker allowed us to see a
little of the woman whose profession must needs expose
her to the most distasteful tasks. When asked if she had
seen enough of the photographs Dahmer had taken of
his corpses, she replied simply, 'I do not care to see any
more.'

The burden of Miss White's cross-examination, which
began on Wednesday morning, 5 February, was that, if
Dahmer could behave lawfully on some occasions, then
he should not be allowed to escape responsibility for those
occasions when he behaved unlawfully. Citing the incidents involving Ernest Miller (murdered with a knife),
Somsack Sinthasomphone (spared because Dahmer had
to go to work), and Luis Pinet (attacked but reprieved
because he was too strong), she repeatedly asked Dr
Becker whether or not they showed that the defendant
was able to conform his conduct to the requirements of
law. It was an otiose line of questioning, because it
skimmed the surface and seemed frightened to tackle the
depths, and because it devised the ludicrous picture of
Jeffrey Dahmer about to murder someone and stopping

to reason with himself, 'I had better not do this, I should be conforming my conduct to the requirements of law'. Those are the words with which the statute is framed, those were the words the jury would have to think about, and those were the words prosecuting counsel would chant until we all knew them by heart. It was insultingly simple-minded – a kind of reasoning by attrition – but the court had thus far demanded no higher level of intellectual debate.

Besides which, the Pinet incident was possibly the most glaring illustration of Dahmer's episodic inability to conform – three times within forty-eight hours. The Somsack offence, on the other hand, was altogether another matter; it seemed to demonstrate a mind functioning rationally with a view to self-preservation.

Dr Carl Wahlstrom, a psychiatrist from Chicago, was the third and last expert witness for the defence. Quietly spoken and deferential, Wahlstrom appeared timid and unsure of himself. He gave so little impression of command that Mr McCann had an easy time diminishing his stature before the court. He had only been out of school a year! The man was a tyro! He had never published a paper on anything, nor addressed the American Psychiatric Association! McCann was misguided, as it happened, for Dr Wahlstrom's report was the most painstaking and thorough of the lot, and if one could hear him (which required an irksome effort), one learnt more about Dahmer's mind than from either of his preceding colleagues.

Wahlstrom was the first to use the word 'psychotic' in his description of the defendant, an important step towards the identification of clinical madness. While there is much difficulty attendant upon the diagnosis of necrophilia, psychosis is universally accepted in medical circles as a severe mental disease. No wonder McCann was bent upon discrediting him.

'Mr Dahmer is a thirty-one-year-old white male with a long history of serious mental illness which was essentially

246

untreated,' stated Wahlstrom. 'His personality structure is extremely primitive', and he has 'bizarre delusional ideas'. This was a reference to his attempt to create a zombie who would remain his personal friend and possession. He had told Dr Wahlstrom, 'If they had their own thought processes they might remember that they had to leave, or lived somewhere else', a remark which, together with his intention to build a power-bestowing temple, led Wahlstrom to the conclusion that the defendant's trouble was of psychotic proportions. The severity of his mental disease 'requires continuous treatment', he said.

In preparing for his examination, Wahlstrom had studied a report by the elusive Dr Smail, who had been the first to meet Dahmer and had declared him fit to plead, but was not scheduled to give evidence. Smail had written that the results of one of the tests he had used indicated 'the possibility of a major mental illness, either of the quality of a schizophrenic disorder or a major affective disorder'. This was the first time that anything of Smail's opinion had been heard, and because he was otherwise silent on the matter, it carried considerable weight. It was therefore this very weight that Mr McCann sought to diffuse in cross-examination, and he went straight to the point. Had not Dr Wahlstrom omitted certain sections of Dr Smail's report? Did not Smail decide that the defendant had a clear perception of reality, that he had a clear perception of conventional morality, that he was at all times competent? Wahlstrom had to admit that this was true, but he was too nervous a witness to repudiate the erroneous impression that one conclusion invalidated the other.

While the District Attorney went on to depict Dahmer as merely 'a hunter', the witness suceeded in holding on to his evaluation of the defendant, supporting it with references to his fascination with the colours of people's insides, and his desire to have sex with the viscera. The impression left was of a man propelled headlong towards explosive dementia. I was reminded of Dr Crowley's so far unquoted opinion; the reader will recall that Crowley had seen Dahmer during the last four weeks before his arrest, when corpses competed for space in his apartment. He had used two mild yet pregnant words to describe his condition: he was 'disabled' and 'immobilised'.

The defence rested its case on 5 February, and court recessed. We were not immediately to hear the prosecutor, however, for there were two more psychiatrists to be called, Doctors Palermo and Friedman, appointed by the court (that is, by Judge Gram) to offer an objective assessment of the defendant's mental state. The implication that doctors engaged by the defence or prosecution were not to be relied upon was a dangerous one, and it went home very neatly. The jury was being told that these two men were independent and therefore trustworthy.

On Thursday, 6 February, George Palermo took the stand. He looked as if he was used to it, that the courtroom was no hostile environment as far as he was concerned, and that he would get this over with nice and quickly. He was relaxed, urbane, smiling, often joking, slightly superior in manner, friendly and patient. Wearing his European sophistication as a natural mark of status, Dr Palermo resolved to impart his wisdom with as much clarity as he could muster. He was patently a nice man and an amusing companion who would make a splendid dinner-guest. He also had an illustrious career behind him, both in his native Italy and in the United States, as teacher and forensic psychiatrist. The jury were reassured by his combination of experience and jocularity.

Invited by Judge Gram to read out his findings, Dr Palermo went over much the same ground as his predecessors but reached startlingly different conclusions. Jeff had been picked on at school and had never defended himself, hence he had internalised his feelings of hostility. Quoting David Dahmer, he said Jeff had been 'withdrawn, never smiling, doing things only when prompted by Mom or Dad, and when angry he would storm out of the house and go to the wooded back yard smashing

wooden sticks against the trees'. Joyce Dahmer had likewise told Dr Palermo that her son had felt inadequate and
inferior. These observations, allied to the young man's
chronic inability to form relationships and his frustrated
desire to be close to another man, marched Dr Palermo
to the conclusion that he was a 'sexual sadist'. No one had
yet suggested this. Dahmer's murders were not to do with
sex, said Palermo. 'Aggressive, hostile tendencies led to
his murderous behaviour. His sexual drives functioned
as a channel through which destructive power was
expressed.' Had Dahmer himself corroborated this diagnosis? 'It was not hate or love,' he told the doctor, 'lust
would be a better word.'

'Strange to say,' added Palermo by way of an aside,
'he's not such a bad person.' Dahmer appeared not to
return the compliment. For the first time since the trial
began, he scribbled a note declaring his irritation with the
doctor, who had not, it seemed, paid any attention to
what he had been saying in their interviews. What most
annoyed him was Palermo's assertion that he was afraid
of going to prison because he might be attacked by black
men.

Having finally told the court that Dahmer was legally
sane at the time of each of the offences, Dr Palermo got
ready to be questioned by Gerald Boyle. Ominously,
Boyle said that he knew and respected Palermo (almost
everyone in this case knew everyone else), and paused.
Palermo was too confident to be intimidated. 'I knew after
four hours that he was not psychotic,' he told Mr Boyle.
'I expected to find a major psychiatric illness, and was
shocked to find nothing of the sort.' That, at least, was
bold.

It was here that Mr Boyle revealed himself at his most
subtle. Rather than attempt to undermine George Palermo, he encouraged him to luxuriate in his eminence; he
humbly sought further guidance; and thus he persuaded
the guileless witness to say some astonishing things. For
a start, Palermo attached no importance to the confession.

'Can we believe that Jeffrey Dahmer all of a sudden becomes 100 per cent truthful after his arrest?' he asked. He did not believe that the drilling of skulls had taken place at all as Dahmer said; they were drilled after death (as Dahmer had at first claimed) to facilitate draining of the brain matter. He did not believe the stories of cannibalism; they were 'unproven' (which, of course, they would have to be). He did not credit the story of the temple. 'He told me spontaneously as I was leaving. I have reason to believe it's not true.' He did not believe that Dahmer killed for companionship, but in order to silence a potential accuser; 'He killed because when they woke up they would be angry with him.' He denigrated the *D.S.M.-III-R* manual with haughty disdain as being no more than a guide-book for the uninitiated. Was there a better guide-book, asked Boyle? 'Yes,' smiled Palermo, 'will-power.'

Not only was this a classic *non sequitur* of a reply, but it betrayed a complacency in the doctor which was beginning to look unattractive. He constantly argued with counsel, as a headmaster might reason with a recalcitrant boy, instead of simply answering questions. Judge Gram did not intervene to direct him. On the question of necrophilia, he steered himself into a muddle and denied there was any evidence for it. Where Berlin, Becker and Wahlstrom had found necrophilia, he had found sadism, and positively declared that Dahmer showed none of the symptoms of a necrophile, which was frankly risible. Finally, Dr Palermo offered his own version of what had been going on in Jeff Dahmer's head. The murders were the result of 'pent-up aggression within himself. He killed those men because he wanted to kill the source of his homosexual attraction to them. In killing them, he killed what he hated in himself.'

This was the kind of simplistic view which should have been discarded some thirty years before. The last time I encountered something like it was in a book no doubt familiar to Dr Palermo, published in 1964, in which A.

Hyatt Williams wrote, 'Certain elements of an intolerable internal situation are projected into a victim, the aim being to get rid of these elements into someone else: then to kill and destroy them in that person in order to prevent any re-entry of them into the self.'[5] Palermo's verdict was virtually a paraphrase of this fanciful logic.

Which is not to say that there is no evidence of suppressed aggression in Jeffrey Dahmer. His calm and monotone manner belies the volcano which may be raging within, and he is (consciously) quite unaware of its presence. Some of the murders clearly indicate the use of force, which must have its epicentre somewhere. Besides which, aggression and sex have ever been interlaced, sometimes with delightful, sometimes with disastrous effects. It is the man whose aggression has been thwarted who should be watched. Aggressiveness is essential to ambition, self-preservation, competition, self-affirmation. The weak man lacking in these initiatives (and it is by now obvious that Dahmer lacked each and every one of them to a remarkable degree) will leave his aggression to fester and pollute his nature. Then it might be that the only expression it has left is through dominant sex. Some of this was surely present in Dahmer's pathology, but that is a long way from the shallow conclusion that he was trying to kill the homosexual in himself.

Michael McCann, taking over from Boyle, declined to ask the witness any questions, but rather delivered an oration which appeared to be a rehearsal for his closing argument. Again, the judge did not intervene.

Dr Samuel Friedman, who next gave evidence for the court, openly disagreed with his colleague on the question of motive. The murders, he said, were not meant to chastise the killer's own homosexuality; they were an effort to continue a relationship. This made much more sense in the light of what we had heard. Dr Friedman, white haired, with a voice like a record playing at too slow a speed, spoke in such a low rumble that the microphone was not sensitive enough to pick out the articulations. He

251

was a kindly man, eager to do well, but afraid of reaching provocative conclusions; he walked the safe road.

Friedman went out of his way to praise Jeff Dahmer as a man: 'Amiable and pleasant to be with, courteous, with a sense of humour, conventionally handsome and charming in manner, he was, and still is, a bright young man.' However, his insight into himself was 'best described as zero' and he more or less 'pleaded' for an explanation. He 'felt helpless'. Dr Friedman spoke like a man who would have been proud, in normal circumstances, to have Dahmer as a grandson, and was moved to pity by the depths into which he had plunged. Several times he said he had been 'impressed' by the testimony of Dr Judith Becker, and was the first witness to express some faith in the possibility of redemption. 'I hope,' he said, 'that something can be done to reconstruct this individual, who certainly has the assets of youth and intelligence.'

Nevertheless, Friedman's habitual rigidity overcame him. He was reluctant to decriminalise illegal conduct or reduce the importance of free choice. He disapproved, for example, of survivors from the Vietnam War alleging post-traumatic stress syndrome as the reason for their descent into criminality, because he did not like making excuses for people who behave badly when they have the opportunity to behave well. (The effect of this digression was to invite the jury to ponder that an insanity verdict might somehow 'let Dahmer off', and it ought properly to have been interrupted by Judge Gram. It was not.) I suspect Friedman's Jewishness might have influenced his opinion; to forgive Dahmer was tantamount to forgiving Hitler.

Gerald Boyle stood up to cross-examine, and invited the witness to agree with the point that it was possible to make elaborate logical plans and choices towards the achievement of an ultimately insane purpose. 'Does not the ability to make decisions render a diagnosis of psychotic behaviour impossible?' Alive to the danger of this line of argument, McCann objected, and was sustained.

Rephrasing his question, Boyle first elicited Friedman's agreement that the exercise of choices did not invalidate a diagnosis of mental illness, and secondly, crucially, he got him to admit that Jeffrey Dahmer's personality disorder did in fact amount to a mental disease. It was not without some hint of triumph that Mr Boyle sat down.

Immediately, Mr McCann asked for the jury to be excused while he placed a motion before the court. 'The defence is marching under the flag of a newly-created mental illness,' he said, and asked Judge Gram to rule that Boyle should restrict himself to alleging mental illnesses which were recognised and not introduce mere personality disorders. Gram denied the motion, and the prosecution opened its case at 1.30 p.m. on Friday, 7 February.

The first witness was Dr Ollson, who confirmed that he had prescribed sleeping pills to Jeffrey Dahmer on seventeen occasions. (The judge asked Dahmer whether he minded the doctor breaking confidentiality to give evidence, and he said he didn't – it was the first time his voice had been heard in court.) He was followed by Raymond Flowers, Luis Pinet and Somsack Sinthasomphone, each of whom had been assaulted by Dahmer to different degrees, telling the stories with which the reader is now familiar. The last two were identified only by initials, and all three were protected by the judge from being photographed or filmed.

The State called the police officer who had arrested Dahmer for indecent exposure, and his probation officer. To these as to the three previous witnesses several questions cropped up with noticeable regularity. They were each asked if Dahmer heard voices or had hallucinations, and whether they believed he was suffering from a mental illness such as would impair his capacity to conform. McCann was anxious to establish that the defendant appeared normal and stable, but as these were not expert witnesses, and could not be expected to assess his mental condition, the questions ought not to have been allowed. Mr Boyle did not object.

In order to expedite the case and avoid having to sequester the jury for too long, the court sat on Saturday, 8 February, to hear the State's first expert, Dr Fred Fosdal from Madison, Wisconsin. He was awaited with some interest, for he had unhappily talked to a journalist before the trial had started and revealed that Dahmer had drilled heads to create 'zombies'. Since the matter was then still *sub judice*, Fosdal could legitimately have been held in contempt of court, but freedom of the press in America has a habit of over-ruling any higher concern. Nonetheless, Dr Fosdal's indiscretion caused him to suffer the biggest fit of nerves in his career. Despite his being a veteran testifier on responsibility issues, his level of confidence on that Saturday morning before court assembled was no more than a kitten's. He paced and prowled, talked to anyone who would listen, spilled a cup of water down his suit, and would clearly have given anything to be anywhere else but in Milwaukee.

In the witness-box, Dr Fosdal appeared frightened to death. He could not stop touching things, fiddling with his tie, the microphone, his glasses, his suit, his glasses, the microphone again, while Mr McCann went through the list of his eminent appointments and achievements. It is customary then for opposing counsel to ask questions which might tend to suggest the witness was not all he was cracked up to be (as had happened with Berlin, Becker and Wahlstrom). It would be the perfect opportunity to make heavy sardonic reference to that indiscreet chat with the journalist. Poor Fosdal prepared himself for the onslaught, but he need not have worried. Gerald Boyle had no desire to exploit his discomfiture. In the most gentlemanly act of the proceedings, he said, 'We've known each other for a long time. I have no objection to Dr Fosdal,' and sat down.

Still the man could not relax. As he started to give evidence, he looked wooden, like a puppet placed in position. He tried to encourage relaxation by crossing his legs, and only looked more unnatural than ever. He sat back, felt it was wrong, sat forward, coughed. His throat was so dry with fear that he coughed at the beginning and end of every sentence, and poured endless cups of water to alleviate the condition. When he knocked one of these all over his papers, nearly drowning the witness-box, he exclaimed, 'Oh shoot! That's the second time I've done that this morning. I'm glad I didn't say something else on interplanetary television.' It was one of the only three laughs of the trial. Even Dahmer smiled.

The burden of Fosdal's evidence was that Jeff Dahmer was odd, but not ill. Prompted by McCann ('He will try to dehumanise Jeff as much as Jeff dehumanised his victims', said a journalist sitting next to me), he depicted a man at once pathetic and cruel. Asked whether he regretted not having a steady lover, Dahmer had told him, 'It might have been nice.' 'What would it have taken to stop you killing?' 'A permanent relationship.' Fosdal painted a sorry picture of the bathhouses, stalked by lonely men looking for the brief comfort of a moment's sex, and a harsh one of the defendant, utterly indifferent to the horror of pouring hot water into Weinberger's head. There was no suggestion of sadism – the doctor accepted that killing was only a means to an end. It was he who told the court that Dahmer had to take a shower with two bodies in the bathtub (possibly decapitated), and he who revealed that Dahmer had prepared six meals with various body parts from his victims.

We were also permitted a glimpse of the twisted morality which moved him. He told Fosdal that his lust overpowered any normal moral choices, but at the same time he really liked Tony Sears and might have been able to form a relationship with him. He strangled him with his bare hands because 'he was very special', then spent the whole of one Monday emptying his skull. Many of these young men died because Jeff Dahmer *liked* them.

Dr Fosdal emphasised that Errol Lindsey and some subsequent victims were handcuffed. It is difficult to see why it should be necessary to handcuff an unconscious man, unless it be that the man might wake up and, manacled, fight for his life, an image too awful to contemplate. Equally possible is the use of handcuffs as an icon of symbolic control. Neither counsel sought to pursue the implications, though it might well have been in the State's interest to do so.

Under gentle but perceptive questioning from Mr Boyle, Fosdal concurred that there was no malingering or deception on the part of Dahmer and that he appreciated the rapport between them. 'He was about as co-operative a defendant as any I have met in twenty years.' Totally at ease with his subject, and knowing full well where he was going, Mr Boyle asked if Dahmer was a necrophile.

'Yes, but that is not his primary sexual preference.'

'Dr Becker said he preferred people in a comatose state, knocked out. What's that called?'

'There's no name for it.' Boyle then went through the various categories listed in the book that 'you folks' use (*D.S.M.-III-R*), getting Fosdal to admit all the disorders which Dahmer did not have and by elimination leaving his obviously very real disorder unidentified. 'I concede that he has a mental disease,' the doctor eventually said, thereby joining Dr Friedman as a second 'convert'. Out of six psychiatric experts so far heard, five had now agreed that there was indeed a mental disease present at the time of the killings. The disease did not, however, in Fosdal's view interfere with his ability to conform. Well, said Boyle, what would interfere with it? Is there any paraphilic disorder which would qualify? Only if it were combined with another disease, said the doctor.

Boyle then asked the witness to consider the hypothesis of a necrophile who went to find corpses daily, obsessively, hundreds of times. Would it still be necessary to find another disorder, in addition to necrophilia, before such a man could be said to be ill and unable to control himself? Mr McCann jumped to his feet with an objection. This was hypothetical and inadmissible. Not so, said Boyle, quoting precedents which allowed hypothetical questions to an expert witness in order to help the jury. (What he was really appealing to was common sense, and that was precisely what McCann could not allow.) A decision seemed to perplex the judge, who had in previous days sustained and over-ruled objections on an apparently whimsical basis, and so he retired to chambers for conference with counsel.

McCann said the jury would be confused as to the issues if such a hypothetical question were allowed; it was irrelevant; Dahmer was accused of murder, not necrophilia. This argument put forward by McCann was, it must be said, either disingenuous or naive. Murder had already been admitted, and was not now an issue; insanity was the matter being tried and necrophilia was a legitimate consideration under this heading. Perhaps Judge Gram had not grasped this essential distinction, for he sustained the objection in the worst decision of the trial. It meant that Mr Boyle would have to proceed without analogy or illustration.

Boyle then turned to Dahmer's proposed altar. Did that demonstrate delusional thinking? Not at all, it was unusual and bizarre, that's all. Well, if it wasn't delusional, what did the defendant hope to gain from it? A source of power. How come? Tell me, doctor, what does delusional mean? Is eating another person delusional? Dr Fosdal was getting more and more uncomfortable as he found himself defending one indefensible position after another, and either hedged or answered in jargon. Boyle chose this moment to spotlight Dahmer's most peculiar ambition.

'What about this desire to create a zombie? Do you consider that to be delusional thinking?'

'No, it was a very practical and reasonable attempt to achieve his aim.'

'Have you ever met a case of home-made lobotomy before?'

'No, I think this is the first time internationally. Mr Dahmer is setting some precedents here.'

257

'It couldn't have worked, could it? You're a doctor, you must know.'

'It's possible.'

'Did you ask him how long he was going to keep the zombie? Do you believe he would have created a zombie and never killed again?'

'Absolutely. That would have been the solution of his problem. Absolutely.'

With this breathtaking answer the psychiatrist was manoeuvred into the position of appearing almost as mad and delusional as the defendant. Zombies are thought in some primitive societies to be corpses reanimated by a magician or witch-doctor and thereafter kept as slaves. The belief has frequently been noted in Haiti, for example, and some studies have attempted to discover whence it derives. It may, astonishingly enough, be realisable by the controlled use of poison, and those identified as zombies may look and behave like distracted creatures because their brains have been damaged. A poison containing tetrodotoxin is administered to the victim, who falls into a cataleptic state, fully paralysed yet aware of what is happening and unable to show it. He is declared dead and is buried. Very soon afterwards, he is exhumed and resuscitated by another hallucinogenic drug, which leaves him in a trance-like and obedient condition.[6]

By this account, Dahmer's dream was not theoretically out of the question. Even more amazingly, the poison used by the zombie-makers is found most prevalently in certain species of the puffer fish, which Dahmer liked above all others. (His delighted description of a puffer fish at the pet shop is in an earlier chapter.) Could Dahmer have known this? Nobody thought to ask him. It is more than likely just another curious coincidence. But Dr Fosdal was not speaking of theory; he was talking of practicality, and seriously supposed that Dahmer might have been able to create a zombie to solve all his problems. Would he have clothed him and fed him? Would he have taken him out for walks? Would he have kept him, ageing, forever? Dr Fosdal did not think far enough to ponder such possibilities.

Having established that Fosdal testified about thirty times a year, scarcely ever for the defence, Boyle concluded by accusing him of having tried to get the defendant to diagnose himself so as to defeat the argument for necrophilia. The doctor's nervous cough returned, and he was released.

With only one star witness yet to appear, several ideas and impressions hovered unexpressed over the courtroom. One was that psychiatrists could assert no monopoly over what constituted insanity. Six of them had had their say, and we were yet not much wiser. Without proclaiming what he was up to, Gerald Boyle was busy sewing the seeds of doubt by suggesting that the definition of insanity did not belong by inviolable right to doctors. He was trying to return the problem to the community (i.e. the jury), the ultimate arbiters of what is acceptable to their fellow citizens.

Secondly, almost nobody (Boyle included) had attempted to fathom what it might be like to be Jeffrey Dahmer. To Dr Berlin he was a theory personified, to Dr Wahlstrom a case history, to Dr Palermo a criminal, to Dr Fosdal a threat. Only Becker and Friedman had looked for the man. Judith Becker had identified the child in him, and Sam Friedman had lamented the waste. Paradoxically, it was the rumbling inaudible Friedman who had come closest to hinting at the profound sense of grief, of loss, that Dahmer might have experienced with every death he caused. His crazy wish to prolong a relationship through murder was obviously doomed, and he was left each time with the evidence of his failure and the confirmation of his isolation. He constantly used the word 'loss' when talking about the aftermath of killing, but nobody had picked it up.

While the psychiatrists needed him for their examination (and most of them appear to have written down everything he said without bothering to ask why he said it), Dahmer also needed the psychiatrists. They were listening to him, they paid attention to him, they noticed him. His talks with them were surrogate relationships, finite both in time and commitment, but better than nothing.

The last abiding impression was that no 'expert' witness dared admit to uncertainty. If only one of them had said 'I don't know', it would have been a powerful pointer to the complexity of human behaviour and would have put the jury at ease, given them comfort in their quandary. They might have thought it was all right not to know, that if the experts could entertain doubts, then their own confusions were not reprehensible.

Everyone had been waiting for the big man from California, Dr Park Dietz, who had testified in the trial of Hinckley for the attempted assassination of President Reagan, and came heralded by an august reputation. We had, however, to wait a day, as Dr Dietz did not wish to make the journey to Milwaukee on his birthday, and the prosecution filled in with several lay witnesses. Two of Dahmer's superiors at the Ambrosia Chocolate Factory were called, plus the manager of the Unicorn Bath Club in Chicago, policemen who had arrested him for offences prior to 1991, the man who cleaned his carpet, and the manager of the Oxford Apartments, Sopa Princewill. The only surprising nugget of information came from this latter, who testified that he was so impressed by Jeff Dahmer that he had once thought of going into real-estate business with him.

Whispers had been circulating for days in the media room that Park Dietz had recorded hours of interviews with Dahmer on video-tape, and intended to show them in court. With the jury out, Mr Boyle argued fiercely that such an unprecedented strategy would undermine the defence's prerogative to decide whether the defendant should himself give evidence – it would effectively make him a witness against his wishes. Mr McCann's view was that it would offer the jury a chance to observe the man's intelligence after the defence had contrived to have him sit in court 'like a dolt'. Judge Gram disallowed the showing of the videotapes; given that the entire proceedings were already being televised 'gavel to gavel', it was the wisest ruling of the trial.

Dr Park Dietz made his appearance in the witness-box on Wednesday, 12 February. It was immediately apparent why he was saved until the last, for there was about him an aura of unassailable proficiency. He was alert, meticulous, fastidious, precise, patiently prepared to suffer the task of explaining difficult concepts to the untutored. Like a reluctantly cynical professor, he had learnt that you have to speak slowly if people are to grasp your meaning, and you have to use simple words. To this end, Dr Dietz gave his evidence as if he were dictating to a shorthand typist, and paused between each sentence to make sure the jury had absorbed its significance. He was also the only witness blatantly to face the jury when delivering his answers, instead of looking at the person who had asked him the question. The jury was his audience, and it was to them that he determined to deliver his lecture.

Dr Dietz gave the impression that he was the one man in the country who could solve their dilemma, for he had dealt with extreme kinds of behaviour all his professional life and trained other psychiatrists in the field. He was now a professor at the University of California at Los Angeles, but had been at Harvard and Virginia before that, had studied law as well as psychiatry and was uniquely competent in marrying the two. He appeared, however, as a cold scientist, a linesman on the periphery of life rather than a scrummer at the heart of it. The *New Yorker* once tartly described him as 'prim'.

Michael McCann hardly needed to ask him any questions. All that was required of the District Attorney was to push the train and watch it roll. It was strange to see McCann rendered superfluous, like a schoolboy given a walk-on part. Obviously, Dietz had told him what the prompt cues were, and he had only to read them out.

From the first Dr Dietz made clear that he would have no truck with subtle interpretations: 'Dahmer went to great lengths to be alone with his victim,' he said, 'and to have no witnesses.' One might have thought that was too obvious to merit a ponderous statement; after all, no murderer wants an audience. But to Dr Dietz it was an essential piece of information. He went on to list all the ingredients of premeditation (killing only at weekends, preparing pills in advance) to indicate that Dahmer was not an impulsive murderer, but a calculating one who had to pump himself into the mood with alcohol because the act of murder was distasteful to him. 'If he had a compulsion to kill, he would not have had to drink alcohol. He had to drink alcohol to overcome his inhibition, to do the crime which he would rather not do.'

The witness then went on to explain exactly what was meant by the dreaded word 'paraphilia', in terms so beguilingly simple that one almost felt grateful to him. A paraphilia was 'a titbit of normal courtship behaviour', in so far as we all like to gaze upon our loved one, telephone her, rub against her, show off to her; the paraphilic distortions of these normal activities were voyeurism, telephonic scatalogia (i.e. obscene calls), frotteurism, and exhibitionism. Such exaggerations of normal activity were not tolerated by our society, and were therefore categorised as paraphilic disorders. The defendant suffered from three of them – necrophilia, frotteurism, and partialism.

Conceding that the acquisition of a paraphilia was not a matter of choice ('we cannot choose what we find sexy'), Dietz insisted that a man so disordered could still choose whether or not to *give in to* his paraphilic urges. 'Most paraphiles never act on their paraphilia in a criminal way. The paraphile is as free as any other human being to choose whether to commit a crime to gratify his wishes. Paraphilia provides no more than the motive for what a person would like to do. If you say paraphiles are compelled, then you have to say we are all compelled to want what we want.'

262

This was a disarming view, disarmingly well put. But it was seriously out of key with informed opinion among experts in sexology, a point upon which Dietz was not sufficiently challenged. John Money has written about the 'paraphilic fugue state', which is a flight from the normal to the altered state of consciousness during which 'a person may engage in activities that appear to be purposeful and voluntary, whereas they are actually robotic and involuntary'. These fugue states are episodic or paroxysmal (much like an epileptic attack) and have nothing whatever to do with choice. Dahmer called them his 'moods' or his 'dark side', when he was acting on automatic pilot (until the night of 22 July, 1991, when the machinery short-circuited). Dr Money goes further than this. Paraphilias are, he says, a brain disease 'brought into being by faulty functioning of the brain's own chemistry'.[7] None of this was mentioned by Dr Dietz, nor was it brought to his attention.

The witness proceeded to tell us to what lengths Dahmer had gone in his attempts to make a person stay with him, including the possibility of freeze-drying an entire body. He told us, too, something we had not yet heard, that Jeff had thought of putting an electric wire through a hole in a live man's head and plugging the other end into the socket to see if an electric charge might keep him going. Dietz related this solemnly, with a straight face. Anyone who dared suggest it was the manifestation of a deranged mind would, one felt, have been stared into silence.

Two more insights were vouchsafed us before the doctor got down to the real business of his testimony – to instruct the jury. Jeff was not a sadist in his view; 'he did not torture and took steps to prevent suffering'. And why did he masturbate while holding a severed head in his hand? 'It facilitated the fantasy of the entire person, the fantasy of the living person to whom the head had belonged, which cut out awareness that the rest of the body was missing and the head was severed.' Again, the voice was level, the demeanour unflustered.

263

For the next several hours, Dr Dietz went through every one of the fifteen counts of homicide with a view to deciding in each case whether Dahmer knew right from wrong at the time of the offence and whether his actions betrayed a capacity to conform to the law if he had wanted to. It was a shameless exercise in jury-control, for these were precisely the two questions the jury would have to answer in the privacy of their room when all the evidence had been heard. Dietz in effect appointed himself their foreman, as he could not trust them to reach the right decision without him, and the questions he asked himself were those of a law enforcement officer, not a detached psychiatric examiner.

He took some extraordinary leaps in his determination to force the evidence towards the proper conclusion. To take just one example, Dr Dietz affirmed that Dahmer met Matt Turner in Chicago and brought him home to Milwaukee; the fact that he did not kill him in Chicago indicated that he was making plans and was not acting on impulse, he said. Dietz took no account of the obvious – that Dahmer had no apartment in Chicago. They went to Milwaukee because that's where he *lived*. Similarly, by drilling holes in Konerak's skull, said the doctor, Dahmer was not a mad scientist making zombies, he actually *was trying* to make zombies, and was therefore sane. Dietz's incorrigible obtuseness was familiar to those who had heard him testify before. In the Hinckley trial, he had asserted that the defendant's goal of impressing film-star Jodie Foster by attempting to assassinate President Reagan was not delusional; it 'was indeed reasonable because he accomplished it'. Did this mean that Miss Foster was impressed? Or did it mean that Dietz had surrendered to the logic of the lunatic?

By the end of the day, as the witness came to consider the last two homicides, even he had to concede that Dahmer was hardly in a state to conform his conduct to law by then. But he ascribed this to alcohol intoxication, not to any mental disease.

On Thursday, 13 February, Mr McCann continued his questioning of Dr Dietz on a surprisingly defensive note. (I now saw the value of the press conference at the end of each day. The questions thrown by journalists were a barometer of doubts being circulated, which could be pocketed and refuted in evidence on the morrow. Nobody appeared to be embarrassed by this flagrant piece of show-business.) He concentrated on establishing two points. Dietz had been prefacing many of his remarks with the phrase, 'Mr Dahmer endorsed the concept to me that . . .', which suggested the doctor had made up his mind first and secured the defendant's concurrence second. It was important now to show that there was nothing wrong with leading questions. Dr Dietz assured us that they were the best technique he knew. That was at least honest; it was a technique which made it easier to believe everything you were told ('*Lui beve tutto*,' muttered the sceptical Dr Palermo).

McCann's second concern was to rid the jury of any idea that Jeff's projected temple, decorated with his human skulls, was in any way indicative of madness. It was not a delusional idea, insisted Dietz, because Jeff did not really believe he would gain powers from the shrine, but only suspected that he might get in touch with some spiritual force or other. In other words, the shrine was an example of superstitious belief, not delusional thinking, and in that regard perfectly acceptable.

Dietz's conclusion was that Dahmer's abnormality of mind did not substantially affect his mental or emotional processes. Anybody who had stayed the course thus far did not require a textbook to see that this flew entirely clear of any impartial view of the evidence. That his abnormality did not constitute a mental disease under Wisconsin law might inevitably be true; that it did not affect his emotional processes was nonsense.

When Gerald Boyle rose to cross-examine Dr Dietz, he was noticeably angry, but inadequately prepared. He had not read all Dietz's papers and pronouncements and was ill-equipped to spar with him on semantics. He did, however, pose one very important question which threw into doubt the crux of Dr Dietz's argument. If, as the doctor ·maintained, Dahmer's alcoholism was alone responsible for his incapacity to control his behaviour in the last month before his arrest, and there was no mental disease which contributed to it, would he have gone on killing had he stopped drinking alcohol before he met Tracy Edwards? Dietz paused for a long time as he weighed the implications, and could offer no satisfactory response. Everyone in court by this time knew that Dahmer would have gone on murdering had he not been stopped. If it was not a mental disease that was driving him, what on earth was it?

That evening, when Dr Dietz had finished his testimony, Jeff Dahmer was reflective. 'Maybe he's right,' he said. 'Maybe I could have stopped it all somehow.' Not one person at the trial had suggested how.

266

Chapter Ten

The Shrine

The closing arguments in an American trial are traditionally moments of theatrical grandiloquence, when the two attorneys move on from evidence as to fact and indulge in a frank appeal to the emotions. Implicitly, they tell the jury that it is not exclusively through the use of the intellect that they may reach truth; that there is another route, through feeling, intuition, and empathy, a route which may be just as valuable. You have heard all the evidence and will have to weigh in your minds the importance of facts presented to you, they say. Now forget the facts for a moment and listen to the promptings of your heart.

In consequence, attorneys may rise to passionate Ciceronian oratory in their bid to sway, seduce, persuade a jury to look further than its collective nose. It was during the closing argument that Clarence Darrow, probably the finest American defence attorney of the twentieth century, reached peaks of eloquence and entered the legal annals with a number of historical verdicts. The closing argument threatens the speaker with a naked moment, too, because a confected passion is transparent, and a spurious appeal boomerangs. Only the genuine article will work. In the Dahmer trial, we were given two prime examples of the *genre*, Gerald Boyle moved by pity for the frailties of mankind and the extraordinary damage done to one man's emotions, Michael McCann horrified by the wickedness perpetrated by that same man and the danger of his going unpunished.

With the burden of proof upon him, it was Boyle who was the first to speak. Facing the jury at a lectern, he asked them sombrely for their undivided attention. 'I serve three roles,' he said. 'I am an officer of the court, an advocate for my client, and a help to you in reaching a decision.' Then, with an imperceptible shift on to their side, he said, 'This will be the most important decision in many of our lives. We have all taken oaths to see that the ends of justice are done, and none of us is going to violate that.'

Of the two matters they would need to consider, the first was already established, since nearly all the doctors agreed there was mental disease; the only matter left for them to resolve was the issue of conformity. Boyle then launched into a truly terrible portrayal of misery and alienation, subtly inviting members of the jury to place themselves in Jeffrey Dahmer's shoes, and confiding with them that he, Boyle, was as bewildered by it all as they were. 'How would you like at age fifteen to wake up and have fantasies about making love to dead bodies? What kind of person would wish that on any human being? Who do you tell it to? Do you tell it to your father? Do you tell it to your mother? To your best friend? I don't know how this paraphilic business works, but none of us can possibly have gotten anywhere near to the fantasy level that this kid was at, at fourteen or fifteen years of age. I would not be Dahmer for one day.

'When your mind is in the gutter and it stays in the gutter, it never gets out of the gutter until something changes it,' continued Boyle. 'He was desolately lonely. His will-power was gone. He was so impaired that he could not stop. He was a runaway train on a track of madness, picking up steam all the time, on and on and on, and it was only going to stop when he hit a concrete barrier or hit another train. And he hit it, thanks be to God, when Tracy Edwards got the hell out of that room.

'You know what happened. He threw in the towel. He

just became helpless in his own mind. And I submit to you that at some juncture along this killing spree one would have to be blinded not to accept the fact that he was so out of control that he couldn't conform his conduct any more. No human being on the face of the earth could do anything worse than what he did. Nobody could be more reprehensible than this man, if he's sane. Nobody. The devil would be in a tie. But if he's sick – but if he's sick – then he isn't the devil.'

It was a powerful performance, and one which, at last, sought to humanise Jeff Dahmer and lift him out of the morass of mystification into which three weeks of theorising had pitched him. There was a feeling in court that Boyle had achieved his purposes, (*a*) to foster at least some measure of identification, and (*b*) to advance the notion that Dahmer was insane by the end. Just one count of insanity would suffice.

When Michael McCann rose to give his closing argument (limited by Judge Gram, as Boyle's had been, to two hours), he knew what he was up against, for he asked the jury not to confuse the defendant with his lawyer. 'There is a killer in this courtroom,' he said, contemptuously jabbing his finger at Dahmer. 'He seeks to escape responsibility for crimes to which he has already pled guilty.' Most of the experts had missed the obvious, McCann maintained, which was that you kill because you are hostile, angry, full of resentment or frustration or hatred. Dr Palermo said Dahmer was hiding all this. Don't let him hide it from you.

'I want to tell you who I identify with,' he said. Holding up portraits of each of the victims one by one, Mr McCann paraded them before the jury with a mounting litany of imprecations. 'Don't forget Steven Tuomi, who died at the Ambassador Hotel with the defendant. Don't forget Doxtator, age fifteen, picked up by the defendant. Don't forget Richard Guerrero, who died at the defendant's hands,' and so on through the list. 'Don't forget Ernest Miller, who was stabbed to death by the defendant because he was becoming conscious . . . don't forget Curtis Straughter, strangled to death by the defendant . . . don't forget Jeremiah Weinberger, who struggled for life for a day and a half before he died at the hands of the defendant.'

It was an emotionally draining experience, particularly when McCann brought home exactly what murder involves. With jerking hand movements and a vicious grimace he simulated pulling a leather strap around somebody's neck. He forced the jury to look at the defendant, telling them that men had been 'strangled by those hands you see on the table'. He countered the argument that Dahmer had been kind in putting victims to sleep before killing them. His voice broken with passion, and almost weeping, he said, 'Please don't drug me, please give me a chance to defend myself, let me fight for my life at least.' Lastly, in a gesture that was almost disgusting, he told jurors, 'It takes five minutes to strangle a man to death. Try it in the jury room. Go try it.'

People died merely in order to afford Dahmer a couple of days of sexual pleasure. That was the price of his not trying to control himself. 'Your life, your life, your life, for my sexual satisfaction.' McCann finished with his own plea to common sense, expressed in triste dignity. 'Don't be fooled by him,' he said. 'He fooled the police in Bath, Ohio. He fooled the West Allis Police. He fooled the Milwaukee Police. He's fooled a lot of people, including the court who gave him probation for sexual assault. Please, please, don't let this murderous killer fool you.'

Gerald Boyle had the last word in a brief rebuttal, during which he invited jurors to imagine themselves parents of such a man as Jeff Dahmer. His actual father was sitting at the back. With this unsettling thought, case number F912542, State of Wisconsin vs. Jeffrey L. Dahmer, closed.

Judge Gram read out all fifteen counts, in a parody of liturgical practice and intonation. It sounded like an entombment. He then gave instructions to the jury, reminding them that the closing arguments of the attorneys should not be considered as evidence. Four instructions with especial relevance to this case stood out, *viz*:

> You are not bound by medical labels, definitions or conclusions as to what is or is not a mental disease.
> You should not find that a person is suffering from a mental disease merely because he may have committed a criminal act, or because of the unnaturalness or enormity of such act, or because a motive for such act may be lacking.
> Mental disease is an abnormal condition of the mind which substantially affects mental or emotional processes.
> An abnormality manifested only by repeated criminal or otherwise antisocial conduct does not constitute a mental disease.

The last of these was included on an erroneous understanding of the statute framed in 1965, and ought properly to have been expanded. As is pointed out in Chapter Eight, the clause relating to 'repeated criminal or otherwise antisocial conduct' was intended to exclude psychopathic offenders from the definition of abnormality, but there was no defence of psychopathic disorder in this case. The clause was therefore wrongly included in the instructions in such a way as to invite inference that repeated paraphilic conduct could not constitute a mental disease, whereas there was no reason in law why it should not, since it manifestly affected mental or emotional processes. The mistake posited a serious possibility of misdirection, but we do not know whether members of the jury paid heed to it or not.

The jury went out on Friday, 14 February, and were expected to deliberate over the weekend. In the event, we received word on Saturday morning that they had already reached a verdict. The court was hastily convened and the

271

jury marched in to take their seats at 4.10 p.m. The fore-man handed over fifteen slips of paper, one for each count in the indictment, and Judge Gram proceeded to read out the answers to two questions posed on that paper. The first was, did the defendant suffer from a mental disease? Only if the answer to that question was affirmative would the second question need to be addressed.

On the first count, the verdict was that Jeffrey L. Dahmer did not suffer from a mental disease. Two jurors signified their dissent. The atmosphere in the packed courtroom was tense and hushed as the judge turned the page over and read out the decision on the second count. It was identical, with the same two dissenters. So it continued for the following three counts. When it came to the death of Eddie Smith in Count 5, his sister Theresa let out a cry of relief and sobbed. Count 10 related to the death of Tony Hughes, and returned a similar verdict. Mrs Hughes lowered her head and wept quietly. Would there be any variation before the end? At the last count, when the same verdict was read out with regard to the murder of Joseph Bradehoft, there came a whoosh of joy from the public seats and victims' families embraced one another. Dahmer, meanwhile, looked progressively more shrunken with each blow. By the end, his isolation from the rest of the community was complete.

Lionel and Shari Dahmer sat stony-faced in their usual seats at the back. Immediately following the last verdict, they left. Lionel came to me one minute later, a shaken man. 'It just doesn't make sense,' he mumbled. 'It just doesn't make sense.' The sense that the verdicts implied was that Dr Dahmer had sired a monster.

Judge Gram publicly thanked the media co-ordinator, Dan Patrinos, the court clerk and stenographer, Vicky and Mary ('How long have you worked here, Mary? Twelve years?'). It uncomfortably resembled the Academy Awards ceremony, and recalled a moment some days before when he had, in faulty German, wished one of the jurors a happy birthday. The judge concluded the day's work with a panegyric to Milwaukee. 'We have a system of justice which cannot be beat anywhere in this country.' Sentencing was postponed until Monday, 17 February.

On Monday morning we were exposed to another American ritual, at once moving and barbaric. The defendant, now the convict, was dressed in orange prison uniform for his last appearance before the world, and a relation of each man he had murdered was invited to address the court in his presence, to bruit his or her grief and anger. The purpose of this distasteful exercise seems to be to influence the judge before he passes sentence, to defy him to be lenient in the face of so much sorrow. To this extent, the practice is an interference with justice as well as a display of pain, and it is surprising that it should be tolerated.

The rough mediaeval spectacle provided some touching moments. 'Eddie Smith tried to be Jeffrey Dahmer's friend,' said his brother, 'and as a result he lost his life.' Looking straight at Dahmer, a relation of Ernest Miller said, 'You took his life like a thief in the night.' Mrs Shirley Hughes was unbearably dignified. 'Is it a thrill to you to know I can't fight back?' she asked her son's killer. 'The whole world will know just how ugly a person you are.' Recalling her lost son, Mrs Hughes held up two fingers and one thumb to make the deaf-mute sign for 'I love you'. Curtis Straughter's grandmother told Dahmer, 'You almost destroyed me. But I refuse to let you. I will carry on.' Richard Guerrero's sister called him *diablo puro*, and David Thomas' mother, 'a sneaking conniving person'; she burst into tears and had to be led away. When the sister of Errol Lindsey, in hysterics, rushed across the courtroom in an attempt to hurl all her hatred at Dahmer in full view of the world's television, bailiffs restrained her and protected him in a weird reversal of roles. It was then that Judge Gram put an end to this hurtful charade.

Gerald Boyle announced that Dahmer himself wished to address the court. The statement he made, in part fashioned by his defence, in part a genuine reflection of what he felt, was listened to in silence. 'Your honour, it is over now,' he said. 'I feel so bad for what I did to those poor families, and I understand their rightful hate . . . I take all the blame for what I did . . . I have hurt my mother and father and stepmother. I love them all so very much. I hope that they will find the same peace that I am looking for. Mr Boyle's associates, Wendy and Ellen, have been wonderful to me, helping me through this worst of all times.' He thanked Boyle for taking on the case and for helping to search for answers. 'In closing, I just want to say that I hope God has forgiven me. I know society will never be able to forgive me. I know the families of the victims will never be able to forgive me. I promise I will pray each day to ask their forgiveness when the hurt goes away, if ever. I have seen their tears and if I could give my life right now to bring their loved ones back, I would do it. I am so very sorry.'

Dahmer resumed his seat to await his sentence. There was just one more unexpected diversion. Judge Gram took it upon himself to tell us all what he thought the killer's motive had been. The information was both gratuitous and revealing. In the judge's view, Dahmer had hated himself for being homosexual and had destroyed what he saw of himself in others. It was the view expressed by Dr Palermo (and no one else), a view thought by some to be facile and superficial.

On the first two counts, Jeffrey L. Dahmer was sentenced to life imprisonment plus ten years, to run consecutively. The remaining thirteen counts carried a sentence of life imprisonment with no eligibility for parole before seventy years, also to run consecutively. This meant the prisoner would have in theory to serve a minimum of over nine hundred years.

Lionel and Shari Dahmer requested a ten-minute private meeting with their son before he was led away, which Gram granted in judge's chambers. They hugged and held one another. Dahmer was straightway taken to the Correctional Institute at Portage in upstate Wisconsin, where the following day the director received nearly two hundred enquiries from authors and mental health experts wishing to interview him. In the coming days he was to receive good wishes from strangers all over the world.

And what, ultimately, had this odyssey taught us, the spectators? There was opportunity enough for probing deep into the human psyche, but perhaps a court of law was not the most appropriate place to do it. The disciplines of legal procedure prevented anyone from straying beyond the obvious, and even the psychiatrists, court-appointed or not, found themselves bound by these restrictions. It was indeed a pity, for the art of psychiatric enquiry would have been the one avenue towards an understanding of those facets of Dahmer's conduct which were hidden even from him, had it been permitted to explore them. Being confined to definitions of sanity and evaluations of criminal responsibility, the psychiatrists were hampered by their collusion with the legal process. Yet the clues were there, in the allegations of cannibalism (or *necrophagy* – the eating of human flesh), and in Dahmer's oft-repeated and usually dismissed intention to create a shrine adorned with the remains of people he had killed. For here we discover a primitive spirituality with roots in the very beginnings of human society.

Psychology and its practical offspring psychiatry, far from debunking religiosity, confirms man as an essentially spiritual being. The aspect of Jeffrey Dahmer which lay untouched by his trial was his embryonic mysticism.

When discussing cannibalism, it is important to remember we are discussing a human activity, one of the age-old practices of humankind which have been successfully stifled by civilisation. To describe a man who eats men as 'bestial' or 'inhuman' is to state the exact opposite of the truth, for few other species have pursued the practice as long or as systematically as we have. As Morris Carstairs provocatively put it, 'If the abjuring of cannibalism is taken as a criterion of cultural advancement, then mankind is surpassed by many animal species in whom a repugnance against cannibalism is innate and does not have to be learned.'[1]

That there is a primal urge which lurks at the heart of the human mind is demonstrated by the unconscious echoes of infantile play. Parents indulge their children at an early stage by getting down on all fours and pretending to be animals about to gobble them up. The child gleefully retaliates with accompanying exclamations of 'I'm a wolf' or 'I'm a lion'. It never seems odd to parents that their little ones should show affection by promising to devour them, for they instinctively recognise that the child's notions of eating and loving are inextricably bound together. It is the initial 'oral' phase of sexuality which is here dramatised, when love and power are transmitted through the mouth.[2] Moreover, the infantile phase is never entirely forgotten, but carried through into adult life in terms of endearment ('I love you so much I could eat you up'), and in such *quasi*-cannibalistic sexual practices as the love-bite and oral sex. The adult who prefers oral sex above other sexual experiences indicates an infantile need for nourishment, a wish to recreate the moment of being mothered. (It may well suppose a lack of such mothering in infancy, but that is another matter; the point here is not why the need is manifested, but how.)

The horror provoked by undisguised cannibalism was well illustrated in the film of Tennessee Williams' *Suddenly Last Summer*, when Sebastian Venable (Montgomery Clift) is pursued and surrounded by a group of menacing adolescents on the beach. They bring him to the ground, overwhelm him, and as his arm thrusts out from beneath the scrum, you realise that they are eating him alive. The elemental nature of the scene is conveyed by a fierce unrelenting sun, the featureless stare on the boys' faces, a disturbing sound-track of rhythmic tribal metallic beats, and above all in the narration by the incredulous eye-witness (Elizabeth Taylor in the best performance of her career). Mingled with disgust we are aware of an unspoken and barely apprehended (*Unbewussten*) fascination with the possibility of it, and that fascination is the faint ripple of the involuntary memory of mankind.

We owe debts to different disciplines for our modern perceptions of what goes on beneath the surface of our mind. Jung famously studied the cross-breeding of mythology and psychology, recognising myth as the theatre of the unconscious, and Frazer traced the history of spiritual feeling in human societies. Cults and rituals have flourished among our species for up to half a million years, the most primitive of them being designed to placate or protect the spirits which inhabited everything in the empirical world. More developed spirituality involved the belief that one could ingest the character and attributes of a respected foe by eating parts of him, and as full-blown religions evolved, so did the idea that one could become spiritual oneself by literally eating the godhead.

Cannibalism is forbidden in civilised societies under such a strict *taboo* that, as we have seen, it is only tolerated in the pretence of child-play. But it has not always been so, and is still not so in some societies which differ from our own. Examples abound. The Basuto tribesmen cut out the heart of a slain enemy and ate it immediately, thinking thereby to inherit his valour. Some of the tribes of South America ate the hearts of invading Spaniards, and the Sioux Indians used to reduce the hearts of their conquerors to powder and swallow it. Some head-hunting tribes eat or suck out the brains, and the Zulus used to think that by eating the forehead and eyebrow of their enemy they could acquire the ability to look unflinchingly in the face of adversity. If a New Zealand warrior killed a chieftain, he would gouge out the eyes and swallow them, believing thereby to pass the soul of the chief into his own body.[3]

Jeffrey Dahmer let slip one relevant remark in his conversation with Judith Becker. 'Maybe I was born too late,' he said. 'Maybe I was an Aztec.' Dahmer mentioned this after relating how he had scalped Anthony Sears, but the reference has another significance. Aztec priests were known to extract the living heart. Explaining his cannibal habit, Dahmer said, 'I suppose in an odd way it made me feel as if they were even more a part of me.'[4]

The belief that eating an enemy or a god would make him 'part of' oneself is so old and profound that it suffuses religion to an embarrassing extent. By eating the body of his deity, the savage would assimilate the deity's power and divinity, sometimes literally. If it was a corn-god (and there were many), then the deity's earthly body was the corn itself, which of course did give the eater of it some strength. If it was a vine-god, then the juices of the grape were his earthly blood, which afforded the drinker of it extra power. 'The drinking of wine in the rites of a vine-god like Dionysus is not an act of revelry, it is a solemn sacrament.'[5] Similarly, Dionysus was thought sometimes to appear in the shape of a bull, and at Dionysian festivals worshippers would eat the raw flesh of the bull thinking they were taking parts of their god into themselves.

All of which is resonant of the dominant religion now obtaining in the Western world. Christianity in fact inherited this basic tenet of paganism, and when Christ exhorted his followers to eat his flesh and drink his blood he was merely following precedent. Thus has primitive cannibalism passed into the mystic ritual of the communion service in Christian liturgy. When the communicant takes the wafer and the wine, it is not enough that he should *believe* he is eating the flesh and drinking the blood of Christ. The doctrine of transubstantiation explicitly states that the wafer and the wine are, at the moment of Holy Communion, literally the body of Christ. Thus a true Christian must be a cannibal, or he is nothing – a mere mouthing dissembler or heretic. And the reverence with which the worshipper eats that flesh is an act of love.

Christianity proclaims its pagan origins even in its iconography, with Christ impaled on a cross and saints penetrated by arrows or disembowelled. It is born from primitive urges. Jeffrey Dahmer grew up with these images lauded as icons of the ultimate good, and yet there was a dangerous ambivalence attached to them, for they were overlaid by Lutheran austerity. He would be expected to imbibe the Christian faith and at the same time deny its pagan extravagance, which is to rob it of its glow and history. Most full-blooded Italians and Spaniards have no difficulty with the blatant violence and sex of Christian imagery, for they accept the pagan element in themselves to which their Church gives expression. They are part of Nature, close to the earth and its origins, with strong links to their distant brutal primitive ancestry. They are a continuity and their Church is the celebration of that continuity. Lutherans, on the other hand, people of the cold north, tend not to be so elemental or dramatic, and are offended by the robust paganism of the Catholics, whose Dionysian excesses they condemn. The pagan yearnings of Jeffrey Dahmer were forbidden by his own contradictory two-way-facing religion; he might have to fashion one of his own to accommodate them.

What might happen internally to a man like Dahmer is illustrated by the strange phenomenon of 'windigo psychosis' among certain North American Indian tribes, particularly in Canada. Its chief characteristic is a compulsive desire to eat human flesh.

The origin of the psychosis is religious. The Indians believe in a giant ravenous monster with a heart of ice called a windigo. He is fearsome to behold, insatiable, and omnipresent. If an individual becomes possessed by the spirit of the windigo, he will be compelled to kill and eat his fellow men, and since there is a harsh tribal taboo against cannibalism, the possessed man is condemned to be an enemy of his own kind, to be ostracised and despised. There is no greater fear than to be taken over by the windigo spirit. Children of the Ojibwa tribe played a game in which one of them pretended to be the windigo while the others ran screaming for cover; if he caught a child he would pretend to eat him. The analogy with our own 'bogyman' games is obvious, as is the legacy from demoniacal possession. A parallel belief in the idea of a 'spirit helper' who will protect the individual from the windigo calls to mind the ancient Greek tradition of the 'daemon' as guide and interpreter.

The relevance of all this becomes clear when psychology investigates the nature of the tribal society which harbours such a belief. It is a society which places greatest store by the exercise of self-discipline; which forbids outward shows of emotion, not only of anger but of joy also; which values huge restraint and fortitude under adversity; which, in short, demands the repression of self to such an extent that every ordinary feeling is driven underground and acute anxiety is the inevitable result. The social rules of these tribes are a sure recipe for mental breakdown.

The male hunter would spend days alone, a weak and isolated man pitted against all the inimical forces of nature and forbidden by his culture to lament his lot. He would therefore be driven to seek a relationship with someone or something outside himself, and this could only be attained through the intercession of an invisible spirit helper. Thus was each man utterly apart from every other, and stoicism the ultimate virtue. It is no wonder that deep distrust, even to a paranoid schizoid level, was often the outcome of such enforced apartness. Spontaneity was banned, extreme wariness encouraged. The need for affection was entirely stifled, with the result that people became introverted and lifeless. In these circumstances, possession by the windigo is relatively easy – the spirit walks into a vacancy where a vibrant person should have been. Already one may recognise the shadow of Jeffrey Dahmer.

The first symptoms of windigo psychosis are a tendency towards abrupt mood changes (the eruption of moods formerly suppressed) and a deep lethargic depression. Since the advent of the white man, alcohol has been available to release those anxieties and suspicions which had lain dormant, and the depressed individual will, in drinking, bring himself ever closer to explosion. He is progressively shunned, until his isolation is confirmed and he withdraws from society to give himself over to the windigo. He might eventually become a windigo himself, emerging from the forest to kill and cannibalise the tribesmen whose company he craves.

One such case came to light in 1879 in Saskatchewan. A Cree Indian called Swift Runner took the white man's police to a grave near his camp. Human bones were scattered about the camp, and it transpired that Swift Runner had killed his wife and eaten her, and forced one of his sons to kill a younger brother and dismember him – he, too, had been eaten. He confessed that he had killed his baby son and his mother-in-law and made food from them. All this, apparently, while there was no shortage of conventional food in the camp, so the motive for cannibalism could not be hunger. Swift Runner was tried in Edmonton. He asked why he was there and the judge told him it was because he had eaten his family. 'You might as well hang me because I'm going to kill lots more,' he said. He appeared indifferent when sentence of death was passed upon him.

Swift Runner's confession resembled Dahmer's, in that it was detailed and co-operative. He had already dissociated himself from the acts he was describing. Attributing his cannibalism to the windigo spirit which possessed him, he was able to hold himself not accountable, in his own mind, for what he had done. He had had no alternative, he was not in control, he had surrendered to the windigo. Those who investigated the case came to the conclusion that 'the profound impact of belief upon behaviour has all the quality of a determining force'.[6]

The thread which unites such disparate analogies as the pagan element in Christianity and the windigo curiosity is that of spiritual power, to be spurned at one's peril, to be courted as best one may. Indian tribes erroneously thought they could keep the windigo at bay by rigorous control of their emotions; Christians have likewise tried to ward off their devil by making themselves invasion-proof, unconquerable, and have achieved the opposite. When it comes to the Christian use of relics to propitiate the deity and gain power from him, we find ourselves moving right into the haunted world of Jeffrey Dahmer.

There are churches in Italy which boast altars or walls festooned with body parts. Model representations of feet, hands, noses and the like are offered by the faithful to their God in the certainty that He will heal them, give them some of His power. The shrine of St Anthony in the Basilica at Padua has pinned to its sides dozens of photographs of people mutilated or otherwise damaged in road accidents, in acknowledgement of Anthony's having saved the victims from something worse. The Virgin Mary is variously credited with having rescued mariners by hauling their ship to safety in her teeth, or stopping the flow of lava from Mount Etna with her foot. Historically, too, sacred relics from the Divine Corpse have had churches built to house them, and when the Bishop of Chalons removed Christ's navel from his church and threw it on the fire, the whole town rose up in fury against him. There was even a sacred relic of Christ's foreskin venerated in mediaeval times.

The potency of these superstitions resided in their promise of power, in the belief that the faithful would benefit from them. Did this amount to delusional thinking? A false idea is factually incorrect, a delusional idea incorrectly attributes power. If I were to maintain that a brass kettle is revolving around the moon, it would most probably be a false idea (though I might persist in believing it and could not have my belief dissolved by reason). Should I expect the kettle to determine the winner of a horse-race it would be a demonstrably delusional idea. Jeffrey Dahmer's shrine was not a false idea. It existed. He had the black table, the griffins to protect it, the skulls to adorn it, two skeletons to flank it. But the power he expected to derive from it was delusional. It was 'a place for meditation, where I could feel I was drawing power from an outside source . . . I was trying to get in contact with the spirits.'[7]

He was deliberately vague when asked what was the purpose or direction of that power, even telling one doctor it might assist him in making money in real estate. I suspect this was not a serious remark, but one intended to demonstrate the hopelessness of the question. You do not interrogate the spirits, you do not channel their energy towards the achievement of earthly ambition. You humbly do their bidding. You summon their power and prostrate yourself before its pulsating fire. Obedience, not manipulation, is your function. Dahmer did not say what he would do with the spiritual power bestowed upon him through his shrine, because he did not know. How could he? The whole idea was a delusion, an absurdity, the construction of a diseased mind. But it was *his* diseased mind, and it was not amenable to literal enquiry. The question was foolish, earth-bound, and the answer, which the doctor assiduously wrote down and reported, was appropriately banal.

On quite another level, the level of pure untouchable madness, Dahmer's shrine was to be his mansion of ecstasy, where he would 'go out of' his quotidian identity and mingle with the spirits who understood him. They might well be the spirits of the people he had killed, people who knew him better than anyone in the world, indeed the *only* people who knew him as he really was. The fact that he would reach these spirits through the relics of sex and murder indicated the fundamental religiosity of his beliefs, for sex, murder, and solitary meditation are all part of the torrid fabric of religion. The Japanese mystic and novelist Yukio Mishima experienced his first orgasm while looking at a painting of the martyrdom of St Sebastian, his body ecstatically pierced by arrows. Mishima went on to dream of slaughtering young white men on a large marble table (just like Dahmer's table – an altar of sorts) and eating parts of their bodies. In 1970 he committed *hara-kiri*, publicly disembowelling himself at an army headquarters in Tokyo. The Japanese dare not call Mishima insane, because he was their greatest novelist as well as their most embarrassing suicide, so they prefer to say nothing about him at all. But his mysticism was clearly born of a disturbed erotic religiosity, immune to mental health classifications; the *D.S.M.-III-R* cookbook would have been just as inadequate with Mishima as it was in defining Jeffrey Dahmer.

Dahmer's crimes permitted him to act, for a moment, at a higher level of intensity than is given to ordinary folk with ordinary joys. His 'windigo' alienation had forged for him a solitary path isolated from the rest of humankind. He was unreachable. Daily life held no meaning for him. Mundane happiness was denied him. His madness evolved from the need to create a moment of bliss, *his* moment, unlike anyone else's. The psychiatrist cannot really enter into such a closed, private world, or if he can, it must be to destroy it. The murderer's separateness is his only identity, in that he has an experience we do not have. The doctor's purpose is to cure him, make him like everyone else, deprive him of that one identity which, insanely, makes him feel he exists. The successful psychiatrist is a killer, for he murders ecstasy.

Peter Shaffer's play *Equus* tells the story of a young man who has unaccountably blinded half a dozen horses at the stables where he is employed. It is based upon an actual incident, but Shaffer uses it to dramatise the conflict between society's need for bland conformist sanity, and the individual's need for transcendence. The boy is examined by a psychiatrist, Dysart, who brutally brings him through the experience by 'abreacting', reliving it under hypnosis. He is then horrified at what he has done. 'He'll be delivered from madness,' he says. '*What then?* He'll feel himself acceptable! *What then?* Do you think feelings like his can be simply reattached, like plasters? Stuck on to other objects we select? *Look at him!* My desire might be to make this boy an ardent husband – a caring citizen – a worshipper of abstract and unifying God. My achievement, however, is more likely to make a ghost! Let me tell you exactly what I'm going to do to him! I'll heal the rash on his body. I'll erase the welts cut into his mind by flying manes. When that's done, I'll set him on a nice mini-scooter and send him puttering off into the Normal world where animals are treated *properly*. . . With any luck his private parts will come to feel as plastic to him as the products of the factory to which he will almost certainly be sent. Who knows? He may even come to find sex funny. Smirky funny. Bit of grunt funny. Trampled and furtive and entirely in control. Hopefully, he'll feel nothing at his fork but Approved Flesh. *I doubt, however, with much passion*. Passion, you see, can be destroyed by a doctor. It cannot be created.'[8]

Shaffer is not suggesting that the passions of a damaged soul should *not* be excised, that it would somehow be acceptable for deluded stable-boys to blind horses at will; he says that the doctor has nothing to put in their place once they *have* been removed. By the same token, nobody would think of proposing Jeffrey Dahmer's strange passion could be excused, still less allowed. He has quite properly been exiled from society and no more young men will fall victim to his depravity. But the source of his compulsion has not been eradicated; the psychiatrists examined him, attempted to diagnose him, but they did not cure him. Nor did they know him. His very blandness, his lack of colour and contour, testify to the total secrecy of his personality. The only people who really knew him are dead.

Dahmer's passion was necrophilic, and it was his alone. His shrine would do honour to it, in the inviolable privacy of his mind. Dr Friedman thought that the shrine answered a need to have something artistic, decorative and creative in the house, but he did not spot the significance of this. The aesthetic sense objectifies, after all; it has to. It loves the static, the seeable, the perceivable, the deadness of immutability. The need to create beauty is in a way necrophilous, for it hankers after stillness and permanence and control. The creator of beauty is a controller. There is no reciprocity in art.

Dahmer's shrine would be his creation, the only one in his entire existence. It would be beautiful, bound by the mystical absolutes of symmetry (as his drawing shows), and it would be his ultimate exercise in control. He knew all about the beauty of things, and nothing whatever of the love which gave them life. Sitting before the table, alone with his relics, he would have control over his life at last, over sex, the world, the past, power through the absolute beauty of death. Those he had killed would be there with him, twelve skulls in front, the skeletons of Lacy and Miller at each side. They were not wasted. He had kept something of them. They were now his companions in the world of the spirit, which that vast uncomprehending and hostile world outside could not touch. He had been chained to that world, an unwilling guest among its horrible disorder. Here before his shrine he would be free at last. Somebody asked, What was it a shrine to? 'Myself,' he said. The self which diverted, the aberrant self. Shockingly, it would be the only place on earth where he could feel his own kind of comfort and ease, for nowhere else would he fit. 'If this had happened six months later, that's what they would have found.'

In the company of flickering lights, incense, ghosts, and silent comforting eyeless grinning skulls, Jeff Dahmer would finally be in peace. It was 'a place where I could feel at home'.[9]

Postscript

THE INSANITY DEFENCE
by Kenneth Smail, Ph.D.

The insanity defence in a criminal trial attempts to introduce morality into the legal assessment of blameworthiness. The defence becomes an examination of good and evil, though these are not the qualities directly assessed and debated by the secular participants in an insanity trial. It arises from the moral consciousness of the community, but is managed within the criminal justice system and examined using concepts of the mental health professions. Mental disease, mental defect, mental capabilities and psychiatric diagnoses are the words which come into play.

But mental responsibility is not only an issue of morality; it is also an issue about reason and emotion. Reasoning processes may collide with the emotional response to crime. Victim and community outrage is a natural consequence of the social disorder and chaos created by criminal violence, but expressions of anger have to be postponed until the insanity question has been deliberated. The defendant may be exculpated for an act he in fact committed, because an abnormal mental state is held accountable. Under those circumstances, the insanity defence may invoke anger because justified wrath cannot be heaped so readily upon something one cannot see or touch.

Moral, rational and emotional understanding about the criminal responsibility of the defendant have their roots in many different disciplines. Observations about psychological abnormality have come from writers, philosophers, theologians and lawyers, whose insights have crossed guild lines and fertilised new associations of ideas. For example, Hamlet's rebuke 'The lady doth protest too much methinks' found its way into Freud's notion of reaction formation as psychological defence mechanism. There is no monopoly on insight and difficult questions require many viewpoints. But the chief resource for the American criminal justice system when analysing insanity issues is the discipline of psychology.

Psychiatrists and psychologists perform insanity evaluations. Courts rely upon them for relevant, candid and accurate assessments of a defendant's mental capability, using the legal standard of insanity. Mental health professionals are at their best when performing their analysis as objective consultants rather than advocates for a particular viewpoint. We should not attempt to prosecute or defend an accused person. Ultimately, decisions about a defendant's criminal responsibility should not be abdicated to psychiatrists or psychologists, but should remain with triers of fact. While mental health professionals may reflect values of the community where the trial occurs, these evaluators are not accountable to the community as would be an elected official or jury. The insanity test which mental health professionals apply is not a product of the mental health sciences but a legislative codification of the community's notion about justice and responsibility.

The test for insanity appears as a single sentence in the Wisconsin Statutes: 'A person is not responsible for criminal conduct if at the time of such conduct as a result of mental disease or defect he lacked substantial capacity to appreciate the wrongfulness of his conduct or conform his conduct to the requirements of the law'. Moral value judgements are clearly embedded in this standard. There is no precise definition of the word 'substantial'. The term suggests something less than total, but more than a little.

The word cannot be understood further without placing it in some value context.

The test does not excuse behaviour merely because a defendant is mentally ill. For example, a person diagnosed with schizophrenia who robs a gas station to obtain beer money may be as accountable as one without such a diagnosis. A lack in *substantial capacity to appreciate* or *conform* must flow from the disease or defect. However, if the robber had delusional beliefs to the effect that he owned the gas station and all its contents, then he might be legally insane. Under those circumstances, the disease resulted in, by way of the delusions, a substantial lack in capacity to appreciate the wrongfulness of his conduct. Additionally, it is true that mere deficiencies in psychological abilities do not satisfy the test. Psychological wounds from troubled lives are not likely to be sufficiently incapacitating. While the test is an instrument used to make a dichotomous decision, people's abilities exist on a continuum. Some people properly found responsible for criminal conduct may have been less able to appreciate or conform than others who are also found responsible. The test is also time, crime and person specific. It does not necessarily follow that once a person is found insane he or she will always be unaccountable for future conduct. Nonetheless, a documented history of psychosis and past judgements of non-responsibility may help reinforce current evidence for insanity. Such was not the case with Jeffrey Dahmer.

The evaluation of Jeffrey Dahmer's mental responsibility was eventually assigned to eight psychiatrists and psychologists. These professionals collectively represented a range of experience working with criminal defendants, and some of them had specialised training with persons suffering from sexual disorders. They also had varied experience in addressing forensic mental health questions. By and large they worked independently. In the proper order of things, there should have been eight opinions, hopefully convergent about Dahmer's state of mind at the time he committed the fifteen crimes charged, and particularly what that state of mind implied about his mental capability to appreciate the wrongfulness of his conduct and his capacity to conform his conduct to the requirements of the law.

Seven of those eight examiners testified at trial. I did not. The legal system attempts to find truth by sharpening distinctions between opposing sides. While an accused person's abilities to conform or appreciate may fall anywhere on a continuum, it is chiefly those experts' opinions which reflect one extreme or the other that are brought to court. As one can see below, my opinions were not sufficiently supportive of the defence position and yet I was a defence-retained expert. Interestingly, the District Attorney, who was alert to the implications from the fact I did not testify during the defence presentation, considered subpoenaing me for testimony. He later explained that he decided not to subpoena me because he would be cutting new legal ground in Wisconsin and did not want to unnecessarily create an issue for an appeal. At the same time, his ongoing assessment of his case was that his experts were doing well.

Among the seven who did testify, the opinions about Dahmer's state of mind seemed more similar than divergent. Most thought he was not psychotic in the sense of sensory disturbance or having significant disorders of thought or affect. Most described severe sexual disorders, marked problems with intimacy and alcohol abuse. The fact that opinions did vary somewhat on a complex topic did not hinder the operation of the insanity defence nor did the differences reflect badly upon the professionals. Among major league umpires, the strike zone will vary somewhat. Here, too, the system can work with less than absolute precision.

The discussion concerning whether Dahmer had a mental disease and the opinions people reached showed greater divergence of thought than did the general description of his mental state. Several of the experts who testified reluctantly affirmed that Dahmer had a mental disease as appropriately defined. One expert steadfastly denied that he did. Ten of the twelve jurors said 'no' as well.

The question that was asked of them was whether Dahmer had an 'abnormal condition of the mind which substantially affected mental and emotional processes' at the time he committed any or all of the fifteen homicides. This is the appropriate definition of mental disease under Wisconsin law. The analysis would appear to be straightforward. The mind is not an anatomical thing, but the confluence of all psychological activity, except perhaps for physical behaviour. Dahmer's psychosexual functioning was well established to reflect severe psychopathology defined as necrophilia. The rarity of Dahmer's mental activity as manifested by his sexual behaviour was as evident to the individual on the street as it was to the mental health professionals. This abnormal condition of the mind greatly affected Dahmer's mental and emotional processes by dictating the erotic thoughts that he would think and the longings and passions he would feel. Dahmer's abnormal condition affected his mental and emotional processes in the same manner that a turned key affects a car motor. The processes themselves were not rendered inoperable, yet that is not the requirement of the definition.

Experts who are not accustomed to forensic work may mistakenly apply a more stringent definition of mental disease, and lay people may intuitively agree with them. By design, however, the insanity defence concept of mental disease is much broader. The issue of mental disease is a threshold question. If one were to give shape to the insanity defence, it would appear as a funnel with the disease being the larger aperture. Many who meet the mental disease criteria eventually fail the test. The definition of the disease is broad enough to encompass nicotine withdrawal, but that condition will not ultimately prevail in an insanity defence. One should also note that the term 'mental disease' in the mental health system is used for a different purpose than it would be in the law.

In one context it is for diagnosis and treatment while the legal system uses it for the purpose of conceptualising conditions potentially suitable for exculpation. The broader definition in law is expressly for the purpose of giving the jury great discretion when considering the insanity issue. Psychosis, implied by the more stringent definition of mental disease, is not irrelevant to the insanity analysis, but it is not a necessary condition at the threshold. The impairments consequent to psychosis are more likely to be critical when mental capabilities are assessed.

Under the law, there are several conditions which are not mental diseases, even though those conditions are abnormal and they substantially affect mental and emotional processes. For example, the state of mind created by the voluntary ingestion of alcohol or drugs, including hallucinogens, will not qualify, even though the mental condition momentarily mimics functional psychosis. This and other exceptions are simply rules based upon the values arising from the moral consciousness of the community. In this example, the value appears to be that one is responsible for intoxicated behaviour if the intoxicated state was voluntarily created. Dahmer's mental state did not fit any one of these exceptions. There were multiple influences upon his behaviour when he committed the homicides, but none of those influences undid the fact or created the fact that he had necrophilia. The jury's refusal to recognise Dahmer's mental disease may have reflected their moral judgement that a new exception to the mental disease definition should be made so that the paraphilia do not qualify for insanity.

The equivocating testimony by some experts regarding the mental disease issue and the jury's ultimate conclusion that Dahmer did not have a mental disease, appeared to be instances when something other than reason was controlling opinions. Perhaps a demand for logic could not hold back the revulsion arising from Dahmer's conduct. Some may have been fearful as to what an acknowledgement of a mental disease would lead to in both this and future cases. If that is what occurred, they failed to understand the rigours of the remaining test. There were also clear instances when experts failed to maintain their roles and were allowed to expand upon their personal views of moral responsibility. The fact that some experts personally believed that it was or was not a good idea to include necrophilia as a mental disease, was inappropriate. Lectures about social policy are not proper material for forensic mental health experts when testifying in insanity trials.

While Dahmer acknowledged that he probably had not invented any new crimes in the history of humanity, he repeatedly stated that his acts were the worst imaginable and that there could be no forgiveness or salvation. For years he had acted outside the most fundamental rules of social behaviour. He was among us only in the most superficial ways. With the revelations of his crimes the line between him and the rest of the community became very clear to all. His mind and his behaviour, in separate yet related functioning, made him different from us. In talking with me, he never held out much hope that he would be ultimately acquitted or that his behaviour would be excused. Yet as the trial approached, he seemed to want to use the test to find acknowledgement that there was something not part of him (a disease) that made him want to commit his crimes. He never expected to be a physical part of the community (i.e., to walk Wisconsin Avenue), yet the disease acknowledgement held out some possibility that some day he could be reaffirmed, find acceptance and re-establish a connection with other people. He knew he had been very far apart from the rest of us and the disease issue became a connecting thread. This time the line of separation would not be drawn by his mind or his behaviour, but by the judgement of the jury. For Dahmer's purposes, he did not fail the test, but the test failed him.

The logic of the jury instructions meant that those

293

representatives of the community would never formally consider the issues of his capacity to appreciate or conform his behaviour. Without satisfying the threshold question, the rest becomes moot. Nonetheless, the testimony did dwell upon those issues and the rigours of those standards meant that his conviction at the end of the trial was inescapable.

In regard to Dahmer's capacity to appreciate the wrongfulness of his conduct, none of the examiners thought he was exculpatorily insane on that account. The framers of the insanity test deliberately replaced the word 'know' with the word 'appreciate' and thereby seemed to embrace additional meaning. The term appreciate is more than cognitive. Most people assert that it implies emotional understanding as well as thinking. In this case, one must recognise that Dahmer's lack of empathy or even sympathy for his victims was astounding. Clearly, his senses must have been seared in order for him to have done what he did. Nonetheless, he did go to extraordinary efforts to conceal his activity. After he was caught, he reported that he knew while he was killing that his actions were wrong and that they were against moral and criminal codes. With these facts, the enhanced concept of 'appreciate' seemed to be no more than a thin veneer over a solid core of evidence, indicating that he knew what he was doing was wrong. The difference between 'appreciate' and 'know' was a distinction without meaning.

The analysis of Dahmer's capacity to conform his behaviour was unsettling because it never appeared entirely satisfactory. At the outset there were fundamental problems as to how one proves that certain behaviour is out of control. What data does one look for? What decision rules should apply? How much data does one need to make a firm decision? What assumptions should one make? How can out-of-control behaviour be reliably (repeatedly) distinguished from reckless or impulsive behaviour? The purpose of raising these questions is to keep the evaluation within the rules of scientific inquiry.

One way to assess the control question would be just to consider Dahmer's behaviour and then attempt to infer control capabilities. There were innumerable instances when Dahmer seemed to alter his intended course of behaviour in order to avoid detection or for some other consideration. Altered behaviour implied influence and influence implied some level of control. Conversely, there were instances when his behaviour showed little caution and was frankly reckless. Those instances might invite the casual conclusion that *only* out-of-control people would engage in such dangerous (apprehension-prone) behaviour. Unfortunately, that would be poor reasoning because the observation does not settle the essential question: did he choose not to control his behaviour or did he try and fail? An analysis of his mere behaviour would not appear to be productive.

Some acknowledged Dahmer's influence over his behaviour but then argued that his actions merely reflected practical decisions carried out in accordance with a higher-level imperative over which he had little or no control. This assertion refocuses analyses directly upon his internal psychological phenomena and would attempt to weigh the strength of his drive to commit the crimes against the resources he possessed to control himself. The question becomes one of a gas pedal versus a brake.

Clearly, Dahmer had an imperfect ability to conform his behaviour. A person who has no urge to have sex with corpses is likely to have a perfect ability to refrain from killing for intimate gratification. The equation is immediately different when there is an urge that needs controlling. Beyond this simple truth, the defence was able to flush out some of Dahmer's limitations. He could find few pleasures to seek other than those he sought with corpses. He was also walled out of the social community. To the extent that conformity is achieved through a socialisation process, Dahmer had long since isolated himself from that process.

While his abilities were imperfect, they were not absent. In fact, they were very evident at an operational level of decision-making. It is relevant here to consider the evidence that his sensory functioning was not impaired; he could think logically and there was no gross impairment in his emotional functioning. He could delay gratification, set goals and problem-solve with relative effectiveness.

The drive that Dahmer needed to control was difficult to articulate because it was difficult to understand. It could not be measured physiologically in any meaningful way. One general assessment of drive found in psychology is that the strength of a drive can be estimated by the amount of work done in order to achieve a particular goal. Dahmer clearly engaged in a great deal of physical, mental and emotional work in order to carry out his crimes, and therefore one could surmise that he had the strong drive to pursue those activities.

Additional considerations reinforce this logic applied and thereby strengthen any conclusions. There is an assumption when conducting psychological evaluations that the subject is 'normal'. The task of evaluation is to observe the person on a relevant continuum and then measure or appraise the discrepancy from that point of observation to 'normality'. For example, 'normal' intelligence may be defined in part in terms of an I.Q. of 100. A person's measured intellectual ability takes meaning from that reference point. When conducting insanity evaluations, the initial assumption is that the accused person retains substantial capacity to appreciate the wrongfulness of his conduct or conform his conduct to the requirements of the law. An accused person's abilities to appreciate or conform have meaning in reference to the abilities of an average person.

There is also a general rule in behavioural science that the amount of data needed to declare that a condition exists contrary to expectation must be significant. The purpose of this rule is to minimise erroneous declarations of deviancy. The assertion that a deviant condition exists must be clearly supportable. Ultimately, the testimony would have to be to a 'reasonable degree of professional certainty', rather than a reasonable degree of personal certitude. The denial that such a condition exists means either that it does not exist or that evidence was not found to prove that it exists. The import of this reasoning is that Dahmer needed to demonstrate significant evidence of his inability to conform his conduct in order for the examiner to confidently advise the court that such a condition existed. When the facts were held against this standard, the conclusion was that Dahmer did not demonstrate a substantial lack in his capacity to appreciate the wrongfulness of his conduct or conform his conduct to the requirements of the law. The evidence failed to prove Dahmer insane.

The analysis of his psychological capabilities is rational and it has practical value because it helped to answer the question about insanity. It does not lead to the only possible conclusion. Non-scientific inquiry may use different assumptions and apply different rules for analysis. There is no assumption here that my conclusion will satisfy all perspectives or always satisfy scientific perspectives. Dahmer's psychological disorders are rare and therefore not frequently examined. Ed Gein committed similar crimes in Wisconsin in the 1950s, while Dennis Nilsen committed strikingly similar crimes in the 1970s in London. Clearly, there is much more to discover about these individuals than is already known and, when more is known, perhaps proof of insanity will be available. Jeffrey Dahmer is now out of free society and confined in a community of serious criminals. We are safe from him but not from his psychopathology. Other similarly disturbed individuals will come. It is imperative that multidisciplinary lines of inquiry focus on people who commit such crimes. The insanity question does not appear to be anywhere near as important as understanding these individuals. To that end, Brian Masters has undertaken an important task in the preceding pages. His insights will encourage psychologists and psychiatrists to consider additional aspects of the complex personality of men like Jeffrey Dahmer.

Bibliography

Books

Anthony, Sylvia, *The Child's Discovery of Death* (Kegan, Paul & Co., 1940).

Clark, Tim & Penycate, John, *Psychopath: The Case of Patrick Mackay* (Routledge & Kegan Paul, London, 1976).

Davis, Wade, *The Serpent and the Rainbow* (Collins, 1986).

Derleth, August (ed.), *Collected Ghost Stories* (1952).

Frazer, J. G., *The Golden Bough* (Macmillan, 1975).

Freud, Sigmund, *Collected Papers*, vol. III (Leipzig, 1924).

Fromm, Erich, *The Anatomy of Human Destructiveness* (Jonathan Cape, London, 1974).

Krafft-Ebing, *Psychopathia Sexualis*, in the modern edition edited by Alexander Hartwich, *Aberrations of Sexual Life* (1951).

Michaud, Stephen G. & Aynesworth, Hugh, *The Only Living Witness* (1983).

Laing, R. D., *The Divided Self* (Tavistock Publications, 1969).

Levin, Jack & Fox, James Alan, *Mass Murder: America's Growing Menace* (Plenum Press, 1985).

Maslow, Abraham, *Motivation and Personality* (Harper & Row, New York, 1954).

Masters, Brian, *Killing for Company* (Coronet Books, 1986).

Norris, Joel, *Serial Killers: the Growing Menace* (Arrow Books, 1990).

Prins, Hershel, *Bizarre Behaviours: Boundaries of Psychiatric Disorder* (Tavistock/Routledge, 1990).

River, J. Paul de, *The Sexual Criminal* (Charles Thomas, Springfield, Illinois, 1956).

Rosen, Ismond (ed.), *The Pathology and Treatment of Sexual Deviation* (Oxford University Press, 1964).

Shaffer, Peter, *Equus* in *Three Plays* (Penguin, 1976).

Schreiber, Flora Rheta, *The Shoemaker* (Allen Lane, 1983).

Stekel, Wilhelm, *Auto-erotism* (Liveright, New York, 1950).

Stekel, Wilhelm, *Peculiarities of Behaviour,* vol. I (Williams & Norgate, 1925).

Stekel, Wilhelm, *Sexual Aberrations* (John Lane, 1934).

Storr, Anthony, *Human Destructiveness* (Routledge, 1992).

Wertham, Frederic, *Dark Legend: A Study in Murder* (Victor Gollancz, London, 1947).

Wilson, Colin, *A Casebook of Murder* (Leslie Frewin, 1969).

Wilson, Colin, *Order of Assassins* (Rupert Hart-Davis, London, 1972).

Wilson, Colin & Pitman, Patricia, *Encyclopaedia of Murder* (A. Barber, 1961).

Journals

Blom, G. E., 'The Reactions of Hospitalized Children to Illness', *Pediatrics,* vol. 22 (1958).

Brill, A. A., 'Necrophilia', *Journal of Criminal Psychopathology*, vols. 2 and 3 (1941).

Brittain, Robert P., 'The Sadistic Murderer', *Medicine, Science and the Law*, vol. 10, no. 4 (1970).

Davenport, H. T. & Werry, J. S., 'The Effects of General Anaesthesia, Surgery and Hospitalization upon the Behaviour of Children', *American Journal of Orthopsychiatry*, vol. 40 (1970).

Levy, D. M., 'Psychic Trauma of Operations', *American Journal of Diseases of Children,* vol. 69 (1945).

Money, John, 'Forensic Sexology: Paraphilic Serial Rape (Biastophilia) and Lust Murder (Erotophonophilia)', *American Journal of Psychotherapy*, vol. XLIV, no. 1 (1990).

Pearson, Gerald H. J., 'Effect of Operative Procedures on the Emotional Life of the Child', *American Journal of Diseases of Children.*

Smith, Selwyn M. & Braun, Claude, 'Necrophilia and Lust Murder: Report of a Rare Occurrence', *Bulletin of AALP,* vol. VI, no. 3.

Symington, Neville, 'Response Aroused by the Psychopath', *International Review of Psycho-analysis*, vol. 7 (1980).

Teicher, Morton I., 'Windigo Psychosis', *International Journal of Parapsychology* (1962).

Other Documents

The State of Wisconsin vs. Jeffrey L. Dahmer, Criminal Complaint 2-291231.

Milwaukee Police Department, file 2472.

Conversations between Jeffrey L. Dahmer and Dr Kenneth Smail.

Notes

In the notes which follow, references to conversations between Jeffrey L. Dahmer and Dr Kenneth Smail are indicated by the initials J.L.D. and the date on which the quoted conversation took place.

1 The Charges

1 J.L.D., 7 and 14 Aug, 1991.
2 Milwaukee Police Department, file 2472.
3 Nilsen Papers, vol. VII, p. 1, quoted in Masters, *Killing for Company*.
4 J.L.D., 10 Aug, 1991.
5 R. D. Laing, *The Divided Self*, p. 25.
6 Colin Wilson, *A Casebook of Murder*, p. 23.
7 Erich Fromm, *The Anatomy of Human Destructiveness*, p. 340.
8 Neville Symington, 'The Response Aroused by the Psychopath', *International Review of Psycho-analysis*, vol. 7, p. 294 (1980).
9 Melanie Klein, *Love, Guilt and Reparation*, quoted in Symington, *International Review of Psycho-analysis*.
10 Colin Wilson and Patricia Pitman, *Encyclopaedia of Murder*, p. 22.
11 Letter to the author, 6 June, 1983, quoted in *Killing for Company*.
12 R. D. Laing, *The Divided Self*, p. 27.
13 J.L.D., 7 Aug, 1991.
14 Camille Paglia, *Sexual Personae*, p. 4.
15 J.L.D., 11 Aug, 1991.

303

2 The Child

1 J.L.D., 10 Jan, 1992.
2 J.L.D., 6 Aug, 1991.
3 J.L.D., 6 Aug, 1991.
4 Flora Rheta Schreiber, *The Shoemaker*, p. 43.
5 Erich Fromm, *The Anatomy of Human Destructiveness*, p. 313.
6 R. D. Laing, *The Divided Self*, p. 133.
7 J.L.D., 26 Aug, 1991.
8 J.L.D., 6 Aug, 1991.
9 J.L.D., 26 Aug, 1991.
10 J.L.D., 14 Aug, 1991.
11 A. Hyatt Williams, *A Psycho-analytic Approach to the Treatment of the Murderer*, read at the 21st Congress of the International Psycho-analytic Association in Copenhagen, Denmark, July, 1959.

3 The Fantasies

1 J.L.D., 14 Aug, 1991.
2 Francisco Goya, Preface to *Los Caprichos*, quoted by Anthony Storr in *Human Destructiveness*.
3 Wilhelm Stekel, *Auto-erotism*, p. 66.
4 Colin Wilson, *Order of Assassins*, p. 61.
5 J.L.D., 26 Aug, 1991.
6 J.L.D., 11 Aug, 1991.
7 J.L.D., 2 Aug, 1991.
8 J.L.D., 26 Aug, 1991.
9 J.L.D., 2 Aug, 1991.
10 J.L.D., 26 Aug, 1991.
11 J.L.D., 26 Aug, 1991.

4 The Struggle

1 J.L.D., 25 Aug, 1991.
2 The State of Wisconsin vs. Jeffrey L. Dahmer, Criminal Complaint 2-291231.

3 J.L.D., 25 Aug, 1991.
4 Wilhelm Stekel, *Sexual Aberrations*, p. 33.
5 Krafft-Ebing, *Psychopathia Sexualis*.
6 J.L.D., 26 Aug, 1991.
7 J.L.D., 13 Aug, 1991.
8 Camille Paglia, *Sexual Personae*.
9 Anthony Storr, *Human Destructiveness*, p. 21.
10 Abraham Maslow, *Motivation and Personality*.
11 Letter to Wisconsin Correctional Service, 3 Oct, 1986.

5 The Collapse

1 J.L.D., 2 Aug, 1991; 3 Aug, 1991; 26 Aug, 1991.
2 J.L.D., 26 Aug, 1991.
3 J.L.D. in conversation with Dr Park Dietz.
4 J.L.D., 26 Aug, 1991. He was reading Leviticus at the time of this interview.
5 J.L.D., 11, 14, 25 Aug, 1991.
6 Robert P. Brittain, 'The Sadistic Murderer', *Medicine, Science and the Law*, vol. 10, no. 4 (1970).
7 Herschel Prins, *Bizarre Behaviours*, p. 35.
8 Joel Norris, *Serial Killers*, pp. 264–5.
9 Stephen G. Michaud and Hugh Aynesworth, *The Only Living Witness*, p. 288.
10 *Confessions*, Book V.
11 Brian Masters, *Killing for Company*, pp. 166–8.
12 A. Hyatt Williams, 'The Psychopathology and Treatment of Sexual Murderers', in *The Pathology and Treatment of Sexual Deviation*, ed. Ismond Rosen.
13 Frederic Wertham, *Dark Legend*.
14 J.L.D., 2 Aug, 1991.
15 J.L.D., 3 Aug, 1991.
16 J.L.D., 11 Aug, 1991.
17 J.L.D., 26 Aug, 1991.
18 J.L.D., 7 Aug, 1991.
19 J.L.D., 26 Aug, 1991.
20 J.L.D., 25 Aug, 1991.
21 J.L.D. to Judge William Gardner, 10 Dec, 1989.
22 Dr Lionel Dahmer to Judge William Gardner, 1 Mar, 1990.

6 The Nightmare

1 J.L.D., 3 Aug, 1991.
2 Milwaukee County Court, 12 Feb, 1992.
3 J.L.D., 26 Aug, 1991.
4 J.L.D., 3 Aug, 1991.
5 J.L.D., 5 and 11 Aug, 1991.
6 J.L.D., 22 Aug, 1991.
7 J.L.D., 13 Aug, 1991.
8 J.L.D., 1, 11, 22, 23 Aug, 18 Nov, 1991.
9 J.L.D., 5 Aug, 1991.
10 Dahmer's confession, pp. 151, 158, in Police Report 2472, Section 5.
11 J.L.D., 19 Sept, 1991.
12 J.L.D., 11 Oct, 1991.
13 J.L.D., 5 Aug, 1991. Dennis Nilsen said he felt 'unclean' when talking about his crimes. See Brian Masters, *Killing for Company*.
14 Erich Fromm, *The Anatomy of Human Destructiveness*, p. 455.

7 The Frenzy

1 Erich Fromm, *The Anatomy of Human Destructiveness*, p. 449.
2 J. P. de River, *The Sexual Criminal*.
3 H. von Hentig, *Der Nekrotope Mensch*, quoted in Erich Fromm, *The Anatomy of Human Destructiveness*.
4 *Ibid.*, p. 451.
5 *Ibid.*, p. 450.
6 Selwyn M. Smith and Claude Braun, 'Necrophilia and Lust Murder: Report of a Rare Occurrence', *Bulletin of AALP*, vol. VI, no. 3.
7 C. M. Eddy, Jnr, 'The Loved Dead', in *Collected Ghost Stories*, ed. August Derleth.
8 A. A. Brill, 'Necrophilia', *Journal of Criminal Psychopathology*, vols. 2 and 3 (1941).
9 J.L.D., 19 Sept, 1991.
10 J.L.D., 19 Sept, 1991.

11 J.L.D., 22 Aug, 1991.
12 J.L.D., 25 Aug, 1991.
13 J.L.D., 11 Oct, 1991.
14 J.L.D., 14 Aug, 1991.
15 J.L.D., 7 Aug, 1991.
16 J.L.D., 14 Aug, 1991.
17 J.L.D., 14 Aug, 1991.

8 The Question of Control

1 Joel Norris, *Serial Killers*, p. 265.
2 J.L.D., 13 Aug, 1991.
3 A. Hyatt Williams, 'Murderousness', in *The Pathology and Treatment of Sexual Deviation*, ed. Ismond Rosen, p. 99.
4 William Shakespeare, *Macbeth*, Act III, Scene iv.
5 Neville Symington, 'The Response Aroused by the Psychopath', *International Review of Psycho-analysis*, vol. 7 (1980), p. 291.
6 Tim Clark and John Penycate, *Psychopath: The Case of Patrick Mackay*, p. 101.
7 G. E. Blom, 'The Reactions of Hospitalized Children to Illness', *Pediatrics*, vol. 22 (1958); H. T. Davenport and J. S. Werry, 'The Effects of General Anaesthesia, Surgery, and Hospitalization upon the Behaviour of Children', *American Journal of Orthopsychiatry*, vol. 40 (1970).
8 *Ibid*.
9 Gerald H. J. Pearson, 'Effect of Operative Procedures on the Emotional Life of the Child', *American Journal of Diseases of Children*.
10 D. M. Levy, 'Psychic Trauma of Operations', *American Journal of Diseases of Children*, vol. 69 (1945).
11 Quoted in *New Yorker*, 2 July, 1984.
12 Jack Levin and James Alan Fox, *Mass Murder*, p. 199.
13 *Ibid*., p. 208.
14 Quoted in *New Yorker*, 2 July, 1984.
15 American Bar Association's submission to the Congressional Committee convened in the wake of the Hinckley trial.
16 American Psychiatric Association Statement on the Insanity Defense, Dec, 1982.

17 Shakespeare, *Macbeth*, Act III, Scene ii.
18 J.L.D., Aug 10, 11, 13, 14, 23, 25, 26, 1991; Sept 18, 1991; Nov 18, 1991; Jan 10, 1992.

9 The Trial

1 Frederic Wertham, *Dark Legend*.
2 Wilhelm Stekel, *Peculiarities of Behaviour,* vol. I, p. 10.
3 John Money, 'Forensic Sexology: Paraphilic Serial Rape (Biastophilia) and Lust Murder (Erotophonophilia)', *American Journal of Psychotherapy*, vol. XLIV, no. 1 (1990).
4 Wilhelm Stekel, *Auto-erotism*, p. 185; *Sexual Aberrations*, p. 348.
5 A. Hyatt Williams, 'The Psychopathology and Treatment of Sexual Murderers', in *The Pathology and Treatment of Sexual Deviation*, ed. Ismond Rosen (1964).
6 Wade Davis, *The Serpent and the Rainbow* (1986). See also a brief discussion in Herschel Prins, *Bizarre Behaviours*.
7 John Money, 'Forensic Sexology', *American Journal of Psychotherapy*.

10 The Shrine

1 G. Morris Carstairs, in *The Pathology and Treatment of Sexual Deviation*, ed. Ismond Rosen, p. 428.
2 Sigmund Freud, *Collected Papers*, vol. III, and Sylvia Anthony, *The Child's Discovery of Death,* p. 149.
3 J. G. Frazer, *The Golden Bough*, pp. 497–8.
4 J.L.D., 11 Aug, 1991.
5 Frazer, *The Golden Bough*.
6 Morton I. Teicher, 'Windigo Psychosis', *International Journal of Parapsychology* (1962).
7 J.L.D., 18 Nov, 1991.
8 Peter Shaffer, *Equus*, Act II, Scene 35.
9 J.L.D., 18 Nov, 1991.